mom,

Wishing you many nites of cuddling up in your chair reading your new book. Enjoy!

We love you

Craig, Kyle & Ryan

# Game of My Life:

# BOSTON RED SOX

## CHAZ SCOGGINS

SportsPublishingLLC.com

Publishers: Peter L. Bannon and Joseph J. Bannon Sr.
Senior managing editor: Susan M. Moyer
Acquisitions editor: Mike Pearson
Developmental editor: Travis W. Moran
Art director: K. Jeffrey Higgerson
Cover/dust jacket design: Kenneth J. O'Brien
Interior layout: Dustin J. Hubbart and Kathryn R. Holleman
Imaging: Dustin J. Hubbart and Kenneth J. O'Brien
Photo editor: Erin Linden-Levy

Printed in the United States of America

Sports Publishing L.L.C.
804 North Neil Street
Champaign, IL 61820
Phone: 1-877-424-2665
Fax: 217-363-2073
SportsPublishingLLC.com

Library of Congress Cataloging-in-Publication Data

Scoggins, Chaz, 1948-
    Game of my life : Boston Red Sox / Chaz Scoggins.
        p. cm.
    Includes bibliographical references and index.
    ISBN 1-58261-992-1 (hardcover : alk. paper)
    1. Boston Red Sox (Baseball team)—Anecdotes. 2. Baseball players—United States—Anecdotes. I. Title.

GV875.B7S364 2006
796.357'640974461—dc22

                        2006000453

*Dedicated to Dick Radatz (1937-2005), the greatest Red Sox relief pitcher of all time, who passed away before he could complete his contribution to this book.*

# Contents

# Foreword

I wish Ted Williams had still been around when this book was written. With so many great Red Sox players recalling their most memorable games, I would have been curious to read what Ted's choice would have been. He had so many great ones—almost every game was a great game for Ted Williams—I don't think it would have been an easy choice for him to make.

I know he wrote in his autobiography that the most memorable hit of his career was the two-out, three-run homer in the bottom of the ninth he hit off Claude Passeau to win the 1941 All-Star Game in Detroit. I wasn't there. I was playing minor-league ball in Louisville that summer and didn't get to Boston until the next year. I've seen the film of Ted clapping his hands as he ran around the bases, though, and he sure looked excited! Bobby Doerr was there, and he said Ted's homer thrilled him, too.

But that was just one hit, not a whole game. I know Ted had an even better All-Star Game in 1946, right in Fenway Park. I was there for that one. Ted went 4-for-4 with two homers and a walk, knocked in five runs, scored four, and we won the game 12-0. The last homer was against Rip Sewell on his Eephus Pitch, which no one ever thought would be hit out of the park because nobody had done it before.

Maybe Ted would have picked that game. Maybe he would have picked the game in Cleveland later that year, when he had the only inside-the-park homer of his career, and it won the game 1-0. We clinched the pennant that night, the only one the Red Sox would win for almost 50 years. I don't know. As I said, he had so many great games.

But if I could pick one for Ted, I know the one I'd pick. I don't even have to think about it. It also happened in 1946. We were playing the Tigers at Fenway, and Fred Hutchinson was pitching for Detroit. Ted always used to tell me: "Get on base, Needle"—that was my nickname because of my long, pointy nose—"Get on base, Needle, and I'll hit one out."

Well, I got on base, and he hit one out. Boy, did he hit one out! I knew it was a home run the moment he hit it, but I had no idea it would go as far as it did. I didn't see where it landed because I was on first base. I was running as soon as the ball was hit, so my back was to the play, but I'm sure I must have been rounding third by the time it came down. When I got back to the dugout, everyone was marveling at how far it had gone. It landed 37 rows up in the bleachers and right on top of a fan's straw hat. He was blinded by the sun and didn't see it coming. Even if he had, he probably wouldn't have believed it. Who could imagine anybody could hit a ball that far? The ball crushed his hat, hit him in the head, and bounced even farther up the bleachers. Later they measured the distance at 502 feet, and you can still see the red seat up there that marks the spot. It's the only red seat in the bleachers.

That was 60 years ago this year, and it's still the longest home run ever hit at Fenway Park—and that's saying something, especially since the hitters are so much bigger and stronger today and hit the ball so much farther, guys like David Ortiz and Manny Ramirez. Yet, no one has ever hit a ball farther in Fenway Park than Ted did that day.

Maybe, taking the passage of time into consideration, Ted would pick that game now. He loved to talk about long home runs. Wherever we went, Ted would always look around the ballpark and say: "Jimmie Foxx hit one way out there," or "Hank Greenberg hit one way up there." I think about all the hitters with great power I've seen since Ted retired— guys like Frank Robinson, Harmon Killebrew, Yaz, Frank Howard, Reggie Jackson, Jim Rice, Mark McGwire, Jose Canseco, Ken Griffey Jr., Eddie Murray, Cecil Fielder, Kirk Gibson, Frank Thomas, and Mo Vaughn—and still none of them ever hit a ball farther in Fenway than Ted did.

Maybe I'm more impressed by home runs because I only hit 17 over my whole career. But whatever game Ted would have picked, I'm sure I wouldn't have quarreled with it. It could be almost any game, because he didn't have many bad ones. A bad day for him was usually 0-for-2 with two walks.

I have been with the Red Sox organization for more than 65 years now, and I either played with, managed, coached, or watched each of the 20 players in this book. I'm sure choosing just one game couldn't have been easy for any of them. It was easy for me, though. I picked a game with one of my 17 home runs. What else? So, I'm curious to see which games the others picked. I'm sure I'll be surprised by some of them—and you probably will, too.

**—Johnny Pesky**
Swampscott, Massachusetts
January 2006

# Preface

About 25 years ago, by some stroke of good fortune, I found myself sitting in the manager's office at Fenway Park, surrounded by several of the greatest hitters in Boston Red Sox history. There was an Old Timers Game scheduled as a prelude to the Red Sox game on that Saturday, and after a lively session of batting practice that morning these former stars, most of them now in their sixties, had gathered in the manager's office to get reacquainted and reminisce before going back out onto the diamond to put on their exhibition for the adoring fans.

I happened to be in there with Peter Gammons and one or two other writers as the old stars began meandering in—Ted Williams ... Bobby Doerr ... Johnny Pesky ... Dominic DiMaggio and several others. The writers were barely noticed or acknowledged. We were just human flies on the wall, and for the next half hour of so, we would listen to and be enchanted by the tales of games played long ago. I didn't take any notes—afraid that the rustling pages of a notebook or the scratching of a pen would distract these diamond greats, who seemed to be blissfully unaware of our presence—and feared they would either throw out the interlopers or move away and continue their conversation in a more private location. We all knew in what low regard Ted Williams held the press!

What struck me most was how vividly these stars, who had played 1000-2000—sometimes even more—games during their distinguished careers could recall the minutest details of contests played 30 or 40 years before. And they weren't always talking about an All-Star Game or a World Series game, or even a game with pennant consequences. They would recall some ordinary June game played in 1940 or in May of 1951 or some other month and year that has long since been forgotten by everyone except those who happened to be there on that particular day.

I hadn't been there. How could I know their memories were accurate? I knew because I could see it in their eyes, which were windows into the past, and I could see exactly what they were seeing, back to a time when ballgames were played in the afternoons, the men in the stands all wore hats and suits, the players used tiny gloves that were left on the outfield grass when their team went in to bat, and the left-field wall at Fenway Park was plastered with advertisements.

"Boy, I remember this game that Hal Newhouser was pitching. ..." Williams might be saying.

"Hal Newhouser! Now *that* was a curveball!" Pesky chimes in.

"... And he starts me off with a fastball, just a little low and off the plate, that I take for ball," Williams continues, ignoring Pesky's interruption. He's in his old batting stance now, holding an imaginary bat. "The next pitch is a fastball in on my hands, and I just get out of the way of it—ball two. Now he throws me a beautiful curve that I take for a strike. The next pitch is a fastball-up that I want, but I can't quite get to it, and I foul it straight back. I'm cursing myself now. *That's* the pitch I should have killed. Newhouser ... he doesn't give you many of those. Now it's 2-2, and here comes a curveball—I mean, a *nasty* curveball— that's on the black, knee-high. I reach out and *just* get a piece of it. Now he comes back inside with the fastball, and I can't get good wood on it. But I get just enough of it to muscle it over Cullenbine's head for a single. Not a bad at-bat. But, man! I wish I had that fastball back!"

The gray or balding heads in the room nod in agreement. They're seeing the same picture, only from where they happened to be—in dugout or on base at that moment. And then it's on to the next anecdote.

I recount this story because I am constantly amazed at the recall powers of ballplayers. Hundreds or thousands of games, thousands of innings or at-bats, tens of thousands of pitches, and still they can isolate them and recite the details decades later. Most of us cannot even remember where we were or what we were doing at a particular hour last Tuesday. In writing this book, I relied heavily on the memories of twenty former Red Sox players, and they seldom needed much of a hint or prompting to relate the details of and the emotions they were feeling on their chosen day.

The difficult part for most of them was not the remembering, but narrowing down hundreds or thousands of games to a single one, for most of the Red Sox players and pitchers in this book had long and highly successful careers. A few, especially the pitchers, immediately picked theirs. Most of the others had to ponder their decisions for several weeks. I didn't envy them having to make their choices, and I was often surprised by the games they ultimately chose, because the games that meant the most to them were frequently not the games for which Red Sox fans remember them best. But as they reveal their innermost thoughts and feelings in this book, you'll understand why they picked the games they did.

Most surprising to me, however, was how many of them chose games the Red Sox lost. The cynics among us, I suppose, will cry: "See? They were just selfish players out for themselves. They never cared whether the Red Sox won or lost."

But as you read this book, I think you'll recognize such a judgment is absolutely false. All the subjects of this book, which spans a period of more than sixty years of Red Sox baseball, played their entire careers during that 85-year period between 1918 and 2004 during which Red Sox did not win a World Series and won just four pennants. So their memories—like those of Red Sox fans—are bittersweet. Losing important games was frustrating to them, too, and there were far too few of them to win or lose during their careers. So while none of them ever reached baseball's pinnacle while wearing a Red Sox uniform, at least some of them got close enough to see the unattainable peak once or twice. After years of trying, just being that close made those games special to them.

Your favorite games involving these 20 Red Sox icons would probably not be the same ones they picked. But for the next few hours, imagine sitting in the manager's office at Fenway Park, surrounded by these 20 players and listening to their tales. I think you'll be as entranced as I was on that Saturday morning a quarter of a century ago.

# Acknowledgments

Only one author's name appears on the jacket of this book. Perhaps I should be acknowledged as the messenger instead of the author, for all I have done is deliver the words and memories of 20 former Red Sox players, each of whom is revered by Red Sox fans. If they hadn't played the games, or if they had not been willing to discuss them with me, this book would not exist. They are the true authors of this book.

The Boston Red Sox were instrumental in making this book possible. The organization was cooperative and supportive in every way and let me rummage unfettered through the club archives. Dick Bresciani, the Red Sox Vice President for Publications and Archives, was always willing and eager to provide assistance, pointing me in the right directions, making useful suggestions, and often serving as a liaison between the players and me. Pam Ganley, the club's Coordinator of Alumni and Archives, was invaluable in providing phone numbers and tracking down the whereabouts of the players I needed. Without the selfless contributions of these two, who had their own everyday tasks to complete, this book could not have been written.

Debbie Matson, Glenn Geffner, Peter Chase, Mark Rogoff, Rod Oreste, Drew Merle, and Kevin Doyle were other members of the club's public relations staff who were never too busy to provide me with assistance on a moment's notice.

My colleagues in the press box were useful as sounding boards and providing advice, notably Rob Bradford, a fellow author and co-worker at *The Sun* in Lowell, Massachusetts; Bob Finnigan from the *Seattle Times*; Alan Greenwood from *The Telegraph* in Nashua, New Hampshire; and Bill Ballou from the *Worcester Telegram & Gazette*. Without the assistance of the *Boston Herald's* Tony Massarotti, neither I nor the Red Sox would likely have been able to track down the elusive Mike Greenwell.

I also need to thank Mike Pearson at Sports Publishing, who sought me out and offered me the opportunity to write this book. He took a chance on an author with one obscure, regionally-published book to his credit, and for that I am grateful.

And most of all, I must thank my wife, Vicki, for her understanding and support during the year it took to research and write this book. We spend little enough time together under ordinary circumstances, with her working a normal job while I work nights and weekends covering sports, and this project cut deeply into our time. I promise to make it up to her.

—CS

# Chapter 1

# BOBBY DOERR

## JULY 13, 1943

For Bobby Doerr, a 14-year, 1,865-game career with the Red Sox from 1937-51 that included playing in the 1946 World Series and eight All-Star Games was highlighted not just by one special game but by one split second.

The son of a telephone company employee, Robert Pershing Doerr was born in Los Angeles on April 7, 1918, and became a baseball prodigy. An older brother, Hal, was a catcher in the Pacific Coast League, and Bobby, already a standout player in American Legion ball, liked to hang around Wrigley Field where the PCL's Hollywood Sheiks played and shag flies during batting practice. Impressed by what they saw, the Sheiks signed Doerr to a professional contract for $200 a month when he was just 16 years old. By the age of 17, Doerr had established himself as a regular, hitting .317 in 172 games.

"There were always a lot of ex-major league players around," Doerr said of the highly competitive PCL. In that era, St. Louis was the westernmost outpost of the major leagues, and many home-grown PCL stars who had played, or could have played, in the majors were more comfortable playing closer to home in pleasant weather that permitted a longer schedule, and they could often earn just as much money. Doerr could learn a lot from these players, and did.

But there wasn't a lot they could teach the kid about playing second base. Doerr could always field, and if there had been a Gold Glove Award in his era, he probably would have won it nearly every year.

"I liked to field," Doerr said. "When I was a boy I'd throw a rubber ball against the front step of my porch and react to what the ball did. I'd do that by the hour, and it softened up my hands. Even when I was in the major leagues, if I started feeling uncomfortable, I'd go out to the left-field wall at Fenway—back before they padded it—and throw balls against it, and that would get me back in the groove."

The Hollywood Sheiks moved to San Diego in 1936 and were renamed the Padres, and one of Doerr's new teammates was a brash local teenager named Ted Williams. Doerr and Williams shared passions for fishing, hunting, and cowboy movies, and the two forged a life-long friendship. Eddie Collins, the Red Sox general manager, came out to California in 1936 to look at the 18-year-old Doerr, who would lead the PCL in hits with 238 and bat .342, and signed him.

"In the first game he saw Bobbie, the kid made four errors," wrote Frederick G. Lieb in his 1947 book, *The Boston Red Sox*. "Even so, Collins was sold on the youth, and when he returned east he was bubbling with enthusiasm, saying, 'I've just acquired the best second baseman in the minors.' And Eddie is something of an authority on second basemen."

Collins had played second base in the majors for a quarter of a century and would be elected to the Hall of Fame three years later. As for Williams, who was only five months younger than Doerr, he wasn't nearly as polished a hitter as Doerr was then. Collins nevertheless recognized Williams's potential and before leaving San Diego extracted a promise from the Padres that the Red Sox would get the first crack at him when it was time to sell his contract.

Williams had a strong year for the Padres in 1937 and was sold to the Red Sox after that season. By then Bobby Doerr was already wrapping up his first year in Boston. Williams, after another year of minor-league seasoning in Minneapolis, arrived in 1939, and that was the year the two 21-year-old future Hall of Famers both established themselves as major-league stars. Williams hit .327 with 31 homers and a league-leading 145 RBI as a rookie. The righthanded-hitting Doerr, generously listed at 5-11 and 175 pounds—four inches shorter and 30 pounds lighter than the Splendid Splinter—hit .318 with 73 RBI and began to unveil his power by hitting 12 homers.

Doerr swatted 37 doubles, 10 triples, and 22 homers for the Red Sox in 1940 while driving in 105 runs, hitting .291, and becoming part of the first

**Boston Red Sox second baseman Bobby Doerr follows the flight of the ball after connecting in a game at Fenway Park.**
*(Courtesy of the Boston Red Sox)*

100-homer infield in major-league history with first baseman Jimmie Foxx (36), shortstop Joe Cronin (24), and third baseman Jim Tabor (21). In 1941 Doerr joined Williams on the American League All-Star team. While Doerr went hitless in three at-bats, he watched in wonderment as Williams blasted a two-out, three-run walk-off homer in the bottom of the ninth off Claude Passeau that beat the Nationals 7-5 in Detroit.

"Just to be there with Ted, all the camaraderie, was really something. And then for Ted to hit that homer ..." Doerr recalled wistfully.

Although Bobby Doerr played on some of the greatest Red Sox teams in history, averaging 87 wins a year and five times winning 93 or more during his career, there would be only one World Series for him and plenty of disappointments, particularly in 1948 and 1949. So the annual All-Star Game became his national stage.

"The All-Star Game was really competitive then. Everyone was bearing down, and it was always a big thrill to beat the National League," Doerr remembered. "It was that way in every All-Star Game. I think it should still be competitive; but now it's more of an exhibition."

Doerr is hopeful that playing for home-field advantage in the World Series, a wrinkle instituted by baseball commissioner Bud Selig in 2003, will restore some intensity to the game.

"I think that was a good move, and that should make the players put a little more effort into it," Doerr said.

Doerr was selected for the 1942 All-Star Game at New York's Polo Grounds but didn't get to play. New York Yankees second baseman Joe Gordon was having an MVP season, and Yankees skipper Joe McCarthy was managing the All-Star team. So Doerr sat and watched the American Leaguers win 3-1.

By 1943 many major-league stars were in the service, and the Red Sox and Yankees were both decimated. Doerr and Gordon were still playing, but they were struggling, even in a watered-down league.

Gordon had hit .322 with 18 homers and 103 RBI for the Yankees in 1942 and won the AL's MVP Award. Doerr had hit .290 with 35 doubles, 15 homers, and 102 RBI for the Red Sox. Now, as the All-Star break approached in 1943, Gordon, already a four-time All-Star, was mired in a season-long slump that would see him finish the year hitting only .249 with 17 homers and 69 RBI. The 25-year-old Doerr was hitting .239 with a mere eight doubles, six homers, and 36 RBI in 76 games in mid-July and had been dropped to eighth in the batting order by manager Joe Cronin. Slow starts with the bat were not uncommon to the Southern Californian and would plague him throughout his career with the Red Sox.

**BOBBY DOERR**
Years with Red Sox: 1937-51
Other Major League Teams: None
Position: Second Base
Bats: Right
Throws: Right
Height: 5-11
Weight: 175
Born: April 7, 1918
Birthplace: Los Angeles, CA
Current Residence: Agness, OR
Current Occupation: Retired

"I didn't play real well in cold weather," Doerr said. "When the weather got warm, I'd loosen up."

Cold weather never affected Doerr's glove, however, and defense was the biggest difference between the American League's two premier slugging second basemen. Gordon had led AL second basemen in errors with 28 in 1942 while Doerr led the league in fielding percentage. At midseason in

1943 Doerr was doing the best fielding of his career to that point, having made only two errors in 434 chances all year. He had recently broken the major-league record for consecutive errorless chances by a second baseman, erasing the old standard set by Oscar Melillo of the St. Louis Browns in 1933, and his streak was up to 307 at the All-Star break. Doerr's last miscue had occurred on May 20, nearly two months before.

The Red Sox finished the first half of the 1943 season on a down note in St. Louis, leaving them in seventh place, eight and a half games behind the two-time defending AL champion Yankees. Doerr had stolen home in the 10th inning to climax a three-run rally that helped the Red Sox to a 6-3 win in the Saturday game at Sportsman's Park, and a sweep of the Browns in a doubleheader on Sunday would get them to the .500 mark at the break. But the Browns won both games on Sunday, July 11. Doerr had gone 0-for-6 in the 8-7, 12-inning loss in the first game. He had accounted for both Sox runs with a two-run homer in the nightcap, a 4-2 setback, but was frustrated with his lack of clutch hitting.

"I've been pretty terrible this season," Doerr told the Boston press. "We would have won every game [in St. Louis] if I'd hit in the pinches."

"I remember I was fussy about being so lousy," Doerr recalled more than 60 years later. "I had been in a heckuva slump for a few weeks. You get in those ruts two or three times a year when you can't seem to do anything about it. And when you didn't produce back then, there was always somebody ready to take your place. You were always looking over your shoulder."

While the other Red Sox players took off for the welcome break, Doerr and pitchers Tex Hughson and Oscar Judd took a train to Philadelphia for the 11th All-Star Game. For the first time, the game would be broadcast live on shortwave radio around the world to entertain the troops. In a letter to baseball commissioner Kenesaw Mountain Landis dated January 15, 1942, President Franklin Roosevelt had urged that the major leagues not shut down for the duration of the war, declaring: "I honestly feel that it would be best for the country to keep baseball going." Roosevelt had also suggested that more night games be scheduled so that Americans toiling in the war industries would be able to attend games after their shifts. So, for the first time, the All-Star Game would be played at night. The 9 p.m. start meant that soldiers in Europe would be crowded around radios in the predawn hours to hear the game, but war did not operate on a nine-to-five timetable anyway. "American boys may be taking off for [the invasion of] Sicily with the description of the All-Star game still ringing in their ears," reported *The Boston Globe*.

There would be six Yankees, including Gordon, on the AL All-Star team. But Joe McCarthy, who would be managing the All-Stars for the sixth time, was overly sensitive to criticism that he had always favored his own players over the stars from the rest of the league. So McCarthy vowed to keep all the Yankees on the bench. It would be the only All-Star Game ever played to date in which no Yankee appeared. Bobby Doerr would get the start at second base ahead of the reigning AL MVP.

"It was strange that he didn't let any of the Yankees play," Doerr said. "But Joe McCarthy was like that. He had kind of an ego, and not too many people criticized him. He was probably thinking: 'I'll show 'em I can win without Yankee players.' I think he was still that way in '48 when he didn't pitch [Mel] Parnell [in the Red Sox' one-game playoff with Cleveland for the pennant]. He wanted to prove he could win without Parnell."

Doerr would go on to play in six more All-Star Games after 1943. But this one, played at Shibe Park, the home of the Philadelphia Athletics, in front of a crowd of 31,938 on the night of July 13, would provide the most memorable moment of his Hall of Fame career.

+++

The National Leaguers struck quickly in the top of the first inning against knuckleballer Dutch Leonard of the Washington Senators. Stan Hack of the Chicago Cubs lined the first pitch of the game up the middle for a single and moments later was perched on third, courtesy of a hit-and-run single delivered by Brooklyn's Billy Herman. A flyball by the St. Louis Cardinals' Stan Musial brought home Hack with the first run of the game.

Mort Cooper of the defending World Champion Cardinals, well on his way to his second straight 20-win season, started for the NL All-Stars, pitching to his St. Louis teammate and brother, Walker. Mort Cooper breezed through the first inning, allowing one baserunner.

But the Cardinals righthander ran into trouble in the second with one out, walking Browns outfielder Chet Laabs and Washington catcher Jake Early. That brought Doerr, batting eighth in the lineup, to the plate.

"I didn't know anything about him," Doerr said of Cooper. He took the first pitch for a strike. Walker Cooper then signaled for a curveball, and his brother tried to comply.

"Mort Cooper threw me a high, hanging curveball," Doerr remembered. "It was one of those pitches that Boo Ferriss used to say that, as a pitcher, you wanted to run out and get it back before it got to the hitter."

"His next delivery Doerr met with that characteristic wrist snap of his," wrote Harold Kaese in *The Boston Globe,* "and lined the ball into the lower deck in left, not much above the screen."

A three-run homer, and the AL All-Stars suddenly led 3-1.

"It was hit pretty good, and it felt good when I hit it," Doerr remembered. "Hitting a home run in that game was quite a thrill … a split-second thrill."

Bobby Doerr would hit 223 home runs for the Red Sox, currently ranking him sixth on the club's all-time list behind Williams (521), Carl Yastrzemski (452), Jim Rice (382), Dwight Evans (379), and Mo Vaughn (230). He would hit a homer in the 1946 World Series and a homer in the 1948 playoff game. But in 13 more All-Star Game at-bats over the next nine years, he would never hit another homer.

"I guess that's the biggest thrill I've got out of baseball," Doerr told the press later that night.

More than 60 years later he still feels the same way about that split second in Philadelphia, an electrifying moment shared with tens of thousands of homesick GIs fighting a war thousands of miles away from Philadelphia.

"Chesterfield sent cases of cigarettes overseas to the soldiers with a label on them commemorating Bobby Doerr's home run," Doerr recalled. "I got a few cartons of them and still have them."

The American Leaguers padded their lead in the next two innings. Doubles by Cleveland's Ken Keltner and Detroit's rookie sensation, Dick Wakefield, made it 4-1 in the fourth. Cincinnati's Johnny Vander Meer, who five years earlier had become the only pitcher in major-league history to throw consecutive no-hitters, was quickly touched for an unearned run in the fifth. But Vander Meer would finish the inning with a flourish, striking out Detroit's Rudy York, Laabs, and Early in succession.

Vander Meer would record six of his eight outs on strikeouts.

"Vander Meer was the fellow who really had the stuff tonight," Doerr said afterward.

While Mort Cooper had been a new challenge, Doerr was familiar with Vander Meer, and when he faced him to start the bottom of the sixth and ran the count full, the Red Sox star lashed a single to left for his second hit of the game.

"We played the Reds a lot in spring training," Doerr recalled. "Vander Meer had a good fastball, but I knew he had a tendency to throw a curveball a lot on 3-and-2. And that's what I hit. Seldom did I guess as a hitter; but on that one I guessed and hit a line drive past third base."

Wakefield would be the only other member of the AL squad to get two hits in the game. Pittsburgh's Vince DiMaggio, the elder brother of the Yankees' Joe and the Red Sox' Dominic—both of whom were by now already in the service—was the hitting star for the Nationals. He ripped three hits and missed hitting for the cycle by a double. DiMaggio tripled and scored off Boston's Hughson in the seventh, then socked a homer off Hughson in the ninth. But the Americans were already well ahead 5-1 by then and won 5-3, their third straight win and eighth victory in the 11 All-Star Games. Doerr, as expected, was flawless in the field, getting three putouts and being credited with three assists on a busy evening.

Ten days after the All-Star Game, Doerr's errorless streak ended at 59 games and 349 chances. In 1946 he set an AL record by handling 28 chances in successive games, and in 1948 he would break his own record by playing 72 consecutive games without an error, handling 414 chances in that streak. On September 25, 1949, the Red Sox turned eight double plays in a doubleheader against the Yankees in the heat of a late-season pennant race. Taken out by a hard slide after turning one of them, Doerr was lying on the ground in pain when he saw Red Sox catcher Birdie Tebbetts standing over him, "C'mon Bobby, get up," Tebbetts urged him. "You don't want all these people in the stands to think you're a Yankee, do you?" Doerr got up and finished the game.

Two weeks after swatting his All-Star homer, Doerr's bat heated up. He launched a career-best 21-game hitting streak and finished the 1943 season at .270 with 32 doubles, 16 homers, and 75 RBI. He hit a career-high .325 in 1944, finishing a mere two points behind Cleveland's Lou Boudreau for the batting title. Doerr did lead the league in slugging percentage with a .528 mark and was named AL Player of the Year by *The Sporting News* but also finished the campaign in a different uniform when he was drafted into the Army in early September.

Doerr returned to the Red Sox in 1946 and drove in 116 runs to help them win 104 games and the AL pennant. He hit .409 in the World Series against the Cardinals.

On June 8, 1950, Bobby Doerr had his most spectacular game in the majors, belting three homers and a single, driving in eight runs, and scoring four times in a 29-4 rout of the St. Louis Browns.

"That was just one of those games when everything you did was right, every time up you'd hit something," he remembered. "But it was one of those games when everyone was hot, and the St. Louis pitchers just couldn't get anybody out. It was such a runaway game."

**Hall of Famer Bobby Doerr, one of the greatest offensive and defensive second basemen in Major League history, attends a fundraiser on behalf of the Ted Williams Museum.**
*(Courtesy of Chaz Scoggins)*

Doerr finished that year with a career-best 120 RBI. It was Doerr's third straight 100-RBI season and sixth of his career, but it would be the last 100-RBI season by a major-league second baseman until Cincinnati's Joe Morgan performed the feat a quarter-century later in 1975. Doerr is the only player in Red Sox history to hit for the cycle twice, and he twice ruined no-hitters by Bob Feller by getting the only hit in each game, one in 1938 and the other in 1946. He also hit two grand slams off Feller.

"I'll bet if you checked my average against Feller, it was probably .150," Doerr chuckled. "I was surprised when someone from *Baseball Magazine* once told me that Joe DiMaggio hit 11 homers off Feller, Ted Williams 10, and I hit nine. I didn't know that. But when I first came up, I remember talking to Cronin behind second base one day, and he told me to cut the plate in half against Feller. Give him the outside half; he was so fast you couldn't cover the whole plate, and you couldn't do much with the outside pitch anyway. So I always looked inside, and that's how I hit him. I remember the second no-hitter I broke up, he had outstanding stuff that day, and I broke my bat and hit a little blooper over second base around the sixth inning. It was a shame to lose a no-hitter on a hit like that."

Chronic back problems limited Doerr to 106 games in 1951, and he retired after that season at the age of 33, having batted .288 with 2,042 hits, 223 homers, and 1,247 RBI in 1,865 games for the Red Sox.

"Bobby Doerr is one of the very few who played this game hard and came out of it with no enemies," praised longtime Yankee rival Tommy Henrich.

Doerr retired to Oregon and owned a cattle ranch for a few years before returning to baseball with the Red Sox in 1957, coaching minor-leaguers. He served as the major-league hitting coach from 1967-69, then retired again to Oregon to work as a fishing guide on the Rogue River. The expansion Toronto Blue Jays lured him out of retirement one last time in 1977, and he was their hitting coach until retiring for good in 1981. He and his wife, Monica, had one son. Monica Doerr, who had battled multiple sclerosis since 1947, died in 2003.

Bobby Doerr was elected to the Hall of Fame in 1986, and the Red Sox retired his uniform No. 1 two years later.

"That is the ultimate achievement of a baseball life," Doerr said of his enshrinement in Cooperstown, "that and having my number retired by the Red Sox in 1988. If I had played on a World Champion, that would have made my life complete."

# Chapter 2

# JOHNNY PESKY

## APRIL 20, 1946

Times in America were tough as the year 1941 drew to a close, but at least times were peaceful. The nation was still trying to extract itself from the grip of the Great Depression, but otherwise it was life and business—and, of course, baseball—as usual for most Americans, unlike life in Europe and Asia, where separate major wars were raging.

The politics of the United States were isolationist, and providing war materials to the Allies under Lend-Lease was about as deeply involved as most Americans wanted to get.

Yet, if one chose to look closely, there were unmistakable signs that the government was preparing for the inevitable. The military draft had been revived in 1940, and a few major-league ballplayers had been called to serve, the most prominent of whom was Detroit Tigers slugger Hank Greenberg, who was inducted into the Army in the spring of 1941. Greenberg, who was less than a month away from his 31st birthday, received an early discharge when Congress decided to release conscripts over the age of 27. The date was December 5, 1941.

Two days later the Japanese bombed Pearl Harbor, and overnight the United States was smack in the middle of the two wars. Greenberg turned right around and re-enlisted in the Army Air Corps, and on January 6, 1942, 23-year-old Bob Feller, the ace of the Cleveland Indians, enlisted in the Navy. The Red Sox quickly lost three players to the draft, pitchers Mickey Harris and Earl Johnson and catcher Frankie Pytlak. It took some time for America's war machine to gear up, however, and as it did, more and more major-league players knew that the day was coming when they'd get that letter with the salutation: "Greetings from the President." Some enlisted right away. Others decided to keep playing while waiting for their draft notices to show up in their mailboxes.

Ted Williams, at the peak of his career and coming off a .406 season the previous summer, knew he would be among the first players to be drafted in 1942 after he was suddenly reclassified from 3-A to 1-A. He successfully appealed the reclassification, arguing that he was the sole support of his divorced mother. But public opinion, isolationist only weeks before and now hot with war fever, turned against the Red Sox superstar. Ever the maverick, Williams ignored the club's advice to enlist and chose to play in 1942. The public howled. Quaker Oats canceled a $4,000 endorsement contract with Williams. Finally, in June, Williams caved in and enlisted in the Navy to be a fighter pilot. He would begin his service training after the baseball season. Williams played out the season and won the Triple Crown, hitting .356 with 36 home runs and 137 runs batted in, then shed his Red Sox uniform and donned the uniform of a naval cadet. When he reported to Amherst College in Massachusetts near the end of 1942 to start ground school, Johnny Pesky, the rookie Red Sox shortstop who had just completed an extraordinary season himself, was right there with him in the same class.

Everyone was wishful that America's entry into World War II would help bring the conflict to a swift and successful conclusion. But no one could predict how long it would last. At the time Pearl Harbor was attacked, the war in Asia had been going on for nine years already, and the war in Europe had been raging for more than two years. As major-league ballplayers began joining the ranks of the military, none of them could be certain that he'd ever play professional baseball again. Even if they weren't killed or maimed in combat, the war might drag on for such a long time that by the time it ended they would all be too old to resume their baseball careers.

Many ballplayers indeed saw combat, but no major-leaguers were killed, and very few were seriously wounded. When the war ended in 1945, all most of them had lost were a few precious years of their baseball careers. Some of the older players worried that their baseball skills had deteriorated while they were in the service, but they were a euphoric bunch who reported to spring training—some of them for the first time in five years— in 1946. They were alive, they were whole, and they were playing baseball. The world was perfect again.

**Boston Red Sox shortstop Johnny Pesky (right) shares the top step of the dugout with Ted Williams before a game at Fenway Park.**
*(Courtesy of the Boston Red Sox)*

Johnny Pesky, playing professional baseball again after three years, was among the celebrants. Playing for the Red Sox in their home opener that year, and becoming a baseball hero instead of a military hero on that April afternoon, would be the most memorable game of a distinguished career.

✦ ✦ ✦

John Michael Paveskovich, the fifth of six children born to Croatian immigrants, was born in Portland, Oregon, on September 27, 1919. His father, Jakov, worked in a sawmill while his mother, Marija, reared the family. When his three older sisters, Anica, Millica, and Danica, and his older brother Anthony, were all old enough to work, they got jobs to supplement the family income. The family was well off enough that even when asthma forced Jakov into an early retirement, John and his younger brother Vincent were permitted to pursue their interest in the strange sport of baseball. Vince would later sign with the New York Yankees and play briefly in the minors.

The ballpark where the Portland Beavers of the minor Pacific Coast League played was only a few blocks away from where the Paveskovich family lived, and teenaged John was hanging around the park so often he was given a job in the visitors' clubhouse. Among the visiting players for whom he shined shoes and ran errands were his future Red Sox teammates, Ted Williams and Bobby Doerr.

Johnny Paveskovich still found plenty of time to hone his own baseball skills and forge his reputation on the Oregon diamonds. He played American Legion ball and for a couple of semipro teams that were sponsored by timber companies. One of them, the Silverton Red Sox, was owned by Thomas A. Yawkey, whose family had made its fortune in lumber.

After he starred for the Silverton Red Sox in 1938 and 1939, the St. Louis Cardinals and Boston Red Sox both sought to sign the 19-year-old Paveskovich. The Cardinals offered far more money, a $2,500 bonus. But the Paveskovich family liked and trusted Red Sox scout Earl Johnson, and even though the Boston team was only offering a $500 bonus, it was an easy decision to sign with the Red Sox. The Red Sox also promised Johnny Paveskovich an additional $1,000 bonus if he played two years in the organization; the Red Sox paid it after just one year.

Paveskovich—his name was shortened to Pesky so it would fit neatly into the box scores—began his minor-league career in 1940 with Rocky Mount in the Class B Piedmont League. Earning $150 a month, he led the league in hits with 187 and in triples with 16 while finishing third in the batting race with a .325 average. Pesky scored 114 runs and made the All-Star Team.

The Red Sox promoted him to Louisville in the Class AA American Association in 1941, and Pesky again hit .325, led the league in hits with 195, and was named its Most Valuable Player.

Red Sox player-manager Joe Cronin, a future Hall of Famer, had hit .311 with 38 doubles, 16 homers, and 95 RBI in 1941. But at the age of 35 he was ready to relinquish his job as the everyday shortstop, and he chose 22-year-old Johnny Pesky as his successor. The 5-9, 168-pound, lefthanded-hitting shortstop turned in a brilliant rookie season. Pesky led the American League in hits with 205 in 147 games while batting .331 and finishing second to Williams in the batting race. Pesky swatted 29 doubles and nine triples, stole 12 bases, and scored 105 runs. He finished third in the MVP voting behind the Yankees' Joe Gordon—the surprise winner— and Williams, who won the Triple Crown. Had there been a Rookie of the Year award in those days, Pesky would have won it in a landslide. *The Sporting News,* then acknowledged as baseball's bible, named him the shortstop on their postseason Major League All-Star Team. Yawkey was so pleased with the performance of his 23-year-old shortstop, who had played for a $4,000 salary, that he gave Pesky a $5,000 bonus at the end of the season. Pesky used the extra money to buy a house for his parents in Portland.

Although Johnny Pesky was the newest Red Sox star in a lineup of stars that included Bobby Doerr, Dominic DiMaggio, and a part-time Joe Cronin, they all knew and accepted there was only one supernova on the team, and the offense revolved around Ted Williams. Their mantra was to get on base, by any means possible, so Williams could drive them in.

"I never paid much attention to my own statistics," Pesky said. "Every day I just tried to get on base for Ted. Sometimes I'd take pitches I knew I could hit, sometimes even a cookie right down the middle of the plate. I always hit with a strike on me, and I got my share of walks."

Pesky and DiMaggio, both of whom were fast, often bunted for basehits. "We'd even bunt with two outs," Pesky said. "The other teams didn't like it much. The reason was we didn't want Williams leading off because then they could pitch around him. They sure as heck weren't going to pitch around me to get to Ted."

Williams, who rarely beat out an infield hit, admired the speed of DiMaggio and Pesky. In 1957, when he hit .388 at the age of 39, Williams did not have a single infield hit. Had he been able to leg out just five groundballs that year—less than one a month—he would have hit .400 again.

"I could run in those years," Pesky chuckled. "Williams used to kid me: 'If I could run like you, I'd hit .400 every year.' And I'd say: 'If I could hit like you, I'd hit .500!'"

The war put Pesky's baseball career on hold after just one season in Boston. He took Navy flight training with Williams but washed out.

"Flying came easy for me," Williams wrote in his autobiography, *My Turn at Bat*. Williams would fly fighters for the Marines in two wars and nearly lose his life crash-landing his shot-up Panther jet in Korea in 1953. "But poor Pesky. He was a great little athlete. A boxer, wrestler, basketball player, he could run like hell and he was a tiger on the obstacle courses. But he couldn't swim a stroke, he'd go right down, and he flew an airplane like he had stone arms."

The Navy sent Pesky to Officers Candidate School, and after graduation he served as an operations officer. While in the Navy he met his future wife, Ruth Hickey, a WAVE who had grown up just outside of Boston.

World War II ended in August of 1945, the soldiers and sailors began coming home, and Johnny Pesky, now 26 years old, reunited with his Red Sox teammates in Sarasota, Florida, at spring training in 1946.

"When we got to spring training that year, we were just all so happy to get there," he remembered. "The guys were all gung-ho. I got to play a little ball in the service, but not that much. So we all took a lot of extra hitting."

The Red Sox had not won a pennant since 1918. They had talented and exciting teams from 1938-42 but could do no better than finish second to the mighty New York Yankees four times in that five-year stretch and never closer than nine games. There was little reason to believe they wouldn't be talented also-rans in 1946. The Yankees were the automatic favorites, and the Detroit Tigers, who had won the pennant in

---

**JOHNNY PESKY**

**Years with Red Sox:** 1942-52
**Other Major League Teams:** Detroit, Washington
**Position:** Shortstop
**Bats:** Left
**Throws:** Right
**Height:** 5-9
**Weight:** 168
**Born:** September 27, 1919
**Birthplace:** Portland, OR
**Current Residence:** Swampscott, MA
**Current Occupation:** Red Sox consultant and special assignment instructor

1940 and the World Series in 1945 with a war-time lineup, were also expected to contend.

But the Red Sox left the entire league in their dust, forging a 15-game winning streak in the early days of the season, winning 41 of their first 50 games, and finishing the year with 104 victories, the second-most in club history.

Johnny Pesky's bat was never livelier than it was during that early-season surge.

The Red Sox opened the 1946 season on the road in Washington and swept the three-game series from the Senators. A festive crowd of 30,466 was on hand at Fenway Park for the home opener against the Philadelphia Athletics on April 20, and Pesky stole the show. It would be the most memorable game of his Red Sox career.

✦ ✦ ✦

Dick Fowler, a big 6-5, 215-pound righthander just back from the war, started for the Athletics that afternoon and struck out Dominic DiMaggio when the Red Sox came to bat in the bottom of the first. Pesky and Williams drew walks, and Bobby Doerr rapped a sharp grounder to shortstop Jack Wallaesa. *Boston Globe* sportswriter Gerry Moore described what happened next:

"The A's tried for an orthodox double play, and while they were just missing, Pesky scored all the way from second, barely beating [first baseman] George McQuinn's ultimate throw to [catcher Buddy] Rosar with a great, teeth-rattling slide."

"I had a good jump at second," Pesky remembered. "I don't know how hard the ball was hit, but they didn't make the double play. Maybe the first baseman had to stretch for the ball. I don't know; I didn't see it because I was running. It was a gamble, and it was a close play. Early in the game you could do those things. With two outs you can be reckless sometimes, and I could run in those years."

It was the second time in four games the aggressive Red Sox had successfully pulled off the stunt. DiMaggio had done it in Washington.

For seven innings, it was the only run the Red Sox would score. In fact, they couldn't even manage a hit off Fowler until the sixth.

Righthander Tex Hughson, also back in a Red Sox uniform after spending 1945 in the military, started for the Red Sox and was shaky, giving up six hits in the first three innings. But the Athletics couldn't push across a run against the stubborn Hughson until the third. Hal Peck singled, and Wallaesa pounded a double off the right-field fence. Peck scored when Sam Chapman grounded out, tying the game at 1-1.

Hughson then found a groove and did not give up another hit until the eighth inning. Fowler, meanwhile, took a no-hitter into the sixth. McQuinn kept it intact by reaching into the hole to rob Pesky of a hit leading off the inning. Rudy York finally broke Fowler's hex on the Red Sox with a two-out single. But it would be the only hit they would get until the eighth.

Hughson, who had been cruising for four innings, ran into trouble again in the top of the eighth. Wallaesa and McQuinn stroked singles, putting Philadelphia runners at first and third with one out. After McQuinn stole second, Red Sox manager Joe Cronin ordered Hughson to intentionally walk Rosar, loading the bases but setting up a potential inning-ending double play. The batter was a 23-year-old George Kell, who was in his third year with the Athletics and about to embark on a string of seven consecutive .300 seasons (that included edging out Ted Williams for the batting title in 1949 by .0001, .3429 to .3428, the closest race in major-league history at the time). Kell would go on to hit .306 in 14 seasons and be inducted into the Hall of Fame. But this early into the 1946 season, Kell had not yet established his credentials as a fine major-league hitter, and Cronin had no reservations about pitching to the kid with the bases loaded in the late innings of a 1-1 game.

Cronin and Hughson got the double play they wanted, but not exactly the way they envisioned it.

"George Kell was with the A's at the time," Pesky remembered, "and they had the bases full with one out. There was a ball hit toward second base, and Bobby [Doerr] went to field the ball. He was about five feet away from the base when the ball caromed off him right to me! I had contact with the bag, and I threw on to first for the double play."

The stalemate preserved, the Red Sox came to bat in the bottom of the eighth against Fowler, who was still working on a one-hitter. Fowler fanned DiMaggio for the second time in the game, and the large crowd became more impatient, wondering if the Red Sox would ever score again.

Pesky, heeding the mantra to get on base any way possible in front of Williams, tried to bunt his way on and fouled off the first two pitches. He then took a ball. Pesky, who had hit only two homers in 620 at-bats during his rookie season four years earlier, swung at the next pitch and poked it into the right-field stands, just beyond the foul pole located a mere 302 feet from home plate.

"When you hit as few homers as I did—I hit 17 in 13 years—I probably remember all of them," Pesky said. "Fowler hung me a slow curveball, and I hit it about 10 feet fair down the right-field line, into the second row. I thought the rightfielder, Peck, would break his arm trying to reach for it."

The Red Sox led 2-1 on a home run from a most unexpected source. Pesky now had three career homers in the majors, one in St. Louis and the other two curled around the right-field foul pole in Fenway Park. Pesky would wrap a few more homers around that foul pole during his seven-plus years with the Red Sox, and over time it became popularly known as the "Pesky Pole."

York's sixth-inning single and Pesky's eighth-inning homer were the only hits the Red Sox managed off Dick Fowler that afternoon, and Pesky scored both their runs, one using his speed and the other using his minimal power. But the Red Sox held on to beat the Athletics 2-1.

"Hitting that home run and making that double play are a couple of the fondest memories I have," Pesky reminisced.

✛✛✛

A few days later the Red Sox launched their 15-game winning streak, and Johnny Pesky was on one of the best personal streaks of his career.

Pesky was playing through an injury, a strained groin muscle, in early May. That didn't prevent him from racing home from first base to score on a Williams double in the seventh inning of a 9-4 victory over the Cleveland Indians on May 3 at Fenway, the eighth straight triumph for the Red Sox. Pesky had hits in each of his last three at-bats in that game.

Fireballing Bob Feller, who had just hurled his second career no-hitter in his previous start against the Yankees on April 30, was scheduled to pitch for Cleveland the next afternoon. Pesky had never hit Feller particularly well—who did?—and Cronin thought it might be a good time to give his shortstop a day off. Pesky declined, telling Hy Hurwitz of *The Boston Globe* that if he didn't play it would look like he was ducking Feller.

"Cronin told me to take the day off. I said: 'Joe, I'm all right. Please let me play. I've been reading about this guy, and I want to see if he's that good,'" a chuckling Pesky related almost 60 years later. "In those days the pitchers warmed up in front of the dugouts. I looked across the field, watching Feller warm up, and it looked like peas going into the catcher's mitt. I said to Bob (Doerr): 'Maybe I should have taken the day off.' Luckily, I got a couple hits off him that day."

Pesky got more than a couple hits off Feller. He went 4-for-4, running his string of consecutive hits to seven. Pesky ripped a two-run single in the second inning, singled and scored the run that put the Red Sox ahead 3-2 in the fourth, and singled and rode home on a Williams homer in the sixth. The Red Sox won 6-2.

A doubleheader with the St. Louis Browns was rained out the next day and rescheduled for the following afternoon, May 6. Pesky singled in each of his first four at-bats in the first game, giving him 11 consecutive hits, one shy of the major-league record held by teammate Pinky Higgins, who had 12 straight hits for the Red Sox in 1938. When Pesky came to bat again in the eighth inning with a chance to tie the record, the Red Sox were leading 6-3 and George "Catfish" Metkovich was aboard on a single. Cronin trusted Pesky and Dominic DiMaggio, the savvy hitters at the top of his batting order, to do the right things without him needing to give signs. Pesky, concerned that the three-run lead might not be large enough, elected to put on a hit-and-run play. Metkovich dutifully took off for second, but the pitch from Browns lefthander Al Milnar was not a good one for Pesky to handle; the best he could do with it was tap the ball to shortstop Vern Stephens, who threw Pesky out at first base. The streak was over. But Metkovich scored moments later, and the run proved to be important as the Red Sox withstood a St. Louis rally in the ninth and won 7-5, extending their winning streak to ten games.

Pesky collected hits in each of his first two at-bats in the second game of the doubleheader, a 5-4 Red Sox victory. If he hadn't given himself up to advance Metkovich in the first game, he might well have set a major-league record with 14 consecutive hits. But extending the streak never entered Johnny Pesky's mind because he wasn't even aware he was on such a streak.

"No, I didn't know. I didn't look at the box scores in those years," Pesky recalled. "I never paid much attention to those things. Every day I just tried to get on base for Ted."

Two days later, on May 8, Pesky became just the second player in modern major-league history to score six runs in a game when the Red Sox outslugged Chicago 14-10 at Fenway. Pesky went 4-for-5 in Boston's 13th consecutive victory while duplicating the feat accomplished twice previously in the National League by Mel Ott of the New York Giants in 1934 and 1944. Pesky's record-tying sixth run almost didn't count. Doerr belted a ball off The Wall with two outs that pitcher Mickey Harris, who was on base in front of Pesky, presumed would be an automatic double. But Doerr was thrown out at second for the final out of the inning while Harris, with Pesky running up his back, was sauntering around the bases. Wrote

Johnny Pesky, who has been involved in professional baseball for nearly 70 years, most of them with the Boston Red Sox, takes a few moments to relax outside the clubhouse following Red Sox batting practice. *(Courtesy of Chaz Scoggins)*

*The Globe's* Hurwitz: Harris "waltzed home and came mighty close to preventing Pesky from scoring his sixth run." Pesky touched the plate an instant before Doerr was tagged out.

Pesky's four hits that afternoon gave him the lead in the batting race with a .429 average. Williams was second at .427, and DiMaggio was hitting .403. Pesky played in the All-Star Game for the only time in his career that summer and finished the 1946 season with a .335 average while again leading the league in hits with 208. Pesky finished second to Williams in runs with 115 and third in batting and in doubles with 43.

He was unfairly singled out as the goat of the World Series when, as the cutoff man, he allegedly held onto centerfielder Leon Culberson's relay too long while Enos Slaughter dashed around the bases to score the run that gave the St. Louis Cardinals the World Championship. Even when he returned home to Oregon after the season, Pesky couldn't escape the notoriety that he had cost the Red Sox the World Series. While attending a sloppily played football game between intrastate rivals Oregon and Oregon State that was marred by fumbles, Pesky overheard one exasperated fan shout: "Give the ball to Pesky! He'll hold onto it!"

Very few fans back then had access to film of the controversial play, and the film clearly shows that Pesky did not linger with the ball for more than a fraction of a second, and even had he gotten rid of it immediately and made an accurate throw to the plate, it wouldn't have mattered. Slaughter would have scored easily. His dramatic but wholly unnecessary slide made the play look far closer than it really was.

But Johnny Pesky shouldered the blame and never complained. Over the decades Red Sox fans forgave him for the transgression he never committed, and his popularity soared to the point where, nearly 60 years later, he is regarded and revered as Mr. Red Sox.

In 1947 Johnny Paveskovich legally changed his name to Pesky, and he put together a 26-game hitting streak that season while again leading the league in hits with 207, batting .324, and scoring 106 runs. Although his batting average fell off to .281 in 1948, Pesky began walking more and scored a career-high 124 runs. He had 100 or more walks in 1949 and 1950 while batting over .300 both years and scoring more than 100 runs. He posted a .437 on-base percentage in 1950. But the Red Sox couldn't win another pennant.

"I had a lot of fun in those years," he remembered. "I thought we would win two or three more pennants, but we never did. Something always seemed to happen."

Pesky hit .313 in 1951, but his production began to slip. Then, 25 games into the 1952 season, the Red Sox traded the 32-year-old Pesky to the Detroit Tigers in a nine-player deal.

"The day I got traded was the saddest day of my life," he said. "But I still continued to follow the team in the box scores."

Pesky wasn't close to being the same player he was in Boston. The Tigers dealt him to the Washington Senators in 1954, and Pesky retired after that season, a lifetime .307 hitter in 10 major-league seasons.

Pesky stayed in baseball, managing in the minor leagues before returning to Boston to manage the Red Sox in 1963. But he found himself constantly at odds with general manager Mike Higgins, his former Red Sox teammate, and he was fired after two losing seasons. Pesky went to work for the Pittsburgh Pirates but returned to the Red Sox to stay in 1969, serving the club in a wide variety of roles. He has been a broadcaster, a coach, an instructor, and an assistant to the general manager. He currently works as a special assignment instructor.

In 2005 Ruth Pesky, his wife of 60 years, passed away. They had a son, David.

Pesky's .313 batting average ranks ninth on the all-time Red Sox list, and his .401 on-base percentage is seventh. He is also ninth in runs scored. Johnny Pesky was one of the charter members of the Red Sox Hall of Fame when he was inducted in 1995.

# Chapter 3

# DOMINIC DiMAGGIO

## OCTOBER 15, 1946

L ate on a mid-October afternoon in St. Louis in 1946, in a span of less than 10 seconds—the amount of time it takes to run from home plate to second base—the elation Dominic DiMaggio had felt leaving the batter's box would dissolve into lifelong frustration.

"The best day of my life," he declared nearly 60 years later, "was also the worst day of my life."

✦✦✦

Dominic Paul DiMaggio, the youngest of nine children of a commercial fisherman, was born in San Francisco on February 12, 1917. Three of the five sons of Sicilian immigrants Giuseppe and Rosalie DiMaggio were destined to become All-Star outfielders in the major leagues. Vince, the eldest of the trio, had been born in 1912. A strikeout-prone hitter in an era when batters still took pride in making contact, Vince nevertheless played 10 years in the majors for five teams from 1937-46 and made the National League All-Star team twice. A .249 lifetime hitter with 125 homers and 584 RBI in 1,110 games, Vince's best season was 1941, when he hit 21 homers and drove in 100 runs for the Pittsburgh Pirates.

Vince's performance that year, however, was eclipsed by that of Joe, the middle of the three ballplaying brothers. Joe DiMaggio, born in 1914, set one of baseball's most cherished records that summer when he hit safely in

56 consecutive games for the New York Yankees and was named the American League's Most Valuable Player. A two-time batting champion and universally acknowledged as one of the greatest and most graceful players in the history of the game, Joe DiMaggio, the "Yankee Clipper," would be an All-Star in each of his 13 major-league seasons from 1936-51. Joe was a .325 hitter over the course of his career with 361 homers and 1,537 RBI in 1,736 games and was elected to the Hall of Fame in his first year of eligibility in 1955.

At 5-9 and 168 pounds, Dom DiMaggio was considerably smaller than either of his older brothers. He also wore glasses, unusual for players at that time, which was part of the reason he was dubbed "The Little Professor." A highly intelligent and articulate athlete, his vocabulary and manner of speech enhanced that nickname. An anecdote from Jim Prime and Bill Nowlin's book, *Tales from the Red Sox Dugout,* captures DiMaggio's character perfectly:

"[An] umpire once called him out on some very borderline strikes. As always, DiMaggio kept his composure and didn't turn around to confront the man in blue. When he got back to the dugout, he rested for a moment with his knee on the top step, then removed his glasses and began methodically wiping them off. He gazed steadily out at the umpire and said in a calm, almost meditative voice: 'I have never witnessed such incompetence in all my life.' Manager Joe McCarthy, accustomed to slightly saltier language from his ballplayers, fell off the bench laughing."

Dominic DiMaggio was not blessed with the raw power his brothers possessed, but otherwise there was nothing small about his skills and prowess on the diamond. Dom would play just over 10 years in the majors, all of them for the Red Sox from 1940-53, and hit .298 with a club-record 34-game hitting streak in 1949. Although he would reach double figures in homers just twice, with a high of 14 in 1942, he would sock 30-plus doubles seven times and collect 50 or more extra-base hits in four seasons. With his keen batting eye, Dom would draw far more walks than either of his brothers and would boast an on-base percentage over .400 in eight of his 10 full seasons. In an era when the stolen base had virtually disappeared as an offensive weapon, he would steal 100 bases during his career and lead the AL, albeit with a modest 15, in 1950. Six times he would score more than 100 runs, leading the league with 131 in 1950 and again with 113 in 1951. A centerfielder like his celebrated brother Joe, Dom was on a par defensively with the "Yankee Clipper," both in his ability to catch the ball and throw it. Seven times Dominic DiMaggio would be a member of the

All-Star team, no small feat considering Joe and Dom played the same position in the same league for nine years.

"Dom could do it all," Ted Williams said in *Tales from the Red Sox Dugout*. "He ran the bases like a gazelle, played a flawless center field, and possessed a rifle arm."

The Red Sox spent somewhere between $75,000 and $100,000 to purchase the righthanded-hitting DiMaggio's contract, along with that of pitcher Larry Powell (who never pitched in the majors), after the 1939 season. DiMaggio had played three years with his hometown San Francisco Seals in the Pacific Coast League and been named the league's Most Valuable Player in 1939 after hitting .360 and leading the circuit in hits with 239 and runs with 165.

An early-season ankle injury and several other bumps and bruises limited the 23-year-old DiMaggio to 108 games as a rookie for the Red Sox in 1940, but he hit .301. In 1941 he fashioned a 22-game hitting streak and scored 117 runs. Shortstop Johnny Pesky joined the club in 1942, and now the Red Sox had a formidable top of the order with DiMaggio leading off, Pesky batting second, and the incomparable Williams hitting third. Williams won the Triple Crown that year, hitting .356 with 36 homers and 137 RBI. DiMaggio scored 110 runs and finished third in the league behind Williams and brother Joe, and he also amassed 272 total bases to finish fourth behind Williams, Joe, and New York's Charlie Keller.

World War II broke up the Red Sox and every other club for the next three years, and Dominic DiMaggio spent his military service in the Coast Guard. When the Red Sox were reunited in 1946, they dominated the league, leading it in hitting, slugging, and runs scored. A 15-game winning streak helped the Red Sox get off to a 21-3 start, and they won 41 of their first 50 games that year. When it was over they were 104-50 and hoisted their first pennant since 1918. They had beaten out the second-place Detroit Tigers by 12 games and left the Yankees in their dust, 17 games behind. Their record in Fenway Park was 61-16.

A war-weary and pennant-starved public reveled in the Red Sox' success. For the first time in their 46-year history, the Red Sox reached the million mark in attendance and then soared past it. The final turnstile count of 1,416,944 at Fenway nearly doubled the previous club record of 730,340 set in 1942, and could have been far higher. "We had to turn away over 25,000 on a dozen occasions," Ed Doherty, the publicity director of the Red Sox, claimed in Fred Lieb's book, *The Boston Red Sox*. "On several Sundays … we had to stop people as far away as Kenmore Square if they didn't have tickets. There were as many fans heading back to the subways

Red Sox centerfielder Dominic DiMaggio plays some pepper before a game at Fenway Park. *(Courtesy of the Boston Red Sox)*

an hour before game time as there were coming to the ball park." Another 1,250,000 fans watched the Red Sox play on the road that year.

Dom DiMaggio, naturally, was a key contributor to the success of the Red Sox. He hit .316, finishing fifth in the league while scoring 85 runs and driving in 73. The Red Sox, who also had the necessary pitching with 25-game winner David "Boo" Ferriss and 20-game winner Cecil "Tex" Hughson anchoring the staff, were installed as heavy favorites to win the World Series, regardless of which NL adversary they played.

The Red Sox, who had clinched the pennant with two and a half weeks left in the season, had to wait awhile to find out who their opponent would be. For the first time in major-league history, two teams had finished the regular season in a tie for first place. The St. Louis Cardinals and Brooklyn Dodgers had identical 96-58 records, and the two teams would have to engage in a best-of-three playoff series for the NL pennant. The Cardinals beat the Dodgers 4-2 in St. Louis on October 1 and 8-4 in Brooklyn two days later to sweep the series and win their fourth pennant in five years. The start of the World Series was delayed four days, and the Red Sox, who had been coasting for more than three weeks and now began to have concerns about losing their edge, decided to fill the time by playing three exhibition games against an ad hoc team of AL all-stars.

The outcomes of those games didn't matter. What did matter was that Ted Williams was hit in the elbow by a pitch thrown by Washington's Mickey Haefner, and DiMaggio reportedly jammed a thumb while catching a line drive. So it was an unnecessarily banged-up Red Sox team that arrived in St. Louis for the first game of the World Series on October 6. Williams, his elbow bruised and swollen, would manage just five singles—one of them a bunt—in the seven games and would not even show flashes of his customary power until the very last one.

The Red Sox won the first game at Sportsman's Park 3-2 in 10 innings on Rudy York's home run, and DiMaggio took the bad with the good. He went 2-for-5 with a double and a single but was thrown out in the top of the eighth trying to stretch the single into another double. In the bottom of the inning, with the score knotted at 1-1 and Whitey Kurowski on first with two out, Joe Garagiola lofted a flyball to center that DiMaggio, whom baseball historian Fred Lieb has described as "the near-perfect outfielder," couldn't track.

"I never saw the ball in the shadows," DiMaggio recalled six decades later. "Everyone was yelling, and I was looking up, but I just couldn't see it." He almost caught the ball on instinct alone, but it ticked off the end of his glove. He recovered quickly and threw out Garagiola trying to stretch the hit into a triple. Kurowski, however, scored to put the Cardinals in front 2-1. Tom McBride retied the game with a last-strike pinch single in the ninth, and York's homer won it.

Lefthander Harry "The Cat" Brecheen, destined to be the unlikely hero of the World Series for the Cardinals after compiling a 15-15 record during the regular season, shut out the Red Sox 3-0 on four hits in the second game. One of them belonged to DiMaggio.

The World Series moved to Boston, where more than a half-million fans had clamored for tickets. To try to satisfy as many of them as possible, the Red Sox broke with tradition and distributed the tickets on a single-game basis instead of selling them in strips. The Red Sox blanked the Cardinals 4-0 in Game 3 on October 9 at Fenway Park as Boo Ferriss twirled a six-hitter. York hit another homer, a three-run blast in the first inning, to provide all the offense Ferriss would require. DiMaggio yanked a double down the left-field line in the sixth and finished 1-for-4 with four putouts in center field.

In the top of the sixth, with the Red Sox still leading 3-0, DiMaggio extinguished any hopes the Cardinals had of staging a comeback. St. Louis pitcher Murry Dickson started the inning with a double, bringing up the top of the Cardinals batting order, and Red Schoendienst lined a Ferriss pitch to center that was sinking fast. But DiMaggio got a quick jump on the ball, made a shoestring catch, and then tossed the ball to shortstop Johnny Pesky to complete a rally-killing double play.

"I had three assists in the Series, and I should have had four," DiMaggio recalled. "I threw out [Stan] Musial trying for second base, but the umpires called him safe. And by the third or fourth game, they just stopped running on me."

The fourth game got away from the Red Sox early. Enos Slaughter put the Cardinals ahead 1-0 with a second-inning homer off Tex Hughson, and Kurowski doubled. Harry Walker's single scored Kurowski as Hughson cut off DiMaggio's throw to the plate and tried to nail Walker in a rundown, but Pesky threw the ball into the Red Sox dugout for an error.

Walker ended up on third, from where he scored on a squeeze bunt by Marty Marion. The Cardinals led 3-0, tacked on three more runs in the third, and went on to crush the Red Sox 12-3 with a 20-hit assault and evened the World Series at two wins apiece. DiMaggio went hitless, although he did score one of the three Boston runs.

The Red Sox bounced back to trim St. Louis 6-3 on October 11. DiMaggio helped the Red Sox, who were leading 3-1, put the game beyond the reach of the Cardinals in the seventh by triggering a three-run rally with his third double of the World Series. After Ted Williams was called out on strikes and York was walked intentionally for the third time in the game, Mike Higgins doubled to chase home DiMaggio. Following another intentional walk to Leon Culberson, an error by shortstop Marion allowed two more runs to score that put the Red Sox comfortably ahead 6-1. DiMaggio finished the game 1-for-3 with a walk and a sacrifice bunt.

Needing only a split back in Sportsman's Park to secure their sixth World Championship in as many tries, the Red Sox, figuring it was more restful to sleep in a hotel bed than in a berth on a train, flew to St. Louis while the Cardinals rode the rails. Red Sox manager Joe Cronin also decided to hold back his two aces, Ferriss and Hughson, who had combined for 45 wins during the regular season, for a one-two punch in Game 7, if needed, and started 17-game winner Mickey Harris in Game 6. St. Louis manager Eddie Dyer wanted to throw his ace, 21-game winner Howie Pollett, in the must-win sixth game. But Pollett, who had started and lost the first game, was laid up with a bad back. So Dyer went with Harry Brecheen, who had shut out the Red Sox in Game 2. Harris was knocked out during a three-run third, and Cronin was forced to waste Hughson in an effort to keep the game close. But Brecheen stymied the Red Sox on seven hits, one of them a single by DiMaggio, who also had five putouts in center field, and the Cardinals won 4-1 to set up a deciding seventh game.

## DOMINIC DiMAGGIO
**Years with Red Sox: 1940-1953**
**Other Major League Teams: None**
**Position: Outfield**
**Bats: Right**
**Throws: Right**
**Height: 5-9**
**Weight: 168**
**Born: February 12, 1917**
**Birthplace: San Francisco, CA**
**Current Residence: Delray Beach, FL**
**Current Occupation: Retired**

✦ ✦ ✦

After a scheduled off-day, the Red Sox and Cardinals clashed for the final time on the afternoon of October 15, 1946. Four thousand miles away, in a defeated Germany, 10 Nazi war criminals were being hanged at Nuremberg. Hermann Goering, Adolf Hitler's chief deputy, cheated the hangman by swallowing a fatal dose of cyanide in his cell.

But in St. Louis, all that mattered to the crowd of 36,143 in Sportsman's Park was rooting for their underdog Cardinals to be the first team to ever beat the Red Sox in a World Series. Not that these Cardinals were slouches, mind you. With much the same cast, they had played in three straight World Series from 1942-44, winning two of them.

"We thought they were a formidable opponent," DiMaggio said. "We did not take them lightly."

For 29-year-old Dominic DiMaggio, today would be both the best and worst day of his Red Sox career.

Not only was he nursing a sore thumb, according to newspaper reports, DiMaggio had pulled a muscle in his thigh three days earlier and skipped the off-day workout in order to give his banged-up body an extra 24 hours to heal. Nearly 60 years later, DiMaggio branded the reports pure nonsense. "I was perfectly fine," he insisted. "I have no idea where those stories come from. When I hit that ball off Brecheen, I was thinking triple, and I wouldn't have been thinking about a triple if my leg was sore."

DiMaggio staked Ferriss to a quick 1-0 lead in the first inning. Wally Moses opened the game with a single off Murry Dickson and raced to third on a hit-and-run single by Johnny Pesky. DiMaggio brought Moses home with a flyball to right. The Red Sox might have had more, but centerfielder Terry Moore ran down Ted Williams's long fly—his best bolt of the World Series—and made a terrific catch to rob him of extra bases.

"We had him on the ropes in the first inning but only got the one run," DiMaggio said. "He must have had good stuff because we didn't do much against him after that."

The Cardinals nicked Ferriss for a run in the second on a flyball by Harry Walker. DiMaggio took a called third strike from Dickson in the third, and the game remained tied until the fifth when the Cardinals picked up a pair of runs. Dickson doubled in the first run and then scored on a single by Red Schoendienst.

The 3-1 deficit loomed larger for the Red Sox as the game wore on. Bobby Doerr had led off the second with an infield hit, but Dickson settled into a groove and did not surrender another hit over the next five innings. DiMaggio was the only Red Sox batter to reach base in that stretch, coaxing a walk in the sixth.

With the Cardinals only six outs away from capturing their third World Series title in five years, the Red Sox bats finally came to life in the eighth. Cronin sent up Rip Russell to pinch hit for catcher Hal Wagner, who was 0-for-13 in the Series, and Russell lashed a single to center to start the inning. George "Catfish" Metkovich pinch hit for reliever Joe Dobson and whacked a double down the left-field line, putting the tying runs into scoring position with the top of the Red Sox order coming up.

Dyer wasted no time going to the bullpen for the lefthanded Brecheen, who had pitched his second complete-game victory of the Series only 48 hours earlier and was ailing. The Cardinals manager didn't care. "All year, Brecheen never failed when the chips were down," he said.

"I was sick when I came out to the park today," Brecheen revealed after the game. "I had a fever from a cold, and my head was about to burst. But I filled up with aspirin, and when I went in my arm felt good."

Brecheen needed just three pitches to dispose of the lefthanded-hitting Moses, who looked at a third strike for the first out. Pesky, another lefthanded hitter, lofted a 1-and-0 pitch to shallow right, not nearly deep enough to score Russell. Four outs to go. The Red Sox rally was dying, and now it was all up to Dominic DiMaggio, who had to be wary of Brecheen's screwball that broke away from righthanded hitters.

"He did a good job with Moses and Pesky," DiMaggio remembered. But this was the sort of clutch situation he always looked forward to confronting. "You have to be relaxed, cool and ready. If you tighten up, you're at the mercy of the competition."

The Cardinals were also concerned about pitching to the quietly dangerous DiMaggio, and the NL champions hastily convened on the mound. While Brecheen had baffled most of the Boston lineup in his two World Series starts, he had not been a mystery to DiMaggio, who owned two of the 11 hits the Red Sox had managed to scratch out against him in 18 innings.

"I enjoyed hitting against Harry," DiMaggio remembered. "He had a good screwball and good control, but he had trouble getting his curveball over, and he couldn't hurt you with his fastball if he hit you between the eyes.

"They had a real long powwow on the mound while I was waiting to hit. Dyer, Brecheen, a whole bunch of guys," DiMaggio continued. "I was wondering what they could be talking about. I knew they weren't going to walk me with Williams coming up, and I didn't think they were going to bring in a righthander to pitch to me. I finally figured out they were not going to give me anything to hit and would try to get me to chase a bad pitch."

DiMaggio took a first-pitch strike and yelped.

"The first pitch I didn't think was a strike, but [plate umpire] Cal Hubbard said it was. I said: 'That ball was high,' and he said: 'Get back in there and hit.' I loved Cal Hubbard. I thought he was a great umpire. But I didn't think he should be talking to me like that. I said: 'You don't have to worry about me hitting.'"

Brecheen's next three pitches darted out of the strike zone. DiMaggio was ahead on the count 3-and-1, and Brecheen hadn't gotten his fastball or curveball over for strikes.

"I looked down to Joe Cronin to see if I would get the hit sign, keeping one foot in the batter's box so Brecheen wouldn't quick-pitch me, and I kept looking down there long after he had given me the hit sign," DiMaggio related. "The whole time I'm trying to figure out what he is going to throw me. I decided it would be a screwball on the outside part of the plate that he hoped I would try and pull and hit a groundball. And that's what I got. Only I took it the other way."

"Now the Cat's left arm swings up and down, and here comes his patented [screw]ball," wrote Jerry Nason in *The Boston Globe*. "But it didn't do the tricks he'd intended. Dom smashed it with authority high up against the wall in right center, 354 feet away ... only the second truly savage hit anybody had made off Brecheen in all the 20 innings of series ball he pitched."

"Right away I knew it was going to be between the outfielders and the game would be tied," DiMaggio said. "It hit the screen, and Slaughter said later that if the ball had been two feet more towards center, where the screen ended, it would have dropped into the seats for a home run."

Russell and Metkovich scored easily to tie the game at 3-3. DiMaggio, representing the go-ahead run, ran hard out of the batter's box.

"I was thinking triple all the way," he recalled. "I knew if I could get to third, they would be pitching Williams tough, and if there was a ball in the dirt I'd be coming home."

DiMaggio barely made it to second base. "As soon as I hit first base, I pulled my hamstring." Almost 60 years later, the intense pain he felt at that pivotal moment in the 1946 World Series could still be detected in his 88-year-old voice.

Now it was the Red Sox' turn to hold a convention, this time at second base. Dominic DiMaggio was desperately hoping the pain would miraculously subside, that it was nothing more than a cramp, and so were Joe Cronin and the rest of the team. But it became obvious that delaying the game for even a few minutes was not going to make a difference.

"I told Joe: 'I don't want to leave.' But he said if Ted hit a single, I probably wouldn't be able to score from second, and it was a big run," DiMaggio related. "It was a terrible decision that had to be made."

He limped off the diamond as Leon Culberson went in to pinch run. Williams, getting his last chance to be a World Series hero, popped up to end the inning. Culberson, a wartime replacement player who had hung on but was nowhere near DiMaggio's equal, grabbed his glove and trotted out to play center field.

Although two of the first four hitters the Cardinals would send to the plate in the bottom of the eighth were lefthanded, Cronin bypassed southpaw Earl Johnson, who had won Game One in relief and limited St. Louis batters to one hit and one run in three and one third innings. Instead he summoned righthander Bob Klinger, who hadn't pitched in nearly two weeks. Klinger had been at the bedside of his son, who had reportedly been stricken with polio.

Lefthanded-hitting Enos Slaughter welcomed Klinger with a single. Klinger retired the next two hitters as Slaughter remained planted on first, and as the lefthanded, slap-hitting Harry Walker approached the plate, DiMaggio, posted on the top step of the dugout, waved to Culberson to move several steps toward the gap in left-center. "But he wouldn't take more than one step," DiMaggio said.

Walker smacked a Klinger pitch into that gap for a double as Slaughter began his famous mad dash around the bases. The only man who could have slowed him down was the man who had put the brakes on the Cardinals' aggressive baserunning tactics early in the World Series, the bespectacled man who now stood helplessly on the top step of the Red Sox dugout. Culberson hustled to cut off the ball, but he did not have DiMaggio's strong arm, and his arching throw to Pesky, the cutoff man, took far too long to reach the shortstop. Pesky has long been vilified for holding onto the ball a fraction of a second too long after receiving it. But films show it wouldn't have mattered had he gotten rid of it immediately; the determined Slaughter would have beaten it even had Pesky's release been quicker and his throw more accurate.

"Chances are," wrote legendary newspaper columnist Red Smith, "the run that got the bully's share of the swag might never have scored if Dom DiMaggio hadn't [been] injured … It is unlikely [third base coach Mike] Gonzalez would have dared challenge Dom's squirrel rifle arm if he'd been playing center instead of Culberson."

"Slaughter said later that the only reason he tried for home on that hit was because he remembered I wasn't in center field anymore," DiMaggio said.

The Red Sox, down 4-3, wasted a chance to tie or win the game in the ninth after Rudy York and Bobby Doerr led off with singles. Pinch runner Paul Campbell reached third with one out, but Brecheen left him stranded by retiring the last two hitters to record his third win of the World Series and bring the title to St. Louis.

Dominic DiMaggio, a perennial All-Star centerfielder for the Boston Red Sox, helps raise funds for the Ted Williams Museum.
*(Courtesy of Chaz Scoggins)*

+ + +

Dominic DiMaggio never got another chance to play in a World Series. The Red Sox came close in both 1948 and 1949. They eliminated the Yankees from the race on the next to last day of the scheduled regular season in 1948 but still needed to beat the Yankees one more time while praying for a Cleveland loss in order to force a one-game playoff with the Indians for the pennant.

As the competitive DiMaggio brothers drove together to Fenway Park, an injury-wracked Joe vowed to play an otherwise meaningless game for the Yankees just for the satisfaction of eliminating the Red Sox. "I'll take care of it personally," Joe said. Dom responded: "I may have something to do with that."

Joe knocked in runs with a single and a double in the first five innings, cutting a Red Sox lead to 5-4. But Dom led off the sixth with a home run, triggering a four-run rally, and the Red Sox won 10-5. Cleveland lost to Detroit but then clobbered the Red Sox 8-3 in the playoff game.

Joe got a measure of revenge in 1949, helping end Dominic's Red Sox-record 34-game hitting streak before he could mount a serious threat to his own record 56-game streak. The streak was terminated when Joe snared Dom's line drive to center off Vic Raschi.

"If I had let the ball go through," Joe consoled his younger brother after the game, "it would have hit me right between the eyes."

The Red Sox, needing only to split the last two games of the year in New York to win the pennant, lost both and finished a game behind the Yankees.

Dom DiMaggio hit a career-high .328 in 1950 and led the AL with 131 runs, then again led the league with 113 runs the following year. But the aging Red Sox were slipping as pennant contenders, and when the club committed itself to a youth movement under new manager Lou Boudreau in 1953, the 36-year-old DiMaggio abruptly retired after just three games.

A shrewd businessman, Dominic DiMaggio did well for himself in private life. He was one of the original investors in the Boston Patriots when the American Football League was formed in 1959, and two decades later, following the death of owner Tom Yawkey, he made an unsuccessful bid to buy the Red Sox.

DiMaggio was among the inaugural group of players inducted into the Red Sox Hall of Fame in 1995. He is one of only seven players to score 1,000 runs for the Red Sox and still ranks among the Top Ten on club lists in games (1,399), at-bats (5,640), hits (1,680), doubles (308), total bases (2,363), extra-base hits (452), and walks (750).

Now fully retired, Dominic DiMaggio and his wife, Emily, divide their time between homes in Florida and Massachusetts.

# Chapter 4

# MEL PARNELL

## JULY 14, 1956

B y 1956 Mel Parnell was at the end of what had promised to be a long and brilliant career with the Red Sox. A series of unfortunate injuries had taken its toll on the 34-year-old lefthander.

In 1953, less than three years before, Parnell had posted his second 20-win season for the Red Sox, a 21-8 mark. His lifetime record by then stood at 111-59, a .653 winning percentage. Only Cy Young (192) and Smoky Joe Wood (117) had won more games for the franchise, and only Wood (.676) and Babe Ruth (.659) boasted a higher winning percentage. Although he had not made his major-league debut until he was nearly 25, Parnell was only 31 and appeared to have more than enough left in his left arm to win 200—perhaps even 250—major-league games.

But on April 24, 1954, while batting in Washington against his former Red Sox roommate, the wild-in-more-ways-than-one Mickey McDermott, Parnell had his left forearm fractured by an errant pitch.

"It was just one of those things. A freak accident," Parnell remembered. The two pitchers had even planned to go out to dinner together after the game. He missed more than half the season and was only 3-7 when he did perform.

"[Red Sox manager] Lou Boudreau coaxed me into coming back too soon," Parnell said ruefully, "and my career went downhill from then on."

"It was an accident, but that didn't make me feel any better," the late McDermott wrote in his autobiography, *A Funny Thing Happened on the*

*Way to Cooperstown.* "Mel had a great southpaw arm and the pitching smarts to go with it. If is an uncertain word, but if it hadn't been for me breaking his wrist, Parnell could have added another 100 or so Ws to his lifetime 123-75 and be in the Hall of Fame today. ... It still hurts when I think about it."

Parnell slipped on the mound while delivering a pitch during spring training in 1955 and wrenched his left knee. He appeared in only 13 games that season and was ineffective, posting a 2-3 record with a 7.83 ERA.

By the mid-1950s, Red Sox fans were restless. The frustrating but exciting postwar teams were gone, and the Red Sox had not finished higher than fourth and closer to first place than 16 games since 1951. When the fans at Fenway Park weren't booing the great Ted Williams, they were spewing their venom at Parnell, who had won all of five games in two years. Parnell, however, never took it personally.

"They were on the ball club really, because we weren't a good ball club at that time," Parnell recalled. "The fans wanted to see you win, and why not? That's why they were paying their money. When you didn't, they weren't happy."

He had given the fans plenty to cheer about from 1948-53. The epitome of the crafty lefty, Parnell wasn't overpowering, and he walked more hitters than he struck out in his career. But he had mastered the art of pitching.

✦ ✦ ✦

Mel Parnell had been born in New Orleans on June 13, 1922. While in high school he often threw batting practice to the hitters on the Pelicans, the city's minor-league team that was affiliated with the St. Louis Cardinals, and he attracted the attention of the great Mahatma himself, Branch Rickey.

"Rickey started coming to my house to talk to my dad, but I told him not to agree to anything with St. Louis," Parnell said. "They had so many farm clubs and ballplayers, you were just a number and not a name in their organization. But I wasn't getting much action from anybody else."

Then one day the Red Sox sent a couple of scouts to New Orleans to check out an outfielder on Parnell's high school team. The scouts, one of whom was Hall of Fame pitcher Herb Pennock, dropped in to say hello to Vincent Rizzo, the general manager of the Cardinals' farm team, and he tipped them off about Parnell.

"Rizzo told them to be sure to see the skinny lefthanded pitcher," Parnell related. "I struck out 17 that day. The Red Sox signed me, and I don't regret it to this day."

Service in World War II set Parnell's career back three years. He was two months shy of his 25th birthday when he finally arrived in Boston in 1947 and got the shock of his life.

"I had mostly used my fastball in the minors, and I had just finished leading the Eastern League in ERA when I got to Fenway for the first time and saw that Wall. Right then I thought I had made a mistake signing with the Red Sox. I knew I would have to change my style of pitching and start throwing more breaking stuff."

Although he appeared in only 15 games for the Red Sox in 1947 and was cuffed around, posting a 2-3 record with a 6.39 ERA, Parnell adapted quickly to pitching in Fenway Park.

"I threw my slider outside and pitched inside with my fastball to keep the righthanded hitters off balance," Parnell explained. "You had to use your breaking stuff, and you had to keep the ball down at Fenway. Righthanded batters saw that Wall, and they thought about that Wall, and they would do one or two things that would throw their swing out of line."

Mel Parnell went 15-8 with a 3.14 ERA in 1948, and many of his teammates believe to this day that manager Joe McCarthy should have given him the ball in the one-game playoff with Cleveland for the American League pennant that year. McCarthy chose washed-up veteran Denny Galehouse instead, and the Indians routed the Red Sox 8-3 to spoil what would have been the only all-Boston World Series in history. The Braves had won the National League pennant.

"Everybody thought Parnell should be the pitcher to go out there," second baseman Bobby Doerr said 57 years later. "Galehouse was a good pitcher, but he hadn't been pitching much."

"I thought it was my ballgame," Parnell said. "I was in bed at nine the night before, and I got to the park late, just like pitchers always do on the day they're pitching and have nothing else to do. But when I went out to get loose, McCarthy came up behind me and put his hand on my shoulder and told me the elements were against a lefthander. The wind was blowing out, and Galehouse had pitched well the last time he had faced Cleveland."

Parnell remembered that the 36-year-old Galehouse "turned ghostly white" when McCarthy gave him the ball. "McCarthy played a hunch, and it backfired."

Parnell led the AL in victories in 1949 with a 25-7 record, the most wins by a Red Sox lefthander since Ruth had won 24 in 1917. He followed up

**Lefthander Mel Parnell warms up in front of the Boston Red Sox dugout before pitching a game against the Philadelphia Athletics at Fenway Park.** *(Courtesy of the Boston Red Sox)*

that brilliant campaign with a pair of 18-win seasons. He beat the hapless Washington Senators 17 straight times from 1948-52.

But the 1953 season would be Parnell's last outstanding one. Among his 21 wins were four shutouts against the New York Yankees, who were in the process of winning 99 games and their fifth straight pennant. Not since Walter Johnson in 1908 had a pitcher shut out one opponent four times in a single season.

"I enjoyed beating them, especially when [Yankees manager] Casey [Stengel] didn't pick me and Bob Porterfield, and Detroit's Frank Lary, for the '53 All-Star Game because we had been beating them. That really motivated me for the rest of that season."

Then came the string of debilitating injuries. Parnell hoped that 1956 would be his comeback season. The Red Sox had tried to trade him to the Chicago White Sox during the winter but had their offer spurned.

"We'll buy him for cash," said White Sox manager Marty Marion. "But we won't give up any player for him. He's just a gamble."

Parnell began the 1956 season in reasonably good health. But on May 12 he severely sprained his left ankle sliding into second base in Detroit and was disabled yet again.

> **MEL PARNELL**
> **Years with Red Sox: 1947-56**
> **Other Major League Teams: None**
> **Position: Pitcher**
> **Bats: Left**
> **Throws: Left**
> **Height: 6-0**
> **Weight: 180**
> **Born: June 13, 1922**
> **Birthplace: New Orleans, LA**
> **Current Residence: New Orleans, LA**
> **Current Occupation: Retired**

"It bothered me the rest of the season," he remembered. "The bag was strapped down in those days, and my ankle got caught in the strap. I heard something pop. Reno Bertoia, their second baseman, said: 'What was that?'"

When Parnell returned to the mound, he struggled to regain his form. At the All-Star break his record was only 2-2, and he had given up 45 hits in 39 2/3 innings while walking 15 and striking out only 16. The fans were booing louder.

"It's a miracle he came back," said Dr. Ralph McCarthy, the Red Sox team physician. "He had one of those bad sprains, and it's possible he has a little chip in his ankle. He's got to be wrapped up tightly every time he puts on his uniform."

✦ ✦ ✦

Mel Parnell hadn't pitched in 10 days when he arrived at Fenway Park on Saturday, July 14, 1956, and he wasn't sure he was going to be able to pitch today, either. He desperately wanted to atone for his last start on the Fourth of July, a 9-4 shellacking by the Yankees in which he had been tagged for 10 hits and seven runs in seven innings. A gloomy morning hadn't improved Parnell's spirits, and now rain was threatening to wash out that afternoon's game with the White Sox, the team that had rejected trading for him six months earlier. But the game would be on national TV, and a good-sized crowd was expected to see the Red Sox, who had won five in a row to hike their record to 42-35 and were hotter than they had been in a while. The Red Sox were nipping at the heels of Cleveland and Chicago in the tussle for second place behind the Yankees, who had already built up a comfortable lead, so the club was willing to wait and see if the weather would clear.

"I thought for sure the game would be called. I remember the umpires sitting in the dugout conferring. I think they wanted the day off. But [Red Sox GM] Joe Cronin said he'd talk to the weather bureau. When he came back, he told the umpires the rain would let up in 30 minutes, and that's what happened. It turned out to be a beautiful day."

After a 68-minute delay, Parnell took the mound in front of a turnout of 14,542. There were a couple of White Sox hitters he had to be concerned about, but he was confident as he took his warm-up pitches.

"Minnie Minoso was a good hitter, a trouble guy. Larry Doby was a trouble guy. You had to keep the ball away from Doby because he'd fall away when a lefthander pitched him inside, and then the barrel of the bat would be right where the ball was. Sherm Lollar was a good hitter."

Parnell set down the White Sox in order in the first. He walked Doby in the second, but Doby was erased in a double play. Sammy Esposito reached on a throwing error by shortstop Don Buddin in the third but was thrown out stealing by catcher Sammy White when Chicago pitcher Jim McDonald struck out into a double play.

Through three innings Parnell had faced the minimum nine batters. But McDonald, a 29-year-old journeyman pitcher with his fifth AL club, had matched Parnell with three hitless innings of his own.

"The first three innings he got us out easily," Parnell recalled. "He had good stuff, and it looked like it would be a game with only one or two runs. Jim had been in the Red Sox organization, a pretty fair prospect. But he never really put it together."

Billy Klaus finally solved McDonald by doubling in the fourth, and singles by Ted Williams and Mickey Vernon brought him in with the first run. Williams scored when Jackie Jensen rapped into a double play.

The Red Sox added another run in the sixth when Klaus singled home Billy Goodman, who had doubled. They upped their lead to 4-0 in the seventh against reliever Paul LaPalme when Jimmy Piersall doubled and rode home on a single by Buddin.

Meanwhile, Parnell had not allowed another baserunner since Buddin's third-inning error and went into the eighth with a no-hitter.

"The fans realized by the sixth or seventh what was going on, and the applause kept getting louder and louder. [Right-fielder]Jackie Jensen came to me in the seventh and told me: 'Don't let them hit the ball to me! I don't want to be the guy to mess it up!'"

No one was worried about jinxing the no-hitter by talking about it in the dugout.

"I hear guys say they don't know when they're pitching a no-hitter, and I don't believe it," Parnell scoffed. "The scoreboard [at Fenway] is right in your face. How can you not know?"

It was an afternoon, Parnell said, when he had "exceptional stuff." But having made his living by allowing batters to put the ball in play, he knew the odds of him pitching nine hitless innings were stacked heavily against him.

"It's something a pitcher always dreams of but never expects to happen," he said. "It's so hard. One pitch that a guy hits in the hole, and it's over."

Parnell had been disappointed before. He had pitched seven hitless innings in a game in Washington back in 1949 only to have that gem broken up. Furthermore, nearly 3,500 games had been played at Fenway in the park's 45-year history, and no lefthanded pitcher, working in the giant shadow of the famous left-field wall, had ever thrown a no-hitter there. Almost 30 years had passed since Chicago righthander Ted Lyons had thrown the last no-hitter in Fenway, on August 21, 1926.

"I knew with all those sinkers Mel was throwing that somebody would nub one through the infield or get one off the end of the bat," his catcher, Sammy White, told reporters after the game.

But the outs kept piling up, and Parnell had set down 17 Chicago batters in a row going into the ninth. Only two balls had been hit reasonably hard off him, a line drive to deep center by rookie Luis Aparicio in the second that Piersall had initially misjudged but ran down in time, and a line drive directly at third baseman Klaus off the bat of Minoso in the seventh.

"The adrenaline started flowing a bit," he recalled. "You know what you have going for you. You know you need three more outs, and you want to be careful."

He walked Esposito on a 3-and-2 pitch to start the ninth, and the free pass may have actually ensured his no-hitter. Billy Goodman, the second baseman, cheated toward the bag in hopes of getting a groundball for a double play. Had he been playing in his usual bases-empty position, he might not have reached the next ball. Aparicio lashed a grounder up the middle that Parnell lunged for but couldn't get. But Goodman dived for it, snared it in his glove, and flipped to Buddin covering second for the force on Esposito. There was no chance to turn a double play on the speedy Aparicio, who would lead the AL in stolen bases in each of his first nine seasons.

"The hardest play of the game was the one Goodie made in the ninth," said Red Sox manager Mike Higgins. "That ball wasn't a foot from second base, and he did a helluva job to get it."

In retrospect, Parnell believes Goodman would have made the play even had he not been cheating. "The ball wasn't hit that hard," he said.

Bubba Phillips pinch hit for LaPalme and bounced a ball to Klaus, who forced Aparicio at second. Parnell was now one out away from a historic no-hitter. "Jungle Jim" Rivera was due up next, but Marty Marion sent up former Red Sox slugger Walt Dropo to hit for him. Dropo topped a sinker to the right of the mound, and Parnell grabbed the ball. But instead of flipping it to first baseman Mickey Vernon, Parnell sprinted to the bag himself and easily beat the lumbering Dropo there for the final out.

"What's the matter, fella? You don't have any confidence in me?" Vernon, who was known for his good glove, asked with a grin as they celebrated the feat.

"Mickey, I have all the confidence in the world in you," Parnell assured him. "I just didn't have any in myself. I might have thrown it away."

In a brisk one hour and 52 minutes, Parnell had faced just 28 batters, one over the minimum. He had walked two, struck out only four, and gotten 16 outs on groundballs. The White Sox hit only five balls to the outfield.

"A no-hitter couldn't have happened to a better guy," White told reporters. "He earned that no-hitter. The fans have been pretty rough on Mel for a couple of years. Real rough, for that matter."

Red Sox owner Tom Yawkey met Parnell at the clubhouse door after the game and presented him with a new contract calling for a $500 bonus.

Mel Parnell, one of the winningest pitchers in club history, is inducted into the Boston Red Sox Hall of Fame in pregame ceremonies at Fenway Park. *(Courtesy of the Boston Red Sox)*

Back home in New Orleans, however, his father missed the national telecast of his son's feat.

"He turned off the TV during the rain delay and went outside to do some chores," Parnell related. "A couple hours later one of the neighbors came running up to him to tell him I had pitched a no-hitter. He said: 'What are you talking about? The game was postponed.'"

Wrote Bob Holbrook in *The Boston Globe* the next morning: "This was the answer to all those dreary days of the past three years when the top flight lefthander ran into more trouble than any ordinary guy has in a lifetime. This was a day when the catcalls were absent."

For one more glorious afternoon, everything was right with Mel Parnell again.

It wouldn't last. He won only four more games for the Red Sox after his no-hitter and retired after the 1956 season.

"I had an elbow operation after the season that didn't turn out so good," he related. "They told me I'd need two more operations, and I said no, that was enough. But if they'd had that Tommy John surgery back then, that could have helped me pitch a lot longer."

Parnell remained with the Red Sox as a scout, minor-league manager, and broadcaster for several more years. He then returned permanently to New Orleans where he became a businessman. He has been married to Velma for 58 years, and they reared four children, all of whom are in the medical profession.

Mel Parnell's lifetime record for the Red Sox was 123-75 with a 3.50 ERA, and he still ranks fourth on the team's all-time win list behind only Cy Young, Roger Clemens, and Tim Wakefield. Parnell's lifetime record in Fenway Park, the fabled "graveyard of lefthanders," was 71-30, a .703 winning percentage. He was inducted into the Red Sox Hall of Fame in 1997.

# Chapter 5

# BILL MONBOUQUETTE

## AUGUST 1, 1962

B ill Monbouquette was sitting by himself on the United Air Lines charter taking the Red Sox from Boston to Chicago on the morning of August 1, 1962, working a crossword puzzle when one of the stewardesses sat down beside him for a moment.

"Hi! How ya doing?" she asked cheerfully.

"Oh, I'm not doing too well in this," the 25-year-old righthanded pitcher replied, putting down his pencil. "And I'm not doing too well in my pitching, either. I'm struggling a bit."

The stewardess, her brief break over, bounded to her feet. "Ah," she told him encouragingly with a wink, "you'll pitch a no-hitter tonight."

Right then, she was probably the only person in the entire world who thought so.

✚✚✚

Monbouquette was struggling mightily. In three straight July starts he had been tagged for eight hits and eight runs in two and two thirds innings at Kansas City, five hits and three runs in one-third of an inning against the New York Yankees, and seven hits and three runs in two and two thirds innings against the Chicago White Sox.

"Three weeks ago it looked as if Monbo was on the beam and was going to have a terrific summer," Red Sox manager Mike Higgins said at the time.

"Bill had won five out of six starts, but he has been getting rapped hard since then."

Monbouquette had been a little better in his last start before the break for the second All-Star Game in late July. He gave up five hits and three runs, two earned, in five innings at Washington, but was saddled with another loss when the Senators pounded the Red Sox bullpen and won 11-2.

At the second All-Star break, Monbouquette's numbers were the worst of his five-year major-league career. He had compiled a 38-36 record with a 3.64 ERA in his first four seasons with a second-division team that had not had a winning record since his rookie year in 1958; but his 1962 ledger now read 8-10 with a 4.57 ERA, and he had allowed 148 hits in 134 innings while striking out only 84. He had been torched for 25 hits and 17 runs in his last 10 2/3 innings covering four starts. He didn't have an explanation.

"My arm wasn't bothering me," he remembered. "But sometimes you go out there, you aren't concentrating on every pitch. It happens to every pitcher. You have to go one pitch, one batter, one inning at a time. That's what pitching is all about. And there wasn't a lot of film in those days, not like there is now, where you can sit down and analyze your mechanics."

One thing Monbouquette knew was that the blazing fastball that had struck out 17 Washington Senators in a game the previous year, setting a Red Sox record and American League night game record at the time, had cooled down. It had been there in his first start of the 1962 season on April 11, when had had flirted with a no-hitter against the Cleveland Indians at Fenway Park. The only hit he had allowed in the first nine innings had been a bloop single to right by the opposing pitcher, Ron Taylor, leading off the sixth. But the game was scoreless after nine, and the Red Sox didn't win it until the 12th when Carroll Hardy belted a walk-off grand slam. Monbouquette went the distance with a four-hitter.

"Four days later I'm pitching in Cleveland, a cold night by the lake," Monbouquette remembered, "and my shoulder felt like it was on fire. I really think that's where I lost the zip on my fastball. I never got that zip back until that night in Chicago. I think it was because of the extra days off."

Before his July slump, Monbouquette had pitched well enough to make the AL All-Star team for the second time in his young career, although he hadn't pitched in the season's first All-Star Game on July 10. He hadn't been picked for the second All-Star Game on July 30, and the break was a welcome respite.

"I had gone to Maine fishing just to forget about pitching," he said.

✦✦✦

Monbouquette took the mound on the evening of August 1 at Chicago's Comiskey Park. His opponent that night was 42-year-old Early Wynn, who was trying to hang on long enough to get his 300th victory. The rapidly fading Wynn had started the year with 292 victories in 21 major-league seasons but had won only five times in the first four months. He desperately needed three more victories, and he would prove to be a formidable adversary for Monbouquette on this night in front of 17,185 fans.

"Pitching against Early Wynn, you knew it was going to be a battle," Monbouquette said. "He'd throw that high fastball, high slider. He was the type of guy you didn't hit the ball up the middle and you didn't bunt on, because he was gonna hurt you. He was a mean old guy, a real throwback."

The White Sox were also the type of team that could give power pitchers like Monbouquette a lot of trouble.

"They were a good contact team," he remembered. "They hit the ball the other way, and they had guys that could run: Fox, Aparicio, Landis, Smith. They were called the Go-Go Sox for that reason."

But right from the start he knew his fastball was back.

"I remember Sherm Lollar saying to one of our guys: 'What's going on with this guy tonight?' The ball was just jumping out of my hand. I would throw two fastballs in a row, and the batter would step out and say: 'Whoa!' Mike Higgins said afterward that was the hardest he'd ever seen anybody throw."

Monbouquette retired the first five White Sox, then went to a full count for the first time against Al Smith. Monbouquette wound up and delivered the payoff pitch, a curveball that Smith started to chase and then checked his swing. Plate umpire Bill McKinley called it ball four.

"That's how much confidence I had in my curve that night," Monbouquette related. "But it was a ball. Would I have gotten the call in the ninth inning? Maybe."

Smith would be the only White Sox batter to reach base all night. The only other Chicago batter to even work the count full was Jim Landis in the fifth, and Monbouquette struck him out with a fastball.

Monbouquette was aware all along that he was working on a no-hitter. But Wynn was almost as tough and every bit as stingy. After seven innings, Wynn, despite giving up five hits, had not permitted the Red Sox a run. Monbouquette was beginning to get concerned that the Red Sox might never score.

Fireballing righthander Bill Monbouquette delivers a pitch for the Boston Red Sox during a game at Fenway Park.
*(Courtesy of the Boston Red Sox)*

"It could have gone on another four or five innings," Monbouquette recounted. "But the thing was, I hadn't thrown a lot of pitches. I think I threw 87 that night. But I was prepared to go whatever it took."

Gary Geiger led off the eighth with a walk, but Wynn struck out Carl Yastrzemski. Higgins flashed the hit-and-run sign to catcher Jim Pagliaroni on a 2-and-1 pitch, but he swung and missed, and Geiger was cut down at second base. Two outs, bases empty.

But Pagliaroni delivered a single to left, and Pete Runnels dumped another single into left. Lu Clinton followed with yet another single to left off the weary Wynn, and Pagliaroni lumbered home from second base, barely beating Smith's strong throw, with the first run of the game. "It was a bang-bang play at the plate," Monbouquette recalled.

> ## BILL MONBOUQUETTE
> **Years with Red Sox: 1958-65**
> **Other Major League Teams: Detroit,**
>   **New York (AL), San Francisco**
> **Position: Pitcher**
> **Bats: Right**
> **Throws: Right**
> **Height: 5-11**
> **Weight: 195**
> **Born: August 11, 1936**
> **Birthplace: Medford, MA**
> **Current Residence: Medford, MA**
> **Current Occupation: Retired**

The score was still 1-0 when the White Sox came to bat in the bottom of the ninth. Monbouquette had flirted with a no-hitter twice before. Besides his first start in 1962, he had pitched a one-hitter against Detroit in 1960. The only hit had been a wind-blown pop-fly double by Neil Chrisley, a .210 lifetime hitter, that had brushed The Wall at Fenway Park. But that hit had come in the first inning, and there had been no drama involved. This was now the closest he had ever come to performing the feat.

"My fastball was still jumping out of my hand. Someone told me later they had me at 97 miles an hour in the ninth inning, and I told him I don't throw 97 miles an hour. I don't know where they got the [radar] gun, because guns weren't prevalent in those days.

"I had lost my good curveball about the fifth inning, but then I found my slider. If I was throwing 92, 93, 94 miles an hour—whatever it was— my slider was coming in at 90, too. They were swinging and missing, swinging over it, hitting it off the end of the bat. It was one of those nights."

By now Monbouquette also had the White Sox home crowd enthusiastically supporting his bid. He fanned Sherm Lollar on three fastballs for the first out. Nellie Fox pinch hit for Wynn. Every time Monbouquette looked at Fox in the on-deck circle while he was disposing of Lollar, the 11-time All-Star with a .293 lifetime batting average was smiling at him.

"I think he was trying to throw off my concentration," Monbouquette guessed. "If you needed a strikeout, you could forget about that with him. If he went to the plate 600 times, what did he strike out? Six? Eight? Ten times?"

Monbouquette got the lefthanded-hitting Fox to chop a high fastball to third baseman Frank Malzone, who threw him out. One out to go.

Now he had to get past five-time All-Star shortstop Luis Aparicio, a future Hall of Famer. Monbouquette quickly got him in the hole 0-and-2 with a fastball and a slider. Monbouquette tried to put him away with a slider on the next pitch, and Aparicio tried desperately to check his swing. Pagliaroni, certain that McKinley would rule that Aparicio had committed himself to the pitch for strike three, bounded from behind the plate and in his excitement stumbled and fell. Ball one, McKinley bawled. He was giving nothing away.

"From my viewpoint, I definitely think he swung," Monbouquette averred. "One of the Chicago fans hollered: 'They shot the wrong McKinley!' I immediately backed right off the mound because I had to chuckle to myself."

As for Pagliaroni's pratfall, which could have been construed as showing up the umpire, Monbouquette thought: "Now I'm really in trouble! I'm not going to get another pitch from this guy!"

Monbouquette knew then McKinley was going to make him earn his no-hitter. "But that's the way it should be. I didn't want a gift."

The slightly embarrassed Pagliaroni trudged back behind the plate and called for a slider off the plate. Aparicio swung feebly and missed the late-breaking pitch by 10 inches, becoming Monbouquette's seventh strikeout victim of the game. This time Pagliaroni stayed on his feet as he led the Red Sox charge to the mound to congratulate Monbouquette on his feat.

"When it happened, I was about five feet off the ground," Monbouquette remembered. "I didn't know I could jump that good."

Bill Monbouquette had come within a checked swing of pitching the major leagues' first regular-season perfect game in 40 years. Charlie Robertson had last performed the feat for the White Sox in 1922. (Don Larsen of the Yankees had pitched a perfect game in the 1956 World Series, and Pittsburgh's Harvey Haddix had pitched 12 perfect innings in 1959 before losing the no-hitter and the game in the 13th.) It was, nevertheless, a masterful performance. Monbouquette had gone to three balls on only two batters and retired the last 22 White Sox in order. There had been only three well-stroked balls to the outfield: Clinton had gloved a Charley Maxwell fly near the wall in the right-field corner in the second, and Yaz had run down an Aparicio drive to left-center in the sixth. Geiger had caught a ball Landis hit to deep center in the eighth. None of them had made Monbouquette hold his breath.

"It would have been nice to have the perfect game," he reflected. "But, really, I was just looking for the win. It had been a while."

Because the Red Sox were on the road, Monbouquette had no conception of how the news of his no-hitter had been received back in Boston and in his hometown of Medford, just outside the Massachusetts capital. When he was told by reporters the next day, before that afternoon's game against the White Sox, that he was about to be made the honorary mayor of Medford, Monbouquette thought it was a joke.

"Hey, Monbo, Lu Clinton drove in the run. How about Lu for honorary police chief?" one Boston writer suggested.

"It's fine with me," the pitcher replied, going along with the gag.

"Pag scored the run," another reporter said. "We'll make him honorary fire chief."

"That's okay, too," Monbouquette said.

So Monbouquette was overwhelmed when he stepped off the Red Sox' United Air Lines charter at Boston's Logan Airport that evening and saw a Massachusetts State Police cruiser with its roof lights flashing and 1,500 fans—including Medford mayor John J. McGlynn—waiting on the tarmac to greet him. Pagliaroni had to whisper to the stunned pitcher to wave to the crowd.

McGlynn greeted Monbouquette at the bottom of the portable staircase, read a proclamation making him honorary mayor of Medford for the month of August, and presented him with a gavel. The cruiser then whisked him to a Medford fire truck parked in front of the UAL hangar, and the city's fire chief gave him a fireman's hat to wear. Monbouquette was plunked down in the front seat, and the engine led a parade of 50 honking cars on the eight-mile trip to Medford. Monbouquette waved at the fans along the parade route to city hall, where he stepped out and humbly thanked a crowd of 600 fans for their support.

He was somewhat embarrassed by all the attention being showered on him.

"I was," he said, "because that's the way I am."

Bill Monbouquette finished his 50 years in professional baseball as a minor-league pitching coach for the Oneonta Tigers in the Class A New York-Penn League. *(Courtesy of Chaz Scoggins)*

✦ ✦ ✦

Monbouquette had a strong finish to the 1962 season, ending at 15-13 with a 3.33 ERA for an eighth-place team.

"Pitching is confidence," he said, "and every time I went out there after that no-hitter, I had a good feeling."

He won 20 games for a Red Sox team that went 76-85 in 1963, and in 1964 he flirted with another perfect game before settling for a one-hitter against the powerful Minnesota Twins.

"On Wednesday I pitched against the Twins and shut them out on two hits. My old roommate, Vic Wertz, got both the hits," Monbouquette remembered. "On Sunday I have a perfect game in the sixth. There's a groundball to Malzone, who throws it over to first, and it goes right between Tony Horton's legs for an error. Up comes Zoilo Versalles, who I had struck out two times. I get him 0-and-2, and he must have fouled off a dozen pitches. Most of them were balls. He even threw the bat at the ball one time when I side-armed him. I'm coming up and in on the next pitch, and I cut the ball. It sailed out over the plate, and he hit into the left-field seats for a two-run homer. I lost that game, 2-1."

Monbouquette also shut out the Washington Senators four times in 1964, including a pair four days apart. "Gil Hodges was the manager, and he said: 'Goddammit, do you pitch against anybody else?'"

The Red Sox traded Monbouquette to Detroit after the 1965 season. He also pitched for the New York Yankees and San Francisco Giants before retiring after the 1968 campaign with a 114-112 record in 11 seasons. He was 96-91 for the Red Sox.

Monbouquette has remained active in baseball ever since, working as a scout or coach. He has been a major-league pitching coach for both the Yankees and New York Mets and a bullpen coach for the Toronto Blue Jays. He worked as the pitching coach for the Oneonta Tigers, a Detroit farm club, in the Class A New York-Penn League for several seasons before announcing his retirement after the 2005 season. He continues to reside in his native Medford with his wife, Josephine. Bill Monbouquette was elected to the Red Sox Hall of Fame in 2000.

# Chapter 6

# FRANK MALZONE

## MAY 19, 1963

Frank Malzone was born in The Bronx on February 28, 1930. He was born either 10 years too late or 10 years too early.

By the time Frank Malzone took over at third base in 1957, the Red Sox were a franchise past its prime. The potent teams of the 1940s and early 1950s, which had won one pennant and missed out on two others by the margin of a single game, were gone, and before long so were hundreds of thousands of fans.

By the mid-1950s the only attractions the Red Sox had left were their three outfielders: Ted Williams, Jackie Jensen, and a loony Jimmy Piersall who could liven up an otherwise dull ballgame with his antics. When they, too, were gone by the end of the decade, Malzone and a young Carl Yastrzemski were the only everyday stars the Red Sox had. After the franchise was rejuvenated in 1967, Yaz would go on to play for some of the best Red Sox teams in history and appear in two World Series. By then Malzone, a six-time All-Star, had retired with the dubious distinction of being perhaps the best long-term player in Red Sox history who never knew what it was like to experience the thrill of a genuine pennant race.

In only Malzone's first two full seasons did the Red Sox even manage to compile a winning record, but neither of those teams finished higher than third or closer to first place than 13 games. For the remainder of Malzone's career the Red Sox were a second-division ball club, finishing an average of 27 games behind in the American League standings. In 1965, Malzone's last year with the Red Sox, the club bottomed out by losing 100 games and finishing in ninth place, 40 games out.

Malzone, however, has few regrets about his unfortunate timing.

"The whole 11 years I was in the big leagues, I enjoyed every minute of it," he reflected nearly 40 years later. "I wish I had got a chance to play in the postseason. I guess I was 10 years too early, because I would have gotten to play in two World Series: '67 and '75.

"It was a big change when Ted retired and Yaz came in," Malzone said. "Yaz played as good as he could at the time, and then in '67 he had one of the best years any player ever had. I was fortunate I played with Ted five years and then with Yaz five years, which was one of the highlights of my career.

"It was kind of a dead era for the Red Sox. But I approached every year with the feeling that maybe we can somehow get lucky, because there is a little luck involved in baseball, no question about it."

But the Red Sox were neither lucky nor good enough. So Frank Malzone's most memorable performances were often given on an empty stage in front of a small and indifferent audience. People who really knew baseball, however, recognized and appreciated his all-around skills. The incomparable Leo Durocher, once asked if he saw any faults in Malzone, could imagine only one. "Dandruff. Maybe," Durocher commented.

✦✦✦

Malzone, the son of immigrant parents from Italy, was attending Samuel Gompers, a vocational school in the Bronx where he was learning to be an electrician, when his talents on the baseball diamond were spotted.

"I never gave a thought to professional baseball until this birddog scout, Cy Phillips, recommended me to the Red Sox," Malzone recalled. "He asked me if I would be interested in playing pro ball, and I said: 'Yes, why not? I'd love to.' You should have seen the expression on my dad's face when the Red Sox offered me a $150 month. He didn't know you could get paid for playing baseball."

The 18-year-old third baseman hit .305 and helped the Milford (Delaware) Red Sox win the Class D Eastern Shore League pennant in 1948. The following summer he was the All-Star third baseman in the Class C Canadian-American League, leading the league in hits with 178 and triples with 27 while hitting .329 and stealing more than 30 bases for Oneonta, New York. He also met his future wife, Amy, in Oneonta. The Red Sox bumped up Malzone to Class A ball in 1950. But in his second

Eastern League game for Scranton he dislocated his ankle sliding into second and was finished for the season.

"I went from being a plus runner to an average runner," the 5-10, 180-pound, righthanded-hitting Malzone said. However, his potent bat hadn't slowed down. Malzone was back in Scranton in 1951, stayed healthy, and enjoyed another productive season. But the Korean Conflict was raging, and the 21-year-old Malzone was drafted into the Army at the end of that summer. He spent his two years playing service ball in Hawaii, where one of his teammates was Don Larsen, destined to later become the only pitcher to throw a perfect game in the World Series. Malzone remembered hitting four home runs in one game and narrowly missing a fifth, settling for a double off the fence in his last at-bat. He enjoyed his time in the Army, and he and Amy got married.

But as far as the Red Sox were concerned, out of sight meant out of mind. And when he returned to the organization in 1954, other prospects had passed him by, and he felt like an afterthought in spring training that year.

"You come out of the Army, nobody knows what you're going to do," Malzone said. "I thought I'd either make the Triple-A club, or they'd let me go."

He made the Louisville club in the Class AAA American Association. "We had a good team and won the Junior World Series," he remembered. "The next year I went to spring training with the Red Sox for the first time, and I played all of one game. I couldn't believe it. It's not like today where everybody gets in. Pinky Higgins was the manager, and he was set on what he wanted to do. So I went back to Louisville and had a good year, hitting .315." He also made the All-Star Team. In a late-season call-up to the Red Sox, Malzone went 6-for-10 in a doubleheader in Baltimore, his major-league debut.

"I thought I was penciled in to be the regular third baseman in 1956. I think the Red Sox planned for me to be the third baseman," Malzone continued.

Then tragedy struck. The Malzones' 13-month-old daughter, their first child, died suddenly and mysteriously on New Year's Eve. The young couple was devastated.

"I went to spring training, and my wife was out of it. We were both out of it, really. I was dropping pop-ups. I started out the year in Boston, alternating with Billy Klaus, and then they sent me back to the minor leagues, to San Francisco. We met a priest out there who settled us down, got us thinking in the right direction. I know it was doing my wife some

Boston Red Sox third baseman Frank Malzone crosses the plate after hitting a home run at Fenway Park. *(Courtesy of the Boston Red Sox)*

good, and that helped me. You never forget it when you lose your first child like that, but thank God I had my first son, Jimmy, who was two months old at the time. It made a difference that we had another child. I never got over it, but at least I could play now."

Malzone had a good year in the Pacific Coast League, hitting .299 for the Seals. But once again he felt like a forgotten man in spring training. He was 27 years old and began to doubt if he would ever make it.

"The first two weeks of games, and I hadn't played yet. I went to my wife in the hotel one night and said: 'Honey, it looks like I'm going to have to make a decision: Do I want to play Triple-A again or go to work for a living?' We talked it over, and she said to give it a shot.

"We went out to San Francisco for some exhibition games, and by now I wasn't even looking at the lineup anymore. Then one day Pete Daley, a catcher and one of my buddies, comes up to me and says: 'You're playing today.' I said: 'C'mon, don't fool around.' But he says: 'It's true. You're playing.' So I look at the lineup, and I'm in there. I went one-for-four that afternoon, and I played every game the rest of the year. Didn't miss a ballgame, and I had a great year, hit .292 and drove in 103 runs."

In fact, it would be 1960 before Frank Malzone would miss another game for the Red Sox. He had six RBI in a game against the Detroit Tigers in June, and in September he had 10 assists in a game. Malzone finished tied for third in the American League in runs batted in with teammate Jackie Jensen. He also led the league's third basemen in putouts, assists, and double plays and won the very first Gold Glove. He also appeared in the All-Star Game.

Malzone should have been an easy winner as the Rookie of the Year. But during the waning weeks of the 1957 season, the Yankees began lobbying hard for their shortstop, Tony Kubek, who hit .297. The rules back then regarding eligibility for the award were sketchy, and the Yankees argued that Malzone should be disqualified because he had played 33 games and batted 123 times for the Red Sox in 1955-56. Although Malzone had outdoubled Kubek 31-21, outhomered him 15-3, outscored him 82-56, and easily outdistanced him in RBI, 103-39, the Red Sox rookie received just one vote. Kubek got the other 23.

The following year was nearly a carbon copy of Malzone's rookie season. Often batting cleanup behind Williams, Malzone hit .295 with 30 doubles, 15 homers, and 87 RBI in a year when only four AL players topped the 100 mark. One of them was Jensen, who led the league with 122 and won the MVP award despite Boston's mediocre 79-75 record. Malzone also led the league's third basemen in assists and double plays and won another Gold Glove.

His two-run homer beat the Orioles 2-0 on May 30. Back in Baltimore for the All-Star Game on July 8, Malzone singled in the sixth inning off Pittsburgh's Bob Friend and scored the winning run on a pinch single by the Yankees' Gil McDougald to provide the AL with a 4-3 victory. Ten days later he clouted a grand slam and had five RBI in an 11-9 win in Detroit.

The Red Sox' record reversed itself in 1959, inaugurating a string of eight straight losing seasons. But Malzone put together another productive year, hitting .280 with 34 doubles—tying him for second in the league in that department—19 homers, 92 RBI, and 90 runs scored while again leading the league's third basemen in assists and double plays and earning his third straight Gold Glove.

On April 20 he beat the Yankees 5-4 with a 12th-inning homer off fireballing reliever Ryne Duren. Duren was a renowned alcoholic who wore thick glasses and averaged 9.62 strikeouts per nine innings during his career while also averaging six walks. Either by design or due to incurable wildness, one or two of his warmup pitches would invariably wind up smacking into the backstop, leaving waiting hitters intimidated. Malzone was never intimidated by Duren.

"I always hit him well, probably because he only threw fastballs, and I always saw the ball well," Malzone remembered. "It's the guys who throw hard who also have good breaking balls that you have to worry about getting hit, because you stand in there an instant too long wondering if the ball is going to break. [Yankees manager] Ralph Houk told me later he saw Duren in the trainer's room after I hit that homer, and Duren was moaning: 'I just can't get that guy out!'"

On July 20, 1959, Massachusetts Senator John F. Kennedy, who was just beginning his campaign for the presidency, and his brother Bobby were sitting and brooding with Malzone's wife, Amy, in the stands at Fenway Park. The Cleveland Indians, with Jim Perry on the mound, had built up a 5-2 lead over the Red Sox by the late innings, and there had been little for Red Sox fans to cheer about.

"The Kennedy brothers were big Red Sox fans, and one of them said to my wife: 'If Frank doesn't do something, then we aren't going to do anything today,'" Malzone related.

The Red Sox loaded the bases against Perry with two outs in the bottom of the ninth, bringing Malzone to the plate. He drilled a double off the Green Monster to clear the bases and beat the Indians 6-5.

"That was one of my greatest thrills, hitting that game-winning double with the Kennedy brothers in the stands," Malzone reminisced.

Two weeks later, on August 3, Malzone was starting another All-Star Game, this one in the Los Angeles Coliseum. These All-Star Games were the only national stages upon which Frank Malzone would be able to attract the spotlight during his career.

The NL scored a run in the bottom of the first inning, but Malzone tied the game in the second by drilling a home run over the screen in left field off Dodgers ace Don Drysdale. The slick-fielding Malzone was also kept busy at third base, making one putout and racking up six assists, and the AL won the game 5-3.

Three days later, back at Fenway Park, Malzone belted two homers, a double, a single, and drove in five runs to power the Red Sox to a 17-6 rout of Kansas City.

Malzone was an All-Star again in 1960 when he hit .271 with 14 homers and 79 RBI and recorded his fourth straight 30-double season. But the Red Sox continued to get worse and won only 65 games. The durable Malzone had his streak of 475 consecutive games ended when he sat out on June 8. It is the third-longest playing streak in Red Sox history.

"At the time I didn't know I had that many in a row. I didn't find out until Dwight Evans was getting close to my streak in 1983," Malzone said. "I'm still not sure why I didn't play that day. But I think I got hit in the face with a groundball, and it swelled up. They took me to the hospital, and I didn't play the next day."

Malzone got off to a tough start in 1961 and was batting .147 at the end of May. But he finished the year at .266 with 14 homers and 87 RBI, and in 1962 he bashed a career-high 21 homers while knocking in 95 runs and hitting .283. His last homer that season was the 100th of his career.

By Opening Day of 1963, Frank Malzone was 33 years old. But he felt like a kid 10 years younger when the Red Sox, under new manager Johnny Pesky, got off to a quick start. Dick Stuart had come over from the National League and would smash 42 homers with 118 RBI, Carl Yastrzemski would win the first of his three batting crowns with a .321 mark, Bill Monbouquette would win 20 games, and flame-throwing reliever Dick Radatz would come out of the bullpen to terrorize AL hitters and save 25 games and win 15 others. Malzone himself hit like he had never hit before. Thirty-two games into the season Malzone, who had come close a couple of times but had never hit .300, would be leading the league in batting with a lofty .356 mark.

Attendance had plummeted nearly 400,000 in the two years since Ted Williams retired in 1960, and only 733,080 fans had bothered to turn up at Fenway Park in 1962. But the fans began to think things might be different in 1963, and attendance was up nearly 57,000 during the first few weeks as the Red Sox began winning with regularity. For the first time in an All-Star major-league career, Frank Malzone felt like he was in a pennant race.

✦ ✦ ✦

The Red Sox were in first place by percentage points on the morning of May 19, 1963. They were 18-12, a .600 winning percentage, and nearly unbeatable at Fenway with a 13-3 record. But the Chicago White Sox and Baltimore Orioles, with identical 20-14 records, were dead even with the Red Sox in the games-behind column and a mere .012 percentage points behind in the standings. It was quite a race. Even the Kansas City Athletics, who hadn't had a winning season since 1952 when they were in Philadelphia, were only a half-game out of first place. The mighty Yankees, winners of three straight pennants and seven of the last eight, were also a half-game behind at 17-12.

"You almost feel like singing a little song," Malzone chirped to the Boston sportswriters at the time. "We've never really been in first place like this since I came to the big leagues. Oh, sure, we've been there for a little bit, but now we're really up there, if you know what I mean. You begin to feel that if you're up in first place now, why can't you be there at the end of the season?"

The Red Sox and Athletics were scheduled to play a doubleheader at Fenway on this spring afternoon, and because of the rare circumstances—the rag-tag Red Sox were in a pennant race!—the first game would be the most memorable game of Frank Malzone's illustrious career.

"I had hit two home runs in a game plenty of times—and I would have had a three-homer game in Cleveland if Minnie Minoso hadn't reached over the fence and taken two away from me," he remembered. "But this time I accomplished something. We won the game 7-3, and I drove in five of the runs. Driving in runs was important to me. I loved to drive in the tough runs in a ballgame. I didn't try to approach it any certain way; I just wanted to put the ball in play and hit it as hard as you possibly can. You hit it hard, and nine out of ten times you're going to get a basehit.

"Dick Radatz—God rest his soul—always said—and maybe he was just blowing smoke—but he said: 'If I want a guy up at the plate late in a ballgame that I'm pitching and I want to win, I want that guy to be you.' And we had some pretty good guys: Yastrzemski, Dick Stuart, and in '64 Tony Conigliaro. But Radatz said he wanted me up there."

Bill Monbouquette started the first game for the Red Sox that day in front of an enthusiastic crowd of 24,153, and the Athletics jumped on him in the first inning for a run when Wayne Causey doubled and Gino Cimoli brought him in with a single.

The Red Sox retaliated with three runs in the bottom of the inning off righthander Dave Wickersham. Successive singles to open the game by Chuck Schilling, Gary Geiger, and Yaz tied the game and brought Malzone, the cleanup hitter, to the plate.

"Wickersham was one of those sidearming righthanders who didn't throw hard but had a good sinker and a pretty good breaking ball," Malzone remembered. "He was one of those guys who liked to throw inside and knock you off the plate. I had had some good success against him, but I never really felt I could hit home runs off him."

Malzone delivered a two-run single, and the Red Sox led 3-1. When Malzone batted again in the third, this time with the bases empty, much to his surprise he belted a home run in the screen above the fabled Green Monster.

Yaz singled in the fifth, and

**FRANK MALZONE**
Years with Red Sox: 1955-65
Other Major League Teams:
  California
Position: Third Base
Bats: Right
Throws: Right
Height: 5-10
Weight: 180
Born: February 28, 1930
Birthplace: The Bronx, NY
Current Residence: Needham, MA
Current Occupation: Red Sox scout

Malzone followed with his second homer of the game into the screen off Wickersham, putting the Red Sox ahead 6-1. It was the 10th two-homer game of his career.

"You always remember the big games you had, and that was one of them," Malzone said. "Those were probably the only two home runs I ever hit off Wickersham."

Wickersham was long gone by the time Malzone came up again in the seventh. He had been unceremoniously lifted immediately after serving up Malzone's second homer. This time Malzone was facing rookie righthanded reliever Dave Thies.

"When I get in the batter's box and see a kid I don't know, you hit off his fastball, because if he got to the big leagues, he has to throw pretty good," Malzone said. "I looked for his fastball, got a good ball to hit, and lined it into left field for a single."

It was Malzone's fourth hit of the game. Lu Clinton hit a groundball that forced Malzone at second, but Clinton came around to score on a double by Eddie Bressoud.

Not until the eighth could the Athletics manage another run off Monbouquette, and doubles by Norm Siebern and George Alusik cut the Red Sox lead to 7-3. Pesky quickly went to the bullpen for Radatz.

"This guy, when he came into a ballgame, I could take it easy for two innings or however long he was going to pitch because no one was going to pull the ball down to me," Malzone recalled fondly. "To me he was, for four years, the best relief pitcher the Red Sox ever had. He not only got 'em out, he struck 'em out.

"I actually said to him one time when he came into a game: 'Hey, Dick! You don't mind if I sit on the bag, do you?' He said: 'Do anything you want. We'll be in the clubhouse in a couple of minutes.' That's how dominant this man was."

Radatz blew away the last five Kansas City batters of the game, three of them on strikes. The Red Sox won, and Malzone had gone 4-for-4 and driven in five of their seven runs. Looking for his fifth hit and maybe another homer, he was left standing on deck when the Red Sox went out in the bottom of the eighth.

"When you're going strong, you always want that next at-bat," Malzone said. "Don't be a satisfied player. I learned that from Mickey Vernon."

Malzone also had two hits in the second game and another RBI, but the Athletics outlasted the Red Sox 9-7 and earned a split of the doubleheader. The White Sox and Orioles also split a doubleheader that day to stay in a virtual deadlock with the Red Sox for first place while the Yankees divided their doubleheader with the Los Angeles Angels to remain tied with the Athletics, a half-game back.

Malzone finished the afternoon with six hits and six RBI. After the doubleheader the league's leading hitter tried to play down his batting achievements to the assembled sportswriters at his locker.

"I've had good pitches to hit, and I haven't been missing them," he explained to them. "There have been other years and other days when you have those same pitches to hit and foul them off or pop them up."

*The Boston Globe* was most effusive in its praise of the Red Sox third baseman in the next morning's editions.

"Among our most sheepish citizens this morning are those who suggested during the winter that the Sox trade Malzone and play Yazzledazzle at third," wrote Harold Kaese. "So far, Yaz has been indispensable in left, Malzone at third. It should never be hard to figure out an award for Malzone: Most Overlooked Player, or Star Most Taken for Granted."

+ + +

Malzone continued to lead the American League in hitting through most of June, and the Red Sox stayed in the race. On June 11 Radatz relieved Wilbur Wood in the seventh inning of a game in Detroit and hurled eight and two-thirds innings of three-hit, scoreless relief while striking out 11 Tigers. Malzone, who was hitting .344, won the game for him in the 15th inning with a three-run homer off Terry Fox, and Dick Stuart followed with a solo homer to cap the 7-3 triumph.

On June 28 the Red Sox were in third place with a 40-30 record, only one and a half games behind the Yankees and White Sox. Malzone, who was hitting .348, learned he had been elected to start the All-Star Game, outpolling Baltimore's Brooks Robinson 184-67 among the players, managers, and coaches who chose the teams in that era.

Only hours before the first pitch of the All-Star Game in Cleveland on July 9, Malzone received the news that Amy had just given birth to their third son, Frank Jr. Malzone celebrated by ripping an RBI single and scoring himself in the third inning, but the NL stars prevailed 5-3.

"Everything I hit halfway decent was a base hit, and I was even getting base hits to right field, which I didn't do too often in my career," he said about his terrific start in 1963. "But when you're leading the league, believe me, the pressure starts getting to you. You start thinking about it too much, and you go to the plate worrying about getting base hits instead of being natural and letting things happen the way they're supposed to happen."

Yaz overtook Malzone in the batting race in July, and the two Red Sox stars continued to rank one-two for most of the month. On July 18 the Red Sox were 50-41 and in fourth place, very much still within striking range of the first-place Yankees, who were six games ahead. But they collapsed, losing 19 of their next 23 games. For Frank Malzone and the rest of the Red Sox, the pennant race was over before the stretch run had even begun. The first three and a half months of the 1963 season had been merely a tease for Red Sox fans, and the club finished a disappointing seventh with a 76-85 record, 28 games behind the champion Yankees. Malzone ended the year at .291 with 15 homers and 71 RBI.

**Frank Malzone, one of the best-fielding third basemen of his era, reminisces about his career with the Boston Red Sox.**
*(Courtesy of Chaz Scoggins)*

"We were off to a good start, no question about it. Everything was going good, and I felt like I let the club down," he said regretfully. "Me hanging in there might have made the difference."

By then in his mid-30s, Malzone's production began to slip noticeably during the next two seasons. The Red Sox, ready to rebuild after a 100-loss campaign in 1965, let their eight-time All-Star third baseman go. After playing 82 games for the California Angels in 1966, Malzone announced his retirement.

Frank Malzone hit .276 in 1,359 games for the Red Sox from 1955-65 with 131 homers and 716 RBI. An outstanding contact hitter, he struck out only 423 times in 5,273 at-bats. He has remained with the Red Sox as a scout, and he and Amy continue to make their home in suburban Boston. He was elected to the Red Sox Hall of Fame in 1995.

# Chapter 7

# RICO PETROCELLI

## OCTOBER 1, 1967

merico Petrocelli was born into a working-class immigrant family on June 27, 1943, in Brooklyn, New York. His father, Attilio, shared a business with four cousins, repairing cutting tools in New York City's garment district. The youngest of seven children, Petrocelli starred in both basketball and baseball at Sheepshead Bay High School, earning All-Scholastic honors in both sports. Because of his pro baseball potential, Rico was excused from having to work the way his older brothers had to in order to supplement the family income.

"I was able to go out and play baseball and become a good athlete," Petrocelli explained to author Ken Coleman in the book *The Impossible Dream Remembered: The 1967 Red Sox.* "It was all because of my brothers. They were working, bringing in the extra money we needed."

The sacrifices paid off for the Petrocelli family when scout Bots Nekola signed Rico to a Red Sox contract on July 2, 1961, just a few days after his 18th birthday. The skinny, six-foot shortstop adapted quickly to pro ball and displayed impressive power for his size by swatting 30 doubles and 17 homers while driving in 80 runs and hitting .277 for Winston-Salem in the Class B Carolina League in 1962. He also earned All-Star honors that season. Playing at Class AA Reading in 1963, Petrocelli's batting average slipped to .239. But he did clout 19 homers and drive in 78 runs while again being named the Eastern League's All-Star shortstop, and the Red Sox brought the 20-year-old prospect up for one game near the end of the season.

Petrocelli spent the entire 1964 season in the Class AAA Pacific Coast League with Seattle, and in such fast company he struggled with the bat for the first time, hitting just .231 with 10 homers and 48 RBI in 134 games and failing to make the All-Star team. Because of the sacrifices his family had made to allow him to play baseball, Petrocelli put enormous pressure on himself to succeed, and he was devastated by what he perceived to be a poor season.

"I always put tremendous pressure on myself," he said. "I wanted, like every player, to be a superstar like Mickey Mantle or Ted Williams. My first year in the Carolina League, when I hit .280 with 17 home runs and 80 RBI, I thought I was a failure. I didn't want to go home. I thought: 'Omigod, how am I going to face anybody?'"

But the Red Sox were not disappointed in the least by Petrocelli's Triple-A performance. All they were concerned with was his defense, and they deemed him ready for the majors.

Veteran Eddie Bressoud was the incumbent shortstop for the Red Sox. He had hit 20 homers in 1963 and was coming off a .293 season with 41 doubles and 15 homers in 1964. But the Red Sox eased the 21-year-old Petrocelli into the position in 1965.

The rookie hit a modest .232 in 103 games but displayed a perfect stroke for Fenway Park and hit 13 homers. It was a terrible year for the Red Sox, however. They lost 100 games for the first time in 33 years and finished in ninth place, 40 games behind the American League champion Minnesota Twins. The club only drew 652,000 fans, its lowest attendance since World War II.

"That team was going nowhere," Petrocelli remembered. "They'd let people in early to watch batting practice, and some of the things said, man, you wouldn't believe! 'Lee Thomas! You stink! Ya bum!' and a lot worse stuff you couldn't print."

The Red Sox had not enjoyed a winning season since 1958, and they had not finished closer than 11 games to first place since 1950. The stars from those exciting postwar clubs had long since retired, and it was difficult for Red Sox fans in 1965 to believe that the club was truly rebuilding. Carl Yastrzemski had already won a batting crown since replacing the legendary Ted Williams in left field, but there seemed to be little talent surrounding him, and many of the fans were far from enamored with Yaz, with whom they engendered a love-hate relationship akin to the one they'd had with Williams.

But one of their promising young kids, 20-year-old rightfielder Tony Conigliaro, a local high school hero from the Boston suburb of Revere, had led the AL with 32 homers in just his second major-league season, and now

**Young Boston Red Sox shortstop Rico Petrocelli takes a few practice swings under the watchful eye of hitting coach Bobby Doerr during spring training in Winter Haven, Florida.**
*(Courtesy of the Boston Red Sox)*

Petrocelli was on the club. Two more talented rookies joined the Red Sox lineup in 1966. Slick-fielding first baseman George "Boomer" Scott bashed 27 homers and drove in 90 runs, and third baseman Joe Foy broke in with 15 homers, 63 RBI, and a .262 average. Petrocelli upped his production slightly to 18 homers and 59 RBI but hit only .238. The Red Sox improved their record by 10 games but again finished ninth, a mere half-game ahead of the once-mighty New York Yankees, who had crashed from their fifth straight pennant to tenth place in only two years. The fans still weren't sold on the notion that the Red Sox were developing into contenders; only 811,000 turned up at Fenway that year.

And then, almost overnight, "The Impossible Dream" became a reality.

The 1967 Red Sox added two more talented rookies, centerfielder Reggie Smith and second baseman Mike Andrews. The average age of their starting lineup on Opening Day was 23 and a half. Yaz, at 27, was the "old man" of the group. They also had a brash young rookie manager in 38-year-old Dick Williams, who was ridiculed when he predicted at the end of spring training that the Red Sox, who had not had a winning season in eight years, would "win more than we lose."

But win they did. Yaz would capture Major League Baseball's last Triple Crown to date, winning the AL batting title with a .326 average while leading the league with 121 RBI and tying for the home run crown with 44 and winning MVP laurels. Jim Lonborg, a 25-year-old righthander who had compiled a 19-27 record in his first two years with the Red Sox, would win the Cy Young Award by posting a 22-9 record with a 3.16 ERA, leading the league in wins and strikeouts with 246. The rest of the cast, including Petrocelli, would come up with clutch hits, clutch plays, and clutch pitching performances throughout that improbable, unforgettable summer.

There were only 8,234 fans scattered throughout the stands on a bitterly cold and windy Opening Day at Fenway Park on April 12, 1967. But Petrocelli muscled a home run through the crosswind and drove in four runs as the Red Sox edged the Chicago White Sox 5-4. Petrocelli got off to a good start, hitting .333 with 10 RBI in 14 games in April, and the Red Sox finished the month with an 8-6 record good for third place, one game behind the Detroit Tigers and Yankees.

Heading into June, they were still holding their own with a 22-20 record, in third place and four and a half games behind the Tigers and White Sox. Petrocelli's bat remained hot; he was fourth in the league in hitting with a .325 average and had six homers and 24 RBI.

It was often difficult for Williams to keep a lineup or pitching rotation together for very long. The war in Vietnam was escalating, and while none of the young Red Sox players was on active duty, many of them were in armed forces reserve or National Guard units. At various times players had to leave the club for weekend or two-week military commitments. All 20 major-league teams had to adjust to the same circumstances, but the Red Sox were so young, the constant shuffling of personnel seemed to be more of a hardship for them than most other clubs.

Although the 23-year-old Petrocelli had no military commitments to deal with, the size of his young family tripled on June 7 when his wife, Elsie, gave birth to twins. As described by Coleman in his book, Rico was "a worrier" and so insecure about his status with the Red Sox that he was afraid to invest in a house for his wife and three children and continued to rent. Third base coach Eddie Popowski, who had spent a lot of time with Petrocelli in the minors, had to constantly reassure him about his ability, and even the gruff Williams found it prudent to give the shortstop an extra pat or two on the back now and then.

In mid-June the Red Sox fans finally began to be convinced that the team was a genuine contender. The turning point came on June 15 after the Red Sox and White Sox had battled through 10 scoreless innings at Fenway. The White Sox pushed across a run in the top of the 11th, and in the bottom of the inning Conigliaro, down to his last strike, belted a two-out, two-run homer to win the game 2-1.

Six days later the Red Sox forged an unbreakable bond at Yankee Stadium. The Red Sox were already ahead 4-0 in the second inning when Yankees pitcher Thad Tillotson beaned Joe Foy, whose grand slam had powered the Sox to a 7-1 win the previous evening. Foy stayed in the game and scored the fifth run. Jim Lonborg retaliated by drilling Tillotson in the shoulder in the bottom of the inning, both benches emptied, and a full-scale brawl broke out. Petrocelli flattened Yankees first baseman Joe Pepitone—a Brooklyn neighbor he had known for years—with a punch to the jaw before being pulled out of the melee by Dave Petrocelli, one of his brothers who was working security at the stadium. Some Yankees swore they heard Dave Petrocelli yelling: "You hurt my brother, I'll break your leg! I'll kill all you guys!"

Amazingly, no one was thrown out of the game. Tillotson responded by hitting Lonborg with a pitch in the third, and again both benches cleared, although this time the altercation was limited to some shoving and a lot of trash talk. Lonborg went back to the mound and brushed back Charley Smith and then beaned Dick Howser—his 10th hit batsman that season. This time the umpires stopped the game, summoned both managers, and ordered the nonsense to stop. The headhunting ceased, but the Red Sox had come together as a team, and they went on to pummel the Yankees 9-2. A loss that night would have left them with a .500 record. Now they were 32-30 and would maintain a winning record the rest of the way to back up Williams's spring training boast.

Petrocelli was hitting .296 with eight homers and 32 RBI when he was hit in the wrist with a pitch thrown by Cleveland's George Culver on June 23. He only suffered a bruise, but it was bad enough to keep him out of the lineup for two weeks. Despite the injury, Petrocelli was picked by Baltimore manager Hank Bauer to start the All-Star Game at shortstop for the American League. Petrocelli's wrist was still sore, however, and he batted only once before being taken out of the game in Anaheim on July 11. He watched the rest of the longest All-Star Game in history from the dugout as the National League won 2-1 on Tony Perez' 15th-inning homer.

The Red Sox went on a tear after the break, winning 10 straight games from July 14-23, and for the first time since 1949, pennant fever broke out

| RICO PETROCELLI |
| --- |
| **Years with Red Sox: 1963, 1965-76** |
| **Other Major League Teams: None** |
| **Position: Shortstop** |
| **Bats: Right** |
| **Throws: Right** |
| **Height: 6-0** |
| **Weight: 185** |
| **Born: June 27, 1943** |
| **Birthplace: Brooklyn, NY** |
| **Current Residence: Nashua, NH** |
| **Current Occupation: Distributor of novelty items** |

in New England. When the team returned to Boston after sweeping a doubleheader in Cleveland, 15,000 delirious fans greeted the flight at Logan Airport. "It was a mob scene," Ken Coleman wrote in his book, "bigger even than the crowd The Beatles drew at Logan the year before." The Beatles may have been, as John Lennon once claimed, more popular than Jesus Christ. But in 1967 the Red Sox were clearly more popular than The Beatles. Before the month was out, they had already drawn one million fans to Fenway Park for the first time since Ted Williams's farewell year in 1960.

"We were circling Logan, and we began wondering what's going on," Petrocelli recalled. "Finally the captain came on the intercom and said there were so many fans waiting, they didn't know what to do. After we landed they put us right on a bus, and we looked at each other and said: 'What are we doing?' Ten, fifteen thousand people came out to the airport to see us, and we're going to dodge them? Not at least say hello? So we said we were going to go through the baggage claim, and the place was packed! You could hardly walk through. There were fathers there with their kids on their shoulders. It was so fabulous! The year before they would have been out there trying to kill us!"

Petrocelli never regained his stroke after the injury to his wrist, and he hit only one homer and drove in just seven runs in July. But he was still getting the job done in the field, and the Red Sox finished the month in second place with a 56-44 record, just two games behind the White Sox. The Twins and Tigers were also right in the thick of things, setting up the most dramatic four-team race in American League history.

The Red Sox lost Tony Conigliaro on August 18 when he was tragically beaned by California's Jack Hamilton. Petrocelli was on deck and was the first Red Sox to arrive at the sickening scene. A doubleheader two days later was gut-wrenching for different reasons. The Red Sox led 12-7 in the ninth inning of the first game when the Angels rallied for four runs and had the tying run on third and the go-ahead run on first with two outs. Bob Rodgers hit a slow chopper to short, but Petrocelli charged the ball hard and threw out Rodgers by half a step to preserve the victory. The Red Sox then trailed 8-0 in the second game before rallying for a dramatic 9-8 win on utility infielder Jerry Adair's homer. After that weekend, Red Sox fans truly believed they were watching a team of destiny. A popular song, "The Impossible Dream," from the Broadway show *Man of La Mancha,* had become the Red Sox' theme.

The Red Sox were in first place by the end of the month with a 76-59 record. But their lead was a tenuous half-game over Minnesota, one over Detroit, and one and a half over Chicago. The four teams would play leap-frog and battle each other down to the final weekend.

The Red Sox, who had just pulled into a tie for first place with the Twins the night before, were locked in a 1-1 tie with the sorry Kansas City Athletics on September 13. Joe Foy was on third with two outs in the eighth inning. Ken "Hawk" Harrelson, whom the Red Sox had signed to replace the stricken Tony C. after A's owner Charlie Finley had gotten in a snit and released the colorful, outspoken slugger, was due up next. Jack Aker walked Harrelson intentionally to get to Petrocelli, who had driven in the only Red Sox run with a fourth-inning single. This time Petrocelli drove a double over the head of centerfielder Jim Gosger, chasing home both Foy and Harrelson. Petrocelli scored on a single by Reggie Smith, and the Red Sox won 4-2.

Heading into the final weekend of the regular season, the pennant was still up for grabs between the four teams, who were still separated by a mere one and a half games. The Twins were 91-69, the Tigers 89-69, the Red Sox

90-70, and the White Sox 89-70. While the other three teams rested on Friday, September 29, the White Sox lost 1-0 to the hapless Washington Senators and were eliminated. The Red Sox and Twins would go head to head at Fenway in the last two games, and the Red Sox had to win them both.

While Detroit was splitting the first of two doubleheaders with California on Saturday, blowing a four-run, eighth-inning lead in the nightcap, the Red Sox beat the Twins 6-4 to pull back into a tie for first. Another win on the final day of the regular season would assure the Red Sox of no worse than a tie for first place with Detroit, should the Tigers sweep their doubleheader with the Angels.

"It was a first-time situation for all of us, the guys who were up from '64 on," Petrocelli said. "We had lost a lot of games, so this was unfamiliar. And we were playing an excellent Minnesota team that had been to the World Series in '65. But we didn't have anything to lose. Even if we lost, it would have been a great year for us."

The Red Sox didn't lose, and that Sunday afternoon game on October 1, 1967, would be the most memorable game of Rico Petrocelli's career.

"I picked this game because when you compare it to what happened in the past, it was such a great year, and it was a new era in Red Sox baseball," Petrocelli explained. "It changed history for the Red Sox. Just being part of that game was one of the big thrills in my life, and I was privileged to make the last catch in that game."

✦✦✦

Fenway Park was overflowing with 35,770 fans crammed inside that afternoon. The Twins sent their ace, 20-game winner Dean Chance, to the mound to oppose 21-game winner Jim Lonborg. The Twins struck first, scoring an unearned run in the first inning when first baseman George Scott threw away the relay on a double by Tony Oliva. Petrocelli singled to center in the second but was left stranded.

The Twins added another unearned run in the third when leftfielder Carl Yastrzemski overran Harmon Killebrew's single for another error, allowing Cesar Tovar to score all the way from first. The Red Sox looked nervous; their two best defensive players—both Scott and Yaz would win Gold Gloves in 1967—had given Minnesota two runs, and the fans were getting restless. Was 1967 going to be a reprise of 1948 and 1949?

"We made the errors, but we were being aggressive," Petrocelli said. "The one thing we had said before the game was that no matter what happened, we had to play aggressive; don't wait for things to happen."

Lonborg started the bottom of the third with a single, but Adair grounded into a double play. Yaz doubled to lead off the fourth but was doubled up on a line drive by Scott right back to Chance. What else could go wrong?

Going into the bottom of the sixth inning, the Twins still led 2-0. Chance had allowed only four hits, and only one Red Sox runner had gotten as far as second base.

"Chance was a tough, tough pitcher," Petrocelli remembered. "He had an excellent sinker and that good curveball that was tough on righties. We knew he was going to be tough."

Lonborg, a .129 hitter going into the game, was due to lead off, and Dick Williams let him bat while the fans in the stands, watching on TV, and listening on the radio second-guessed the strategy. Lonborg dropped down a bunt and beat it out for his second hit of the game.

"That caught us by surprise. Lonborg wasn't too good a hitter," Petrocelli said. "But how a bunt can pump everybody up was incredible. We needed something to pick us up, and Jimmy made a perfect bunt.

"A veteran team would calmly say: 'Okay, here it comes.' A rally was expected. For us it was: 'All right! We got a hit! Come on guys, let's go!' Like a rah-rah college team," he related. "I can never remember us calmly saying: 'Okay, here we come.' We didn't have that swagger. We were more like kids. We were the underdogs playing a good team, and every hit was 'Yay!' Jimmy got the bunt down, and we were jumping up and down in the dugout like Little Leaguers."

Singles by Adair and Dalton Jones loaded the bases with still nobody out, and the crowd came alive. Yaz kept the rally rolling by lashing another single up the middle, tying the game while Jones raced to third. Harrelson bounced a ball to deep short, and Zoilo Versalles foolishly tried to get Jones at the plate. The throw was late, and the Red Sox led 3-2.

"It was fun! Bang! Another hit. Then another. And all of a sudden we're ahead, and it was a great feeling," Petrocelli recalled.

Al Worthington relieved Chance and uncorked two wild pitches, allowing Yaz to score and pinch runner Jose Tartabull to scramble to third. Worthington fanned Scott for the first out of the inning, but Petrocelli drew a walk. First baseman Killebrew booted Reggie Smith's grounder for an error as Tartabull dashed home with the fifth and final run of the inning.

The Twins countered with a run in the eighth on Bob Allison's two-out single, but Yaz short-circuited the rally by gunning him down at second when he tried for the extra base. It was still 5-3 when the Twins batted in the ninth. Ted Uhlaender led off with an infield hit, but Rod Carew rapped into a double play. The Twins were down to their last out as Rich Rollins pinch hit for Russ Nixon.

"Rollins being a righthanded hitter and Lonborg a good sinkerballer, you had to think the ball was coming to the left side," Petrocelli recalled. "Dalton Jones was at third base, and I yelled over: 'Roomie!'—We were roommates—'Be ready! I think this ball may come our way! At that point you want the ball hit to you. Make the out. Get it over with. Lonborg's ball was tailing in, he hits Rollins on the hands, and it's popped up to me … but not very high. I made sure I went back and saw the ball, and boom! in the glove.

"I squeezed it, and I went down, and it just didn't hit me right away. And then when I looked up, there was Dalton Jones yelling: 'Roomie! Roomie! We did it!' And then I said: 'Holy Jeez! Wow!' And I started jumping up and down, I was so excited."

The fans flooded out of the stands and onto the field to celebrate, and nobody was going to try to stop them.

"I went to give Jim Lonborg the ball, but by that time the fans had taken him out to right field on their shoulders," Petrocelli related. "The people on the field were so excited. It was so nice to see them happy and not coming after us with axes."

Petrocelli finally gave the ball to Lonborg in the clubhouse, where pandemonium was also reigning. Finally the team settled down to listen to the Angels-Tigers game on the radio. So far all the Red Sox had done was clinch a tie for first place. The Tigers had already won the first game in Detroit to keep their chances alive, and the second game was being piped in. Another Detroit win and there would be a one-game playoff for the pennant. The Tigers bolted to an early 3-1 lead, but the Angels came back and won the game 8-5.

The Red Sox had won the pennant for the first time since 1946.

✦ ✦ ✦

The Red Sox again played the St. Louis Cardinals, who had beaten them in seven games back in 1946, in the World Series. Petrocelli, who had led AL shortstops with 17 homers and 66 RBI while hitting .259 during the regular season, belted two homers in Game 6 as the Red Sox won 8-4 to force a seventh game. The Cardinals won that one 7-2, but the World Series loss did little to diminish what the Red Sox had accomplished by going from ninth place to winning the pennant. The euphoria generated by the "Impossible Dream" Red Sox has continued unabated for nearly 40 years.

Rico Petrocelli, who held the American League record for home runs by a shortstop for three decades and played in two World Series, recounts the highlights of his career. *(Courtesy of Chaz Scoggins)*

"We put so much energy into the season, into the last game, and it takes a little out of you," Petrocelli said. "The Cardinals were a great team, and [pitcher Bob] Gibson was too much. When it was over, we were disappointed. But what a great year it was! It brought the fans back, and it made so many new fans. It would have been nice to win the World Series, but at least it was the start of something new and good, and I'm happy to have been a part of it."

The Red Sox would not win another pennant, however, until 1975, when Petrocelli was near the end of his career. Petrocelli set an American League record for shortstops in 1969 by blasting 40 homers, breaking the standard of 39 set by another Red Sox shortstop, Vern Stephens, in 1949.

"I was getting concerned toward the end of the season," he remembered. "I was running out of games. Then, in Washington, I got a hanging slider from [Jim] Shellenback. I hit a line drive to left that I thought was gone, but I forgot big Frank Howard was out there. Thank God he could only jump about three-quarters of an inch off the ground, and the ball went over his head."

Petrocelli's record would endure for nearly 30 years, until Alex Rodriguez of the Seattle Mariners erased it by swatting 42 in 1998. Petrocelli also finished second to Reggie Jackson in slugging percentage in 1969 with a .589 mark and set a Red Sox record for shortstops by playing 48 straight games without an error.

Petrocelli had 29 homers and a career-high 103 RBI in 1970, then moved to third base in 1971 and hit 28 homers while playing 77 straight games without committing an error at his new position. He won another pennant with the Red Sox in 1975, hitting a home run in their three-game sweep of the three-time defending World Champion Oakland Athletics in the ALCS and then hitting .308 with four RBI in the World Series against Cincinnati. Petrocelli retired after the 1976 season at the age of 33. He finished his 1,553-game career with 210 homers and 773 RBI while batting .251. He still ranks seventh on the Red Sox all-time list in RBI and eighth in homers and was inducted into the Red Sox Hall of Fame in 1997.

Since retiring as a player Petrocelli has worked in TV and radio as a broadcaster and managed in both the Red Sox and Chicago White Sox minor-league systems. He presently runs a novelty item business. Rico and Elsie Petrocelli, the parents of four grown sons, reside in Nashua, New Hampshire.

# Chapter 8

# FRED LYNN

## JUNE 18, 1975

F ew ballplayers ever made the game look easier than Frederic Michael Lynn. Fred was born in Chicago on February 3, 1952. But when his father, who was in the linen supply business, was transferred to Southern California two years later, the Lynn family settled in El Monte. A three-sport star in high school, Lynn was a second-round draft pick by the New York Yankees after his senior season. The offer from the Yankees was a generous one, but the naturally gifted Lynn had been recruited to the nearby University of Southern California—on a football scholarship.

"My dad said it would take a lot of money for me to forgo college," Lynn recalled. "I was going to be the first one in my family to go to college, so it was very important to us."

Lynn excelled in baseball under the coaching of the legendary Rod Dedeaux at USC, and the Trojans won three straight College World Series titles while he was there. Lynn earned All-America honors during his sophomore and junior years in 1972 and 1973, and the scouts began touting him as a sure-fire first-round draft pick when he led the nation's collegians with 14 homers as a sophomore. But after a comparatively disappointing junior season at USC, the ardor of the scouts cooled, and Lynn was still available late in the second round of the 1973 draft.

"I hit seven of those 14 homers in the NCAA Tournament," Lynn related. "But the Pac-8, as it was called then, had a lot of tough lefty pitchers my junior year. I still hit over .300 but didn't hit as many home runs, and the scouts started saying I couldn't hit lefties. But home runs—no matter what level I was at—always came in streaks for me.

"I thought the Dodgers would take me in the second round. They were sure I would last that long," Lynn continued. "But Boston got up just before them and drafted me. I had never seen a Boston scout. I didn't know anything about Boston. But I thought the world of my coach and talked to him. Dedeaux said it was a good organization, and I had done everything I could at the college level."

Despite receiving Dedeaux's blessing, Lynn still had doubts about signing with the Red Sox, especially when their contract offer was loaded with incentives instead of guaranteed money. "I said no, give it all to me now," Lynn remembered. To keep Lynn from returning to USC for his senior season, the Red Sox caved and gave him an up-front $40,000 bonus, which was first-round bonus money in those days.

The Red Sox started him immediately in Class AA ball at Bristol, and while he collected 19 extra-base hits and 36 RBI in 53 games, he batted only .259. Lynn had a stronger season with Class AAA Pawtucket in 1974, swatting 21 homers and knocking in 68 runs in 124 games while batting .282. But he was overshadowed by Pawtucket teammate Jim Rice, the Red Sox' first-round pick in 1971 who was a year younger than Lynn. Rice won the International League Triple Crown, hitting .337 with 25 homers and 93 RBI before earning a mid-August promotion to Boston. Lynn arrived in early September with much less fanfare and got only got three at-bats in the first 10 days while the Red Sox desperately tried to climb back into the American League East Division race they had led by seven games on August 23. With the Red Sox in third place and two and a half games behind on September 15, manager Darrell Johnson finally gave Lynn a start in center field against the Milwaukee Brewers.

"Darrell threw me in there because no one else was hitting," Lynn remembered. "I knew I would never embarrass myself defensively—defense has always been the best part of my game in any sport I played—but when I started out hitting, he kept me in there. And I said to myself: 'You know what? You can do this.' It was just a matter of doing it every day."

Lynn homered and doubled in his first two at-bats off Jim Slaton that day. Although the Red Sox lost to the Brewers 9-5 and ended the season in third place, seven games out, Lynn hit .419 with two homers and 10 RBI in 15 games.

Great things were expected of rookies Rice and Lynn in 1975, and neither was a disappointment as the Red Sox rolled to their first pennant since 1967. In almost any other year, Rice would have easily been the AL's

**Boston Red Sox centerfielder Fred Lynn cocks his bat and waits for a pitch during a game at Fenway Park.** *(Courtesy of the Boston Red Sox)*

Rookie of the Year. But Lynn turned in a phenomenal campaign that made him the first player in history to be Rookie of the Year and Most Valuable Player in the same season. Not until Ichiro Suzuki won both awards for the Seattle Mariners in 2001 would Lynn's feat be duplicated.

Lynn hit a pair of homers and scored three times in a 4-2 triumph over the Yankees at Shea Stadium—Yankee Stadium was undergoing renovations—on April 16, then went 3-for-3 and homered again two days later in a 9-7 loss to the Baltimore Orioles at Fenway Park. On April 23 he helped rally the Red Sox from a 7-3 deficit against the Yankees by drilling an RBI single and scoring during a five-run rally in the seventh, then putting the game out of reach with a three-run double in the eighth as Boston won 11-7. Lynn was off to a .429 start with 13 RBI in 10 games.

On May 22, Lynn began a three-week spree. He went 3-for-4 with a three-run homer in a 6-3 loss to the California Angels that night and homered again in a 6-1 triumph over the Angels the next night that put the Red Sox one and a half games behind the first-place Brewers. Lynn didn't start the next game against tough California lefty Andy Hassler and went 0-for-1 after entering the game as a defensive replacement in Boston's 6-0 win that put the Red Sox into first place. Lynn launched a 20-game hitting streak the following day that would hike his average from .333 to .348 and help keep the Red Sox on top of the division. Although Darrell Johnson had two future Hall of Famers on his team in veterans Carl Yastrzemski and Carlton Fisk, the manager had such faith in his two rookies that Lynn was batting cleanup against righthanders while Rice was occupying the slot against southpaws.

"Darrell had seen us in the Triple-A playoffs when he was managing Pawtucket in 1973," Lynn said. "We had been called up from Bristol for the playoffs and done well, so Darrell had seen what we could do in the pressure of a playoff situation. So it wasn't a big deal for Darrell to put us in there."

On June 7 Lynn singled, doubled, homered, and drove in two runs in a 3-1 win over the Minnesota Twins, extending his hitting streak to 11 games. Lynn clubbed his 10th homer, a three-run shot, in a 10-4 romp over Kansas City in the first game of a doubleheader on June 13, then hit another three-run shot in a 4-3 win over the Royals the next night. Lynn ran his hitting streak to 20 games on June 15, the longest by a Red Sox hitter in 11 years. The Royals and Red Sox were tied 4-4 in the eighth when Lynn ignited a four-run rally with a single, and the Sox held on to win 8-7.

Lynn had plenty of opportunities to keep his hitting streak alive in Detroit the next night. The game lasted 12 innings before the Red Sox pulled out a 6-2 win, but Lynn went 0-for-5. Lynn rebounded with a single, scored a run, and drove in one in a 7-6 victory over the Tigers in the following game. The Red Sox were 34-24 and leading the AL East by one and a half games. Lynn was hitting .337 with 11 homers and 40 RBI. He was fourth in the league in hitting behind three-time defending batting champ Rod Carew of Minnesota, who was hitting .395 and flirting with .400; 1974 Rookie of the Year Mike Hargrove of Texas, who was hitting .356; and Thurman Munson of the Yankees, who was at .339. Lynn was slugging .585 and boasting a .402 on-base percentage, but he was still smarting over the end of his streak 24 hours earlier.

"I had had plenty of chances to keep it going and didn't, and I was disappointed with my swing," Lynn recalled 30 years later. "I didn't sleep well that night, and I was up at five a.m. and walking the streets of Detroit—which probably wasn't a real good idea in those days. I went out to the ballpark early to take extra BP—which was something I rarely did—and Dwight Evans threw to me."

"I don't think I helped very much," laughed Evans 30 years later. "Throwing BP isn't easy when you aren't used to doing it. Freddie was yelling and cursing at me the whole time."

But a few hours later, on the evening of June 18, 1975, 23-year-old Fred Lynn would experience the most astonishing—and memorable—game of his Red Sox career.

✦ ✦ ✦

Joe Coleman, Jr., a 28-year-old righthander and two-time 20-game winner, started on the mound for the Tigers in front of a turnout of 13,029 at Tiger Stadium. He retired the first batter of the game, Juan Beniquez, on a flyball to center but was then tagged for a triple by Rick Burleson and a double by Carl Yastrzemski that put the Red Sox ahead 1-0. Lynn came to the plate.

"I didn't know Joe from anybody, except that he had been around," Lynn said. "But I had talked to the veteran guys on the team, like I always did when I was going to face an unfamiliar pitcher—and as a rookie most of them still were—and they told me he was a sinker-slider guy. So what does he throw me? A forkball!"

Lynn smashed it into the upper deck in right-center for a two-run homer.

"I thought it was a sinker at the time and said so after the game," Lynn recalled with a chuckle, "and later I read where Joe grumbled about 'some kid who doesn't even know what pitch he's hitting.'"

The Red Sox tacked on another run on a Rico Petrocelli single before Coleman could get out of the inning. The Tigers answered with a run in the bottom of the inning, but the Detroit ace ran into more difficulties in the second. Burleson and Yaz stroked two-out singles, and Lynn belted another homer, a three-run shot this time, that put the Red Sox in front 7-1.

"The second one was also a forkball, and I hit it off the façade of the roof in right-center," Lynn said. "I was a good low-ball hitter, and he kept throwing the ball in the wrong place."

Lerrin LaGrow replaced Coleman at the start of the third and was also ineffective. Petrocelli started the inning with a single and moved up on a passed ball. After Denny Doyle walked, Tim Blackwell bounced into a double play. Beniquez kept the rally going by singling home Petrocelli, and Burleson walked. Detroit manager Ralph Houk went to his bullpen again, this time for hard-throwing righthander "Bullet" Bob Reynolds. Yaz greeted him with a single that scored Beniquez and brought up Lynn for the third time in as many innings. This time Lynn took a pitch to left-center, and it barely missed clearing the wire fence 400 feet from home plate. By the time the ball was retrieved, Lynn was on third with a two-run triple that upped the score to 11-1.

"Reynolds threw hard, and you could really see his ball move," Lynn recalled. "The ball was moving away from me, so I went the other way with it, and it came within inches of going out. I just didn't get it high enough. Normally, it would have been a double. But it took a funny bounce, and that's why it was a triple."

Lynn trotted home when shortstop Tom Veryzer booted Rice's grounder for an error.

In 1975 there was no ESPN, and cable TV was in its infancy. Except for the crowd inside Tiger Stadium and fans of the Tigers and Red Sox listening on local radio or watching the game back in Boston on a local UHF TV station, few other baseball fans had any clue what Fred Lynn was accomplishing on this late spring evening in Detroit.

"A reporter called my dad after the third inning and began telling him what I was doing," Lynn said. "Three innings, seven runs batted in. He kept on calling."

With the game well in hand and ace Luis Tiant on the mound for the Red Sox, pitching against a team that was destined to lose 102 games, Johnson began making substitutions but kept Lynn in the lineup.

"I was just a rookie. In those days you took the older guys out, but the young guys don't come out. That's just the way it was," Lynn explained. "But I don't think I would have let him take me out of the game anyway. A night like that? I wanted to see what else was going to happen.

"But," Lynn added with a laugh, "I think most of the older guys saw my last homer on TV at the Lindell A.C. down the street." The Lindell A.C. was a popular sports bar located a couple of blocks away from Tiger Stadium.

Lynn didn't bat in the fourth but in the fifth hit the ball hard again off Reynolds. This time, however, it was a line drive that was snagged by second baseman John Knox. It would be the only time Tigers pitchers would retire Lynn all night.

"I hit it right on the nose, but he jumped up and caught it, or that would have been a double, and I would have hit for the cycle. Just the rub of the green," reflected Lynn, who would get that elusive cycle five years later against Minnesota on May 13, 1980.

> **FRED LYNN**
> **Years with Red Sox: 1974-80**
> **Other Major League Teams: California, Baltimore, Detroit, San Diego**
> **Position: Outfield**
> **Bats: Left**
> **Throws: Left**
> **Height: 6-1**
> **Weight: 190**
> **Born: February 3, 1952**
> **Birthplace: Chicago, IL**
> **Current Residence: San Diego, CA**
> **Current Occupation: Promotions for John Hancock and Major League Baseball**

Reynolds, meanwhile, had found a little groove and retired 10 of the last 12 Red Sox batters he faced. Lynn didn't bat again until the eighth. Tom Walker, another righthander, had relieved Reynolds at the start of the inning, and Lynn opened the frame by beating out an infield hit, his fourth hit of the game.

"That was just a cue shot in front of the plate, and I legged it out," Lynn said. "Although I always ran pretty well, I never got many infield hits because my swing prevented me from getting out of the batter's box quickly."

Dwight Evans pinch hit for Rice and struck out, but Rick Miller singled and Bob Heise walked to load the bases. Lynn was forced out at the plate on a groundball by Doyle, and Walker escaped the jam without allowing a run.

Walker wasn't as fortunate in the ninth. Doug Griffin and Cecil Cooper drilled one-out singles, and Lynn stepped up to the plate for the final time on this glorious evening. He yanked another three-run homer into the upper deck in right to make the score 15-1, and that's the way the game ended.

"That was a breaking ball, and that's why I pulled it more, and it went into the second deck," Lynn recalled. "When I was running around the bases, I'm adding 'em up, and that's 10 RBI! I'd never done that in my life. It was a surreal feeling.

"It's the one game for me, offensively, that will stand out forever," Lynn reminisced. "Ten RBI in one game? It's a pretty exclusive group. Not many have done that. That game is so far above what a player could expect. It was like a Little League game. The last time I had hit three homers in a game had been at the end of my Little League career, and I think I had four RBI. But 10 RBI? No one can do that!"

Yet Fred Lynn had. In 75 years of Red Sox history, only two other hitters had ever accomplished the feat: Rudy York had driven in 10 runs against the St. Louis Browns in 1946, and Norm Zauchin had repeated the feat against the Washington Senators in 1955. Not until Nomar Garciaparra drove in 10 runs against the Seattle Mariners in 1999, nearly a quarter of a century after Lynn, would another Red Sox player match his performance.

Before that night in Detroit, few fans outside of New England and maybe Southern California knew who Fred Lynn was. By morning, when baseball fans around the country opened their morning newspapers and read the box scores and accounts of the rout in Detroit, they all knew who Fred Lynn was. He had gone 5-for-6 with three homers, a triple, and a single and tied an American League record with 16 total bases. His RBI collection was one short of the AL record for a game set by Tony Lazzeri of the Yankees in 1936 and two shy of the major-league record set by Jim Bottomley of the St. Louis Cardinals in 1924. Lynn had become the first Red Sox player to hit three homers in a game since Joe Lahoud in 1969. He was hitting .352 with a .413 on-base percentage and slugging .648 with 14 homers and 50 RBI in 54 games. For the remainder of the 1975 season, the nation's fans closely followed the exploits of this gifted, graceful ballplayer, and he would do nothing to diminish their growing admiration.

"I got more attention, and so did the team after that," Lynn remembered. "Maybe people expected more from me after that, but I had high expectations anyway. I was shy in those days, and the attention made me uncomfortable. But on the field I was always relaxed. I was used to playing with high expectations. We were always expected to win the national championship at USC, so being in first place and winning the pennant felt natural to me. That was supposed to happen."

+ + +

In late July the Yankees, rejuvenated after a decade of neglect, were in second place and had illusions of overhauling the Red Sox after winning the first game of a four-game set at Shea Stadium that pulled them within seven games of the top. But the bat, feet, and glove of Fred Lynn, the erstwhile Yankees draft pick, ensured that the Yankees would have to wait another year before commencing their run of three straight pennants that would culminate in two World Championships. The Red Sox shut out the Yankees in a Sunday doubleheader 1-0 and 6-0, knocking them 10 games behind and out of the race. Lynn dazzled the Yankees in the first game.

"I got a basehit against Catfish [Hunter], stole second, and Rick Miller drove me in. That's how we got the run," Lynn remembered. He remembered his game-saving ninth-inning catch off Graig Nettles even more fondly.

"Bill Lee was pitching, and Nettles hit a ball to left-center that was tailing away from me. I felt like I was running for days. I always knew whether I was going to catch a ball or not, and on that one I just wasn't sure. Finally I dove, went flat-out, and caught a snow cone. Jimmy Rice was playing left, and, fortunately, he jumped over me, or I'd still be pressed into the turf out there at Shea. That killed the Yankees."

The Red Sox won the AL East by four and a half games, finishing with a 95-65 record. Lynn wrapped up his rookie season with a .331 average, 21 homers, and 105 RBI. He had finished second to Carew's .359 mark in the batting race but led the league with a .566 slugging percentage, 103 runs, and 47 doubles. He finished third in RBI, fourth in total bases, and fifth in on-base percentage. Lynn continued to star in the postseason, hitting .364 as the Red Sox swept the three-time defending World Champion Oakland A's in the playoffs and hitting .280 with a homer and five RBI in their seven-game loss to the Cincinnati Reds in the World Series.

"The World Series would have been different if we had had Jimmy," Lynn lamented. Rice, who had hit .309 with 22 homers and 102 RBI, broke his wrist during the last week of the regular season when he was hit by a pitch.

Then the awards flooded in. In addition to winning the league's MVP and rookie honors, Lynn was named Male Athlete of the Year by both the Associated Press and United Press International and won a Gold Glove for his fielding excellence.

+++

With Lynn and Rice forming the nucleus, the Red Sox thought they had the makings of a dynasty for the remainder of the decade. But 1976 turned out to be a huge disappointment for everyone. The Messersmith Decision had ended 100 years of reserve clause servitude, creating free agency, and Lynn, Carlton Fisk, and Rick Burleson became embroiled in bitter contract disputes that lasted well into the summer. The Red Sox were never in the race and were under .500 until the final days of the season. Lynn, who had refused to sign for $30,000 and had had his contract unilaterally renewed at $22,000 before coming to terms with the Red Sox on a seven-figure deal in August, hit .314 but had only 10 homers and 65 RBI.

"Seventy-six was the toughest season for me," Lynn admitted.

The Red Sox rebounded to win 97 games in 1977 but finished two and a half games behind the Yankees. Lynn tore up his ankle in spring training, opened the season on the disabled list, and hurt the other ankle by favoring the first. He rushed himself back into the lineup on May 13 in Seattle and homered in his first two at-bats. He limped all year and finished with 18 homers but batted only .260. A healthier Lynn hit .298 with 22 homers and 82 RBI in 1978, and the Red Sox won 99 games but lost a one-game playoff to the Yankees for the division title.

The 6-1 Lynn had played at 185 pounds during the first four years of his career with the Red Sox. But he discovered Nautilus training during the off-season between 1978 and 1979, and it was a bulked-up, almost unrecognizable Lynn who reported to Winter Haven, Florida, for spring training.

"Each second half of the season I'd wear out. I'd start the season at 185 and be 175 at the end," Lynn explained. "I looked at Jimmy, and he was big and strong and never wore out. I had no clue, no supervision. I did something called the executive workout, and the change was so gradual I never even noticed until I got to spring training and would hit a ball and say: 'That's going nowhere.' And it would be a home run."

Lynn went on to have his best major-league season in 1979, winning the batting crown with a .333 average while blasting 39 homers, knocking in

Fred Lynn, the first player in Major League history to win Rookie of the Year and Most Valuable Player honors in the same season, now promotes the game of baseball in a variety of ways.
*(Courtesy of Trinity Products Inc./Rose Goetz)*

122 runs, and scoring 116. Lynn also lashed 42 doubles, fashioned another 20-game hitting streak, and led the AL in slugging with a .637 mark while posting a .426 on-base percentage. He also had a two-homer, six-RBI game against Minnesota that season. The Red Sox won 91 games—their third straight 90-win season—but finished third behind the Baltimore Orioles and Milwaukee Brewers.

Lynn shed the bulk that winter. "I still did the workout the next year," he said, "but I also started running eight miles a day with one of my neighbors, and I guess I ran off all that muscle."

A variety of nagging injuries limited Lynn to 110 games in 1980, and he hit just 12 homers with 61 RBI while batting .301. The Red Sox won only 83 games, finished fourth, and were broken up after that season.

"If there had been a wild card, we might have won it all four times in the seven years I was there," Lynn mused. "If we had still been there when [Roger] Clemens and [Bruce] Hurst came along, what a ball club we would have had!"

Lynn, a lifetime .308 hitter, was looking at free agency again after the 1981 season, and on January 23, 1981, the Red Sox traded him to the California Angels for washed-up outfielder Joe Rudi; Frank Tanana, a lefthanded pitcher who had lost his blazing fastball; and journeyman righthanded pitcher Jim Dorsey. Red Sox fans were led to believe that Lynn had never been comfortable playing in Boston and yearned to play back home in sunny California. Lynn insists he wanted to finish his career in a Red Sox uniform.

"It was devastating for me," he said of the trade. "That I wanted to leave Boston and go back to California was the furthest thing from the truth. I hit .350 lifetime in Fenway! Why would I want to leave?"

Lynn had some productive years over the remainder of his career but never one resembling his glory years with the Red Sox. Playing for the Angels, Orioles, Tigers, and San Diego Padres until retiring at age 38 after the 1990 season, the nine-time All-Star never hit .300 again, slugged more than 25 homers in a season, or drove in as many as 90 runs.

Fred Lynn finished his 17-year career with a .283 average, 306 homers, and 1,111 RBI in 1,969 games. Since retiring as a player, Lynn has worked for ESPN and Fox as an analyst and currently works for Major League Baseball and John Hancock Insurance in a promotions capacity. Lynn and his wife, Natalie, continue to make their home in the San Diego area. Lynn's .520 slugging percentage ranks sixth on the club's all-time list, and his .308 batting average ranks 10th. He was elected to the Red Sox Hall of Fame in 2002.

# Chapter 9

# LUIS TIANT

## OCTOBER 11, 1975

Spring training was over, and Luis Tiant was in his Orlando, Florida, hotel room packing his suitcases for the trip north to start the 1971 season with the Minnesota Twins when he was summoned to the room of Howard Fox, Minnesota's traveling secretary.

"I'm sorry to tell you this, Luis," Fox informed him, "but I have to give you your unconditional release."

Tiant was stunned. He was only 30 years old and three years earlier had been one of baseball's most dominant pitchers. He had been off to a 6-0 start for the Twins the previous season when a freak injury—a fractured shoulder blade—put him on the disabled list in June. Only two months later he was pitching again, though ineffectively, valiantly trying to help the Twins sew up the American League West Division title. And now, having been given less than a year to recover fully from such a catastrophic injury, the Twins were telling him he was through.

Fox, a good and gentle man performing a thankless task, tried to sound optimistic.

"Wherever you go from here," he said, "I hope you win 20 games."

"Don't give me that baloney," Tiant snorted. "If you think I can still win 20 games, why don't you keep me here?"

Two years later Luis Tiant was a 20-game winner again, this time for the Red Sox. He would be a 20-game winner for the Red Sox three times in a four-year period, and in 1975 he would reach baseball's pinnacle by pitching in the World Series and shutting out the mighty Cincinnati Reds.

✦ ✦ ✦

Luis Clemente Tiant, an only child, was born in Havana, Cuba, on November 23, 1940. His father, also named Luis, was one of the island's most celebrated pitchers in a career that lasted from 1926 until 1948. Baseball in the United States was segregated until after World War II, and the lefthanded Tiant pitched for the barnstorming New York Cubans against Negro League clubs during the summer and then for local teams in Cuba during the winter months. With his wife, Isabel, and little Luis to support, the elder Tiant retired from baseball at the age of 42, purchased a truck, and went into the furniture-moving business.

Little Luis, although righthanded, soon acquired his own reputation as a pitcher. Bobby Avila, a former second baseman and by then a scout for the Cleveland Indians, saw Tiant pitch and recommended him to the Mexico City Tigers, and in 1959 the 18-year-old hurler was signed to a Mexican League contract for $150 a month. Tiant pitched for the Tigers for three years and met his wife, Maria, in Mexico. But Cuba was in turmoil during this period; Fidel Castro's communist rebels had taken control of the government, and the situation was getting uglier and more unstable at home. Just before the 1961 Mexican League season ended, Tiant's father spoke to him on the telephone and told him not to return to Cuba. Tiant reluctantly took his the advice, and 15 years would pass before he would see his father again.

Cleveland had purchased Tiant's contract from the Tigers, and in 1962 he began his minor-league career in the United States. The 5-11, 190-pound fireballing pitcher led the Class A Carolina League in strikeouts in 1963 and threw a no-hitter against Winston-Salem, and after getting off to a 15-1 start for Class AAA Portland with a 2.04 ERA and 154 strikeouts in 137 innings in 1964, he was called up to Cleveland.

Tiant went 10-4 as a rookie for the so-so Indians, who were 79-83 that year. By 1967 he was emerging as one of the American League's most dominant pitchers, posting a 12-9 record with a 2.73 ERA and 219 strikeouts in 214 innings for 75-87 club.

In 1968 Tiant turned in one of the greatest seasons by a pitcher in major-league history. He hurled nine shutouts and compiled a 21-9 record while leading the AL in ERA with a 1.60 mark. In 258 innings he allowed just 152 hits and 73 walks while fanning 264 batters.

Boston Red Sox righthander Luis Tiant rears back to throw a pitch
during a spring training game in Orlando, Florida.
(Courtesy of the Boston Red Sox)

On July 3 he pitched his career masterpiece against the Twins. Tiant had 16 strikeouts after nine innings, but the game was still scoreless. Minnesota threatened in the top of the 10th when Rich Reese led off with a double and was sacrificed to third with Frank Quilici reaching first on the desperate and late throw to third. Tiant reached back and fanned John Roseboro, Rich Rollins, and pitcher Jim Merritt, running his strikeout total to 19. The Indians scored in the bottom of the 10th to win the game 1-0. Amazingly, he threw only 135 pitches, and 101 of them were strikes. The 19 strikeouts were an AL record for a 10-inning game, and with 41 strikeouts in his last three starts, Tiant set another league record.

The Indians, despite an offense that averaged barely three runs per game and ranked eighth in the league, finished a surprising third with an 86-75 record. But Tiant didn't win the Cy Young Award that year because Denny McLain went 31-4 for the American League and World Champion Detroit Tigers, becoming the first 30-game winner since Dizzy Dean in 1934 and baseball's only 30-game winner in the last 70 years. Tiant couldn't even get a vote from the Cleveland writers; McLain won the award unanimously.

Too many tough pitches in low-scoring games for the punchless Indians had taken a toll on Tiant in 1968. He reported to spring training in 1969 with a sore shoulder, and it never really got better. He went from a 20-game winner to a 20-game loser, finishing at 9-20 despite a 3.71 ERA. That winter the Indians traded him to Minnesota, where his shoulder blade cracked while delivering a pitch in May.

Now the Twins were telling Luis Tiant he was through. The Atlanta Braves signed him to a 30-day minor-league contract, and he was released after putting 39 runners on base in 23 innings at Class AAA Richmond and posting a 6.26 ERA. But Darrell Johnson, managing the Red Sox' Triple-A team at Louisville, had seen Tiant throw and was convinced he had a chance to make a comeback. Johnson recommended that the Red Sox sign him, and they did.

After just four games with Louisville, Tiant was back in the majors with the Red Sox. They stuck him in the bullpen, and he showed flashes of his old self during the summer of 1971. But with a 1-7 record and a 4.88 ERA at the end of the season, there were plenty of skeptics in Boston who thought Tiant was at the end of the line.

Red Sox manager Eddie Kasko wasn't among them. He was determined to give Tiant one more shot in 1972, and he got his way. Tiant pitched well enough in the spring to make the club as a reliever, and in late June and early July he picked up three wins—one of them in a spot start—and two saves in a five-game stretch.

By August the Red Sox unexpectedly found themselves in the thick of a pennant race. When Sonny Siebert was scratched from a start, complaining of dizziness, Kasko gave the assignment to Tiant, who threw a complete-game victory against Baltimore. Rewarded with another start against the Orioles, Tiant flirted with a no-hitter for six innings and beat them again. In his next start, against the Chicago White Sox, Tiant came within four outs of a no-hitter and won 3-0.

That was the first of four consecutive shutouts for Tiant, and by now Red Sox fans had fallen in love with him and his quirky windup and multiangled delivery. Fans at Fenway would begin chanting: "Loo-ie! Loo-ie!" as soon as he left the bullpen after warming up, and the chants would continue throughout the evening as he posted yet another complete-game victory. Tiant went 11-2 with a 1.19 ERA after August 1 and ended the season with a 15-6 record and his second ERA title with a 1.91 mark. The Red Sox, unfortunately, missed out on the division title by a half-game, the consequence of an uneven schedule dictated by a 13-day players' strike at the start of the season.

**LUIS TIANT**

**Years with Red Sox: 1971-1978**
**Other Major League Teams: Cleveland, Minnesota, New York (AL), Pittsburgh, California**
**Position: Pitcher**
**Bats: Right**
**Throws: Right**
**Height: 5-11**
**Weight: 190**
**Born: November 23, 1940**
**Birthplace: Havana, Cuba**
**Current Residence: Southboro, MA**
**Current Occupation: Red Sox Spanish Radio analyst, special assignment instructor**

"It took me a year and a half to come back from that 90 percent," Tiant said of his broken shoulder, "but I did. I was different than a lot of other people. All my life I pitched with pain, in my legs, in my back, in my arm. Pain doesn't bother me. It has to be really bad to shut me down. I never liked to miss a start. Three days watching games without pitching, that's enough. I used to get crazy watching games."

The blazing fastball that had highlighted his days in Cleveland was gone forever. But Tiant still had plenty of other weapons—and tricks—in his arsenal that would make him one of the premier pitchers in baseball for the remainder of the decade. He was a valuable addition to the Red Sox clubhouse even when he wasn't pitching, keeping a notoriously tight team loose with his pranks and irreverent humor.

He became a 20-game winner again in 1973, finishing at 20-13 with a 3.34 ERA and 206 strikeouts. In 1974 he was the leading candidate for the Cy Young Award with a 20-8 record in late August and the Red Sox in first place. But the team stopped hitting, and Tiant got one unearned run of support in his next four starts. He finished the season at 22-13 with a 2.92 ERA while throwing 311 innings, and the Red Sox faded to third.

The Red Sox won the pennant in 1975, but it was a difficult and emotional campaign for Tiant, whose victory total slipped to 18 while his ERA rose to 4.02. He didn't miss any starts, but he was bothered by tendinitis in his right shoulder and a sore back for much of the second half. Tiant was also anxiously awaiting good news about his parents.

Massachusetts senator Edward Brooke learned that fellow South Dakota senator George McGovern, the former presidential candidate, was planning to make an unofficial visit to Cuba in the spring of 1975. The United States had no diplomatic relations with the communist-controlled island, but McGovern would be meeting with Fidel Castro. Brooke asked McGovern if he'd deliver a compassionate letter to Castro asking him to let Tiant's parents leave the island for a visit with their son. The letter was delivered, and Castro, a former pitcher with one-time professional aspirations of his own, granted the request.

But diplomatic wheels turn slowly. There was a lot of paperwork involved and visas to be issued, and the process dragged on for several months. Not until August 20 did Tiant finally receive word that his parents were en route to Boston. His mother had been able to visit him once in Mexico, but he had not seen his father since the winter of 1960-61. The emotional reunion took place at Boston's Logan Airport.

"It was the biggest thing that happened in my baseball career," Tiant remembered 30 years later. "I didn't see my father for 15 years. When I left Cuba, he was an old man, and I didn't know if I would ever see him again. When they came here, it was my dream to have my mother, my father, my wife, and my children all watch me pitch."

What they all saw was vintage Luis Tiant. He mastered the three-time defending World Champion Oakland Athletics with a three-hitter in the first game of the American League Championship Series at Fenway Park, and the Red Sox swept the series to capture their first pennant since 1967. Now they had to confront Cincinnati's Big Red Machine in the World Series.

Although Rick Wise had led the staff with 19 wins during the regular season, Darrell Johnson named Tiant to pitch Game 1 on October 11. For

Tiant it would be the most memorable game of his illustrious Red Sox career.

Babe Ruth has been credited with restoring the nation's faith in baseball after the "Black Sox" World Series scandal in 1919. By the mid-1970s baseball was in trouble again, albeit for different reasons. Fans found the games boring and were shifting their attention to other sports. The American League had introduced the designated hitter in 1973 as a way to inject more offense into the game, but purists were offended, and the National League continued to play the game the old-fashioned way.

The 1975 World Series would captivate the public, inaugurating a new boom in baseball's popularity. And Tiant would set the dramatic tone for that World Series in the very first game.

"That was like a new era in baseball history," Tiant explained. "It was one of the best World Series played in the history of baseball, and I was proud to be in there. We were the underdogs that year. Nobody was thinking we would win. They had the best team, no question. But we had a good team, too. The only thing was we had a lot of young players, and Cincinnati had been killing everybody for four or five years in a row.

"But if we could win that first game," Tiant said, "we would show Cincinnati we can beat them. If you put that in the back of their minds, I don't care how good a team you are; the underdogs are going to chew you up."

✦ ✦ ✦

It was a gray, damp, 60-degree day when the sellout crowd of 35,205 began filling the seats at Fenway Park on that Saturday afternoon. The Red Sox, with the aid of the designated hitter, had actually outhomered the Reds 134-124 during the regular season. But the fans had never seen the Red Sox put on a show like this during batting practice. Every Red who stepped into the cage seemed capable of blasting pitches deep into the overcast. It was easy to see how the Reds had won 108 games during the regular season and toyed with the Pittsburgh Pirates in the NLCS. How could Luis Tiant, as good as he was, beat them?

Tiant wasn't intimidated.

"To tell you the truth, I liked the good hitters hitting against me, the 40-home run hitters," he said. "I want to fight with them, get them out, and I put more emphasis on those guys than the punch-and-judy hitters. Those are the ones that hurt you most of the time. You make a mistake to the big hitters, yeah, they make you pay. But the judy hitters? It's tough to get them out. They have good bat control. Big righthanded hitters? I never had that much of a problem getting them out."

As Tiant took the mound in the first inning to the cheers of the adoring crowd, he felt euphoria like he never had before.

"It was a thrill for me, a thrill that my mom and dad were here, and my family," he remembered. "Everybody was watching, and this was my chance to show the world what I can do."

Tiant retired the first 10 Reds he faced with surprising ease. But when Joe Morgan, the NL's MVP who had hit .327 with 17 homers and 94 RBI and stolen 67 bases, singled with one out in the fourth, Tiant had to pitch from the stretch for the first time. Cincinnati manager Sparky Anderson had been making an issue of Tiant's unorthodox delivery, claiming he balked every time he threw the ball. With a National League umpire, Nick Colosi, at first base, everyone was waiting to see what would happen. Sure enough, Colosi called a balk and awarded Morgan second base. Naturally, Tiant and Johnson vehemently protested the ruling.

"It upset me in a way, but there is nothing you can do. I know I don't balk, because that's my motion all the time," Tiant said. "But I knew they were going to call it because their manager, that's all he talked about before the game.

"I went to the first-base umpire, and I tell him it's bull-this and bull-that. I cuss him out good," Tiant recalled with a squeaky laugh. "But when he told me: 'You better get back over there, or I'm gonna kick your ass out of the game,' I said, 'Okay, thank you very much,' and I walked away. I just knew I had to get the next guy, and I did."

Tiant retired Johnny Bench on a foul and struck out Tony Perez. And he wasn't called for a balk again in the World Series.

The game was still scoreless after Tiant set down the Reds in the sixth. Lefthander Don Gullett, Cincinnati's ace who had compiled a 15-4 record with a 2.42 ERA during the season, was working on a shutout, too.

The Red Sox had almost scored in the first inning after Dwight Evans had led off with a single and been sacrificed to second. But when Evans tried to come home on an infield hit by Fred Lynn that had trickled into the outfield, he was cut down by shortstop Dave Concepcion.

The Red Sox threatened again in the bottom of the sixth, loading the bases with one out on a single by Lynn, a double by Rico Petrocelli, and an intentional walk issued to Rick Burleson. Cecil Cooper, who had replaced the injured Jim Rice in the Red Sox lineup, lofted a flyball to medium center field, and when Lynn tried to dash home after the catch, he was gunned down by Cesar Geronimo.

The Reds threw a scare into Red Sox fans in the top of the seventh. George Foster led off with a single, and leftfielder Carl Yastrzemski made a tumbling catch of a blooper off the bat of Concepcion to deny him a hit. Foster then tried to steal second and was tossed out by Carlton Fisk. Ken Griffey followed with a double, and Tiant intentionally walked Geronimo to get to Gullett, who hit a soft line drive that second baseman Denny Doyle ran down before it could reach the outfield.

"It wasn't an easy inning," Tiant recalled. "Those guys can hit, and they hit anybody. But I was lucky enough I made my pitches when I needed them, and I got them out. But I didn't consider it a bad inning. A bad inning is when you can't get them out, and they score three or four runs. They don't score, it's a good inning. I don't care if a guy has to jump over the fence to make a catch, that's still a good inning.

"So I shut them out that inning, and I said: 'Hey, you know what? I have a chance to win this game. I want to win this game. We have to win this game.'"

And Tiant immediately set out to make certain the Red Sox did when he led off the bottom of the seventh. Tiant had enjoyed some success as a hitter. He had batted .406 for the Twins in 1970 and had even connected for five homers in the majors. But he had batted only once since the advent of the designated hitter three years earlier, and he had struck out and walked in his first two plate appearances against the hard-throwing Gullett. But when Gullett tried to sneak a breaking ball past him, Tiant pulled it through the hole into left field for a single. The next few minutes would be an unforgettable adventure on the basepaths for both Tiant and Red Sox fans.

Evans was ordered to sacrifice, and he bunted the ball right back to Gullett, who decided to try to nail Tiant at second. It was more of a roll than a slide into second by the portly pitcher, and the ball ended up in center field. Tiant had momentary illusions of going to third, but after taking a few steps in that direction, looked back and noticed Geronimo already had the ball. Tiant hustled back to second, just beating the tag.

"You forget how to do things when you don't do them for a long time," he said about his hitting and baserunning skills. "I got the basehit, and then I see the bunt sign, and I say: 'Oh, man! They're trying to kill me!' But I have to get to second base, and I don't care how. And I get there, and I see the ball get away a little bit, and I start to think about third base, went a little way, and then I almost broke my neck getting back to second."

Doyle ripped an 0-and-2 pitch from Gullett into right field for a single, and now the bases were loaded with still nobody out. Yaz dumped another single into right, and Tiant lumbered home but missed the plate.

"I know I missed it, but the ball wasn't there. I think somebody cut it off, Morgan or Tony Perez," Tiant recalled. "And I hear Johnny [Bench] yelling: 'Give me the ball! Give me the ball!' So he knew I missed it, too. Fisk is yelling: 'Go back! Go back and touch home plate!' But he didn't have to tell me; I knew what I did."

Tiant sneaked back, touched the plate with his toe, and then trotted happily to the dugout. The Red Sox were ahead 1-0.

"The main thing is I don't get hurt," he laughed about his tour of the bases, "and I can come back and continue to pitch."

It would be a while before Tiant would get back on the mound. The Red Sox would score five more times before the inning was over.

Clay Carroll relieved Gullett and walked Fisk, forcing in the second run. Lefthander Will McEnaney fanned Lynn for the first out, but Petrocelli drilled a two-run single, and Burleson singled in another before Cooper capped the rally with a sacrifice fly.

Armed with a 6-0 lead, Tiant set down the final six Reds in order, polishing off a five-hit shutout in his World Series debut.

✢ ✢ ✢

Cincinnati won the next two games by one run. Tiant wonGame 4 in Cincinnati and wasn't nearly as sharp as he was in the opener. He again singled and scored during a five-run rally in the fourth inning, then shut out the Reds over the final five innings in a gutsy performance. Tiant threw 163 pitches and surrendered nine hits and four walks, but he went the distance to record his second complete game of the World Series and even it at two wins apiece.

Tiant also started Game 6 but had to be relieved after falling behind 6-3 in the eighth. The Red Sox pulled it out on a three-run pinch homer by Bernie Carbo and Fisk's famous 12th-inning homer off the foul pole. The Reds then won the deciding seventh game, 4-3.

Tiant compiled a 21-12 record with a 3.06 ERA for the Red Sox in 1976 before slipping to 12 victories in 1977 when he had 12 no-decisions. He went 13-8 for the Red Sox in 1978 with 11 no-decisions and threw a two-hit shutout at the Toronto Blue Jays on the last scheduled day of the season in his final appearance for them. That win, coupled with a New York loss, set up a one-game playoff for the AL East title the next day.

Luis Tiant, a three-time 20-game winner for the Boston Red Sox, relaxes in the stands several hours before a game at Fenway Park. *(Courtesy of Chaz Scoggins)*

The new owners of the Red Sox, Haywood Sullivan and Buddy LeRoux, let the 38-year-old Tiant become a free agent after that season. In the eight years since the Twins told him he was through, Tiant had rolled up a 122-81 record with 26 shutouts. Only Cy Young and Mel Parnell had won more games in a Red Sox uniform, only Young had struck out more batters, and only Young and Smoky Joe Wood had hurled more shutouts.

Tiant pitched two years for the Yankees before ending his career in 1982 after brief stints with the Pittsburgh Pirates and California Angels. He retired at the age of 41 with a 229-172 record, 49 shutouts, and 2,416 strikeouts.

After being out of the game for ten years, Tiant returned to baseball in 1992 as a minor-league pitching coach in the Los Angeles Dodgers system. He served as the pitching coach for Nicaragua in the 1996 Olympics, then joined the Chicago White Sox as a minor-league pitching in 1997. Tiant accepted the job coaching baseball at the Savannah College of Art & Design in 1998 and held that position for four years before rejoining the Red Sox in 2002 as the pitching coach for the minor-league Lowell Spinners. He is currently a special assignment instructor and ambassador for the Red Sox.

Tiant was inducted into the Red Sox Hall of Fame in 1997. He still ranks fourth on the club's all-time list in shutouts and innings pitched and fifth in victories and strikeouts.

Luis Tiant and his wife, Maria, have three grown children and reside in Southboro, Massachusetts.

# Chapter 10

# DWIGHT EVANS

## OCTOBER 14, 1975

D wight Evans is like so many Red Sox players over the decades whose most memorable moments are often intertwined with disappointment and are therefore bittersweet. But few, if any, of them, had to deal with the tribulations Evans did, especially off the field, and few, if any, of them experienced the frequent setbacks Evans suffered for so many years before turning his career around at the age of 28 to become one of the greatest players in Red Sox history. Had the first seven and a half years of his major-league career been anywhere near as spectacular as the last 11 and a half years, he would have been a lock for induction into the National Baseball Hall of Fame.

It is perhaps because of so many disappointments in the early years of his career, when success came far too seldom, that his occasional moments of glory were so much more vivid than later in his career when his heroics were performed on what seemed to be a daily basis and by then taken almost for granted. Perhaps that's the reason Evans remembers most fondly a World Series home run he hit when he was still only 23 years old.

✦✦✦

Dwight Michael Evans was born on November 3, 1951, in Santa Monica, California. He spent his early childhood in Hawaii and did not start playing baseball until the age of 10 when his family moved back to

Southern California. The baseball scene in the San Fernando Valley was highly competitive, and Evans was unable to make the high school varsity as a tenth grader at Grenada Hills. When the Evans family moved to nearby Chatsworth, however, he was good enough not only to make the high school team as a third baseman and pitcher but soon began attracting the attention of pro scouts. The Red Sox drafted him on the fifth round in 1969 and sent him 3,000 miles away to Jamestown, New York, to begin his pro career in the New York-Penn League. He was only 17 years old, and not only was he a long way away from home for the first time in his life, he was bewildered by the fierce survival instinct of pro ballplayers.

"Joe Stephenson, the scout who signed me, put me on a plane," Evans remembered. "I figured I would get there, put on a uniform, and play. But the team was on the road, and I had to work out by myself in jeans and a red shirt I bought because I thought red would be the team color. It wasn't; it was blue.

"Anyway, the team came back, but I didn't start playing for a week until they started releasing some guys. Jackie Moore was my first manager, and he put me at third base. Don Nolan, a 24-year-old guy just back from Vietnam who had tattoos of black panthers on both his arms, was the third baseman. When I finished taking my swings in batting practice and ran around the bases, he spit on me. I just kept going. When I hit my first home run, no one congratulated me when I got back to the dugout. It was a dog-eat-dog world. Then when our rightfielder broke his ankle, I went out there and I stayed out there for almost my whole career."

Evans hit .280 in 34 games at Jamestown and found himself rapidly ascending the minor-league ladder. By 1972 he was barely out of his teens and already playing in Triple-A at Louisville. As one of the youngest players in the league, playing against men several years older, Evans was overmatched for the first time in his life.

"I was hitting .174 at the All-Star break," Evans recalled. "Darrell Johnson, who was the manager, came up to me and said I had seven days to get it going or Boston was going to send me back to Double-A.

"Stan Williams, the pitching coach, took me out for a couple of days and threw me curveballs, everything he had," Evans continued. (This is the same Stan Williams who had a well-deserved reputation for intimidating hitters when he pitched for the Dodgers and who as a pitching coach was known for throwing at the heads of hitters who dared hit a homer off him in batting practice.) Williams worked patiently with Evans and got him over the hump.

Boston Red Sox rightfielder Dwight Evans watches a ball sail into the distance during a game at Fenway Park.
*(Courtesy of the Boston Red Sox)*

"I went 42-for-63 right after the break," Evans remembered, "and that got me all the way up to .240! But I hit .400 the rest of the way."

Evans ended up hitting .300 with 17 homers and a league-leading 95 RBI. At the age of 20, he was named the International League's Most Valuable Player. He also earned himself a September promotion to Boston, where the Red Sox were in a tough three-way battle with Detroit and Baltimore for the American League East title.

"The day I joined the Red Sox they were playing in the old Yankee Stadium with the low fence in right and the monuments in center," Evans recalled. "I didn't play. But when we got back to Boston, I got in the lineup and was there the rest of the way. I only hit .263, but I remember getting some big hits for us."

But the Red Sox fell short, losing the division title to the Tigers by a mere half-game because of an unequal schedule that gave Detroit one more game after the start of the season had been delayed by a players strike. The Tigers had an 86-70 record while the Red Sox finished at 85-70.

But Evans, the 20-year-old rookie, had received his baptism in the pressure cooker of a pennant race, and pennant races would be a regular occurrence for him for much of his Red Sox career. Still, he had a lot to learn about hitting. He played in 119 games in 1973 but hit only .223 with 10 homers and 32 RBI. Evans seemed to be on the brink of stardom in 1974 when he hit .281 with 10 homers and 70 RBI in 133 games and had a carryover 191-game errorless streak in right field.

In 1975 Evans was joined by two other young outfielders, 23-year-old Fred Lynn and 22-year-old Jim Rice, and that gave the Red Sox one of the most enviable outfields in baseball. Lynn hit .331 with 21 homers and 105 RBI and won both the MVP and Rookie of the Year awards, and Rice hit .309 with 22 homers and 102 RBI. Evans contributed 13 homers and 56 RBI while hitting .274, and he piled up 15 assists while leading the league's outfielders with eight double plays. The Red Sox won 95 games, finished first in the AL East, and met the three-time defending World Champion Oakland A's in the playoffs.

"We had lost Jimmy [to a broken wrist] in Detroit, and we were concerned about playing without him," Evans remembered. "I don't think anything fazed us, though, because we had come so far as a team that year and done so much. But I never thought we would beat them three straight. We surprised ourselves."

After upsetting Oakland in the ALCS, the Red Sox found themselves huge underdogs in the World Series against the mighty Cincinnati Reds, who had averaged 100 wins over four seasons and had compiled a 108-54 record in 1975 while winning the National League West by 20 games over Los Angeles and then outscoring Pittsburgh 19-7 while sweeping the Pirates in the NLCS.

"Now here comes the Big Red Machine," Evans said. "The people who said we didn't have a chance against Oakland never thought we could beat Cincinnati. It was just a matter of how many games it would take them to beat us."

It would turn out to be an exciting seven-game Series that revived the national interest in baseball.

The Reds put on a spectacular hitting display in batting practice before the first game at Fenway Park on October 11, drawing oohs and aahs from the early-arriving sellout crowd of 35,205. The pregame show Red Sox hitters put on paled by comparison. There didn't seem to be any way the Red Sox could beat the Reds.

Then Luis Tiant took the mound and shut out the Reds on five hits, igniting a six-run rally himself in the seventh inning with a single off Cincinnati ace Don Gullett. The Red Sox won 6-0, and Evans had a hit and scored a run. The Reds scored a pair of runs in the ninth to beat the Red Sox 3-2 in the second game, and the World Series moved to Cincinnati. The first game in Riverfront Stadium, played on October 14, 1975, would be the most memorable game of Dwight Evans's career.

Righthander Gary Nolan, who had compiled a 15-9 record with a 3.16 ERA during the regular season, started for the Reds that night in front of a highly partisan crowd of 55,392. The 27-year-old Nolan had once been a fireballer but had appeared in only two games in 1973-74 while recovering from arm surgery that robbed him of his fastball.

"Nolan was just a control pitcher with a good breaking ball. Not overpowering by any means," Evans remembered. "He tried to move the ball around. The most important guy on that team was behind the plate: Johnny Bench. He was a master at calling pitches, and he had a great arm."

Evans found that out the hard way in Game 2 when Bench picked him off second base.

"I took a lead off second, and the next thing I knew the ball was in [second baseman] Joe Morgan's glove, and they got me at third," Evans related. "Bench was intimidating, and he could do whatever he wanted at the plate. He beat us in the second game with a double down the right-field line when we were playing him the other way."

Carlton Fisk started the second inning with a homer off Nolan. Evans batted later that inning and fouled out to right. Rick Wise, meanwhile, held Cincinnati hitless until the fourth when Tony Perez drew a two-out walk, and Bench followed with a homer to put the Reds ahead 2-1.

"Wise could be overpowering. He won 19 games for us that year," Evans said. "But we knew a 1-0 lead wasn't enough against those guys."

Nolan removed himself from the game before the start of the fifth, complaining of a stiff neck. Cincinnati manager Sparky Anderson went to the bullpen for rookie righthander Pat Darcy, who had won 11 games as a rookie in 1975. Evans was the first batter he faced.

"He threw pretty hard and had a great sinker, a very, very heavy ball," Evans remembered. Evans grounded out to short, the Red Sox didn't score, and the Reds shelled Wise in the bottom of the inning.

Shortstop Dave Concepcion and centerfielder Cesar Geronimo, who had combined for all of 11 homers during the regular season, smacked back-to-back bombs. Pete Rose ripped a one-out triple, chasing Wise, who had given up four hits in a span of six batters for 15 total bases. When Morgan brought home Rose with a sacrifice fly off reliever Jim Burton, the Reds had a 5-1 lead.

The Red Sox were far from discouraged. "We felt if we could hold them, we were going to come back," Evans said. Relievers Reggie Cleveland and Jim Willoughby held the Reds in check, and in the sixth the Red Sox began their comeback.

Darcy walked Carl Yastrzemski and Fisk, then uncorked a wild pitch. Lynn stroked a sacrifice fly to left, and the Red Sox picked up a run without benefit of a hit.

Evans started the seventh by grounding a single up the middle, the first hit off Darcy. Anderson, whose nickname was "Captain Hook" because of his impatience with pitchers, immediately yanked the rookie in favor of veteran Clay Carroll, who got Rick Burleson to rap into a double play. But Bernie Carbo, a former Red who had been drafted ahead of Bench, pinch hit for Cleveland and slashed a homer to left, cutting Cincinnati's lead to 5-3.

"That was a huge home run that really picked us up," Evans said. "Bernie had had a lot of big hits for us all year, and now it was a two-run game."

The score was still 5-3 when the Red Sox came to bat in the ninth with lefthander Will McEnaney, Cincinnati's fourth pitcher of the night, on the mound. McEnaney struck out Lynn, but Rico Petrocelli lined a single to center, bringing Evans, representing the tying run, to the plate. Anderson hastily summoned hard-throwing righthander Rawly Eastwick from the bullpen. Eastwick, a 24-year-old rookie, had led the NL in saves with 22 and given up just six homers in 90 innings. He was unscored upon in three postseason appearances, including a two-inning stint in Game 2 of the World Series when he caught Evans looking at a third strike.

"I wanted to face McEnaney real bad. He was lefthanded, and he had just given up the hit to Rico," Evans related. "All I really knew about Eastwick was that he was their closer, and he had had a good year. So I went up there looking for one pitch: a fastball."

Eastwick's first pitch was low, and Evans took it for a ball. The next pitch was in his wheelhouse, and Evans swung and connected, driving the ball to left field.

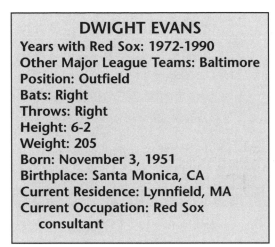

**DWIGHT EVANS**
**Years with Red Sox: 1972-1990**
**Other Major League Teams: Baltimore**
**Position: Outfield**
**Bats: Right**
**Throws: Right**
**Height: 6-2**
**Weight: 205**
**Born: November 3, 1951**
**Birthplace: Santa Monica, CA**
**Current Residence: Lynnfield, MA**
**Current Occupation: Red Sox**
**    consultant**

"He got the pitch up, but I thought I got under it a little, and I wasn't sure it had enough to get out of the ballpark," Evans recalled. "I saw [George] Foster going back to the fence, and it looked like he was going to catch it."

But Foster ran out of real estate, and the ball disappeared over the fence.

"It went out just about the time I reached first base, and I jumped about as high as a human being can jump," Evans remembered. "It was one of the biggest home runs I would ever hit in my career. We had just tied the ballgame, and I thought for sure we were going to win it now."

But the drama was far from over. The game went into the 10th inning still deadlocked at 5-5. When Geronimo led off the bottom of the inning with a single off Willoughby, Ed Armbrister was sent up to pinch hit for Eastwick and put down a sacrifice bunt. Armbrister bunted the ball straight down, and it bounced high in front of the plate. Armbrister took a step or two toward first, then hesitated, and was muscled aside by Fisk as he rushed out for the ball. Fisk's throw to second sailed into center field, and Geronimo wound up on third and Armbrister on second.

Fisk and Red Sox manager Darrell Johnson argued strenuously with plate umpire Larry Barnett that Armbrister should be called out for interference and Geronimo returned to first base. But Barnett ruled that the contact was unintentional—even though intent is not mentioned in the rulebook—and the Reds had runners at second and third with nobody out.

Roger Moret relieved Willoughby, walked Rose intentionally to fill the bases, and struck out pinch hitter Merv Rettenmund. But Morgan lofted a fly over the head of a drawn-in Lynn in center field for a single, and the Reds won one of the most controversial games in World Series history, 6-5.

"Whether it was interference or not, I don't know," Evans admitted. "I'm not sure to this day if it was. All I know is everything broke down right then. Except for the Morgan hit that won Game 7, not winning that game was the biggest disappointment of the World Series."

And yet at the same time the fondest memory of his career.

✛ ✛ ✛

The Red Sox rebounded the next night behind a courageous performance by Tiant, who went to the mound with marginal stuff and threw 163 pitches while authoring a complete game in a 5-4 triumph.

"If you have a heart like Looie's, it doesn't matter how many pitches you throw," Evans said. "Tiant was a thoroughbred. He always wanted the ball, and he never wanted to give it up."

The Red Sox scored all five of their runs in the fourth inning off Fred Norman. Evans had the biggest hit in the inning, a two-run triple, and scored himself on a double by Burleson.

The Reds beat the Red Sox 6-2 in Game 5, the only lackluster game of the entire Series, and needed only one more win in Boston to wrap it up. Rain prevented Game 6 from being played for five days, but it was well worth the wait. Many observers, even 30 years later, still believe it was the most exciting World Series game ever played, and Dwight Evans had a memorable role in it.

The Reds seemingly had it wrapped up with a 6-3 lead in the eighth. But Carbo's second pinch homer of the Series, a three-run shot off Eastwick, tied it up and sent it into extra innings. Cincinnati had its best chance to win in the 11th when Morgan belted a Dick Drago pitch destined for the grandstand in right field with Ken Griffey on base. But Evans came up with an over-the-shoulder catch in front of the fence that ranks as one of the greatest catches in World Series history and then wheeled and doubled up Griffey to end the inning. Fisk won it in the 12th with his famous homer off the foul pole off Darcy.

"That was the most important catch but not the best I ever made," Evans said. "I actually played it wrong. I turned to look over my right shoulder, because the ball always hooks that way off the bat of a lefthanded hitter. It was one of only three times I can ever remember the ball not hooking and staying straight. Tony Oliva hit one of them, and Cecil Cooper hit the other. So now I had to turn the other way and take my eye off the ball, and for about two seconds I didn't know where it was. It was the scariest moment of my baseball career. I just stuck my glove out, and the ball fell into my glove."

Morgan won the World Series for the Reds the next night with a two-out bloop single in the top of the ninth that beat the Red Sox 4-3. Evans hit .292 in the Series with a homer and five RBI.

"We really felt like we didn't lose. But someone had to win," Evans reflected 30 years later. "We thought we would be in the World Series three or four more times. I couldn't believe it took us another 11 years to get back. With the teams we had, that never should have happened."

Dwight Evans had his own ups and downs during the rest of the decade. He was winning a string of Gold Gloves for his play in right field, but his offensive production was maddeningly inconsistent, and he was often injured. There were also serious issues to deal with at home. One of his three children was afflicted with neurofibromatosis, a rare and devastating disease, and needed constant and special medical attention. Who could blame Evans if he was sometimes worried or distracted?

"Nobody was in my shoes. Nobody else in baseball had to go through what I had to go through in those years," Evans said in 2005. But he never complained back then, nor did he ever use his family's health issues as an alibi.

By 1980, however, Evans's baseball career was at a crossroads. He wasn't hitting at all, and by mid-season he had been benched by manager Don Zimmer. His batting average stood at .192 on July 10 when he asked Walter Hriniak, the bullpen coach who was a disciple of hitting guru Charlie Lau, to help him out. Just as Stan Williams had put his career back on track in Louisville eight years before, Hriniak was his savior this time.

"He turned me around," a grateful Evans said. "I was one who was always changing my stances and trying new theories, and none of them was working. But I believed in Walter, he believed in me, and I never looked back."

Evans would emerge as one of baseball's most feared and productive hitters during the 1980s. He hit .317 over the final 80 games of the 1980 season and was off to a terrific start in 1981, hitting .341, when the players went on strike for seven weeks in mid-season. Evans finished the year hitting .296 while tying for the AL lead in homers with 22 in 108 games and driving in 71 runs. He led the AL with 85 walks and 215 total bases, becoming only the fifth player in AL history to lead the league in both walks and total bases in the same season. He finished third in the MVP voting and won his fourth Gold Glove.

Evans followed that up with a .292 campaign in 1982 with 37 doubles, 32 homers, 98 RBI, and 122 runs while drawing 112 walks and leading the AL in on-base percentage at .403 and winning another Gold Glove. Following an injury-plagued year in 1983, Evans bounced back in 1984 to hit .295 with 37 doubles, 32 homers, and 104 RBI while leading the league in runs with 121. On June 28 that year he hit for the cycle, capping his performance with a three-run homer in the bottom of the 11th to beat Seattle.

Evans continued to be productive, and in 1986 the Red Sox returned to the World Series for the first time since 1975. Evans was magnificent, hitting .308 and driving in nine runs in the seven games against the New York Mets while smacking two doubles and two homers. But blowing a two-run 10th-inning lead in Game 6 and then losing Game 7 tarnished his memories.

"Losing the '86 World Series was more disappointing than '75 because of the way we lost it," Evans related. "I really thought we were going to win it right up until the 10th inning of the sixth game."

At the age of 35 Dwight Evans hit .300 for the only time in his major-league career, finishing at .305 with 37 doubles, 34 homers, 123 RBI, 109 runs, and 106 walks in 1987. He finished fourth in the MVP balloting that year.

Evans drove in 111 runs in 1988 and had the most productive game of his career on August 13 when he belted two homers, a triple, and a single to drive in seven runs as the Red Sox routed the Detroit Tigers 16-4. The victory was the 24th straight at home for the Red Sox, setting an AL record, and the team would go on to win the AL East title for the second time in three years.

Despite battling sciatic nerve problems in his lower back in 1989, Evans recorded his third straight 100-RBI season and reached the 20-homer mark for the ninth straight season. From July 10, 1981, through the end of 1989 Evans hit .283 with 251 homers and 878 RBI, and no major-league hitter had more extra-base hits during the decade.

But his production slipped noticeably in 1990, and the 39-year-old Evans became a free agent after that season. After playing one year for the

Dwight Evans, a perennial Gold Glover and one of the greatest sluggers in Boston Red Sox history, was the club's hitting coach in 2002 and is now a minor-league consultant and instructor.
*(Courtesy of the Boston Red Sox)*

Baltimore Orioles in 1991, Dwight Evans retired. In 20 major-league seasons Evans hit .272 with 483 doubles, 385 homers, 1,384 RBI and 1,470 runs. He ranks fourth on the all-time Red Sox lists in homers, runs batted in, hits, and total bases; third in runs, doubles, extra-base hits, and walks; and second in games played and at-bats. He is also eighth in triples and won eight Gold Gloves during his career.

After his playing career ended, Evans worked as an instructor for two years for the Chicago White Sox and then served one year as the hitting coach for the Colorado Rockies. Evans then retired completely to spend more time with his three children before they all grew up and left home. He returned to the Red Sox in 2001 as a minor-league hitting instructor, and served as the hitting coach for the major-league team in 2003. Evans is now a consultant to the team.

In 2000 Dwight Evans was inducted into the Red Sox Hall of Fame. He and his wife, Susan, divide their time between their homes in Lynnfield, Massachusetts, and Fort Myers, Florida.

# Chapter 11

# BERNIE CARBO

## OCTOBER 21, 1975

S everal years after his playing career ended, Bernie Carbo was invited to play in one of the Old-Timers Games sponsored by Equitable Insurance. He found himself seated in the dugout next to Jimmy Piersall, who had played center field for the Red Sox 20 years before Carbo arrived in Boston. Two of baseball's most famous flakes were side by side for the first time.

"Piersall says to me: 'You know, the only reason you're here today is because of that one home run,'" Carbo related with a chuckle. "And I said: 'Yeah, but I'm here, aren't I?'"

Bernie Carbo's game-tying pinch three-run homer in Game 6 of the 1975 World Series will always be a permanent part of Red Sox folklore and is enshrined in the Red Sox Hall of Fame as one of the team's Memorable Moments. That Carbo should have had a longer and better major-league career is not in dispute, especially from Carbo himself. But of all the tens of thousands of big league players who ever played the game, how many of them could say they were a hero in what many observers believe was the most exciting World Series game ever played?

✦✦✦

Bernardo Carbo was born in Detroit, Michigan, on August 5, 1947. An only child, his youth was far from idyllic; his father, Joe, was a philandering alcoholic whose own baseball career had petered out, and he constantly belittled his talented son out of envy, and his mother, Carmen, felt trapped in an emotionally abusive marriage. She eventually committed suicide in 1989.

Bernie found his outlet in sports, starring in baseball and football at Livonia Franklin High School in Michigan. But his dysfunctional home life led to him becoming an alcoholic himself by the age of 16, and he would battle substance abuse problems for the next 30 years of his life.

The Cincinnati Reds thought highly enough of his abilities to select him in the first round of the 1965 draft, ahead of future Hall of Fame catcher Johnny Bench, whom they took in the second round.

"When I met Johnny Bench for the first time in Tampa, he asked me what I got for a bonus, and I told him $30,000," Carbo remembered. "He stomped away, and I don't think he talked to me the rest of the year. I think he got $5,000, a mitt, and a pair of spikes."

A lefthanded-hitting third baseman who stood six feet even but weighed only 175 pounds, Carbo struggled in his first pro season, hitting .218 in 71 games for Tampa in the Class A Florida State League. His hitting improved at Class A Peninsula in 1966 as he led the Carolina League in doubles with 30, belted 15 homers, and drew 108 walks in 132 games while batting .269. He also led the league's third basemen in errors with 41.

The Vietnam War was reaching its peak in 1967, and Carbo received his draft notice from the Army. The Reds got him into an Army reserve unit, but he was limited to 93 games at Class AA Knoxville and hit only .201 while leading Southern League third basemen in errors with 31.

Several years later, when he was playing for the Red Sox, the author noticed Carbo taking batting practice with an unusual bat and asked him what brand it was. Ever the flake, Carbo stared at the label and replied: "It's a Worth bat. Like Fort Worth. You know, where they keep the gold."

Carbo had been posted at Fort Knox, where the nation's gold reserves were actually stored, while on active duty with the Army.

Back in Double-A for a second year in 1968, Carbo found a desperately needed father figure in his manager, Sparky Anderson. The Reds, convinced he would never hit or be able to handle third base, wanted to convert Carbo into a pitcher. But he didn't want to pitch. Anderson put him in the outfield, and he responded by hitting .281 with 20 homers.

"I thought he hated me at first. He was so mean to me," Carbo said of Anderson. "But he spent hours working with me, made me dress a certain way, and made me get to the ballpark on time."

Boston Red Sox outfielder Bernie Carbo slides across the plate before New York Yankees catcher Thurman Munson can tag him out in a game at Fenway Park. Carl Yastrzemski gets a close look at the play. *(Courtesy of the Boston Red Sox)*

At Class AAA Indianapolis in 1969, Carbo had a breakout year, leading the American Association in hitting with a .359 average while tying for the league lead in doubles with 37 and swatting 21 homers. He was named the league's MVP and earned a September promotion to Cincinnati.

Reunited with Anderson, who was now managing Cincinnati, the 22-year-old Carbo fit right in with the Big Red Machine in 1970, earning National League Rookie of the Year honors from The Sporting News while hitting .310 with 21 homers and 63 RBI and helping the Reds win 102 games and the pennant. He was hitless, however, in 14 post-season at-bats, and the Reds were beaten in the World Series by Baltimore.

His career took a downturn in 1971. Denied a raise he felt he deserved, Carbo punched Cincinnati general manager Bob Howsam and held out during spring training. Carbo played only 106 games and hit .219, and after he held out again in the spring of 1972, the Reds traded him to the St. Louis Cardinals. He hit .258 and .286 for the Cardinals during his two seasons in St. Louis but showed little power.

"Nobody can play without spring training. I don't care who you are," Carbo said in retrospect.

Red Sox scouts noticed that his inside-out swing was perfect for a lefthanded hitter in Fenway Park to take advantage of the Green Monster, and he was included with righthanded pitcher Rick Wise in the trade that sent outfielder Reggie Smith and pitcher Ken Tatum to St. Louis after the 1973 season.

"There was a park near my home that eight of us went to play in all the time when we were kids," Carbo said, explaining the development of his swing. "I was the only lefthanded hitter, and when it was my turn to hit, nobody wanted to switch to the other side of the field. So I learned to hit to left."

As expected, Carbo thrived in Fenway, at least initially. At the end of May he was hitting .285 with nine homers and 35 RBI and was on a pace for a 25-homer, 100-RBI season. But he fell into a lengthy slump, found his playing time cut, and finished the 1974 season at .249 with 12 homers and 61 RBI in 117 games. Incredible hot streaks and endless slumps would be a hallmark of Carbo's career with the Red Sox. So was his flaky behavior.

On road trips his constant companion was a large stuffed toy gorilla named Mighty Joe Young that had been given to him by Scipio Spinks, a pitcher with the Cardinals.

Carbo got off to another fast start in 1975, hitting .311 in April and May with eight homers and 18 RBI in just 90 at-bats. But when he plunged into another inevitable slump that coincided with the stellar play of rookie outfielders Fred Lynn and Jim Rice, Carbo's playing time for the remainder of the regular season all but evaporated. He had only 98 at-bats after the All-Star break, including a mere 17 during the month of September. In spite of his limited playing time, Carbo nevertheless drew 83 walks and led the team in on-base percentage with a .412 mark while hitting .257 with 15 homers and 50 RBI.

Four of those 17 September at-bats came on the final day of the regular season, after the Red Sox had clinched the AL East title the previous night. Carbo got a rare start, batted cleanup, and went 2-for-4 with a walk and two RBI in a meaningless 11-4 loss to the Cleveland Indians.

He did not appear in any games as the Red Sox upset three-time defending World Champion Oakland in the American League Championship Series, sweeping the Athletics in three straight games. He sat on the bench when the Red Sox beat the Reds 6-0 in Game 1 of the World Series at Fenway Park. When he pinch hit in the ninth inning and lined out to left in a 3-2 loss the next afternoon, it was his first game action in two weeks.

Back in the familiar confines of Cincinnati's Riverfront Stadium two days later, Carbo watched from the dugout as the Reds built up a 5-2 lead after six innings of Game 3. Then the Red Sox began to stir.

Dwight Evans led off the seventh with a single, knocking reliever Pat Darcy out of the game. But when Clay Carroll got Rick Burleson to rap into a double play, things looked even bleaker for the Red Sox. Manager Darrell Johnson sent up Carbo to pinch hit for pitcher Reggie Cleveland with two outs and the bases empty, and he drove a Carroll pitch the other way that cleared the fence for a home run—his first since August 1 and only his second homer since the All-Star break.

The Red Sox tied that game in the ninth on a two-run homer by Evans, then lost it 6-5 in 10 innings after a highly controversial umpiring decision that went against them when catcher Carlton Fisk collided with Cincinnati's Ed Armbrister while fielding a bunt.

"Clay Carroll was one of my roommates when I was in Cincinnati, and before the World Series he gave me a photograph of himself and wrote on it: Good luck in the World Series, Bernie," Carbo related with a chuckle. "After we lost that game, I went into the clubhouse, and my locker was all torn up, like a tornado went through it. My stuff was all over the floor, and Carroll's picture was ripped up. I asked the clubhouse guy what happened, and he said Carroll came in and did all that."

The Red Sox split the next two games in Cincinnati, beating the Reds 5-4 before dropping a 6-2 decision. Carbo did not play in either game, and the World Series returned to Boston with the Reds holding a 3-2 advantage.

Game 6 was delayed by three days of torrential rain, but it turned out to be well worth the wait. The Red Sox worked out at nearby Tufts University while waiting for the rain to stop.

"I didn't know where Tufts was, so I didn't go. I just stayed home," Carbo said. "So I hadn't had batting practice in about a week."

On October 21, a warm and humid 64-degree evening, the World Series resumed in front of a sellout crowd of 35,205 at Fenway Park. Luis Tiant, 2-0 with a 2.00 ERA in the Series, took the mound for the Red Sox, opposed by Gary Nolan.

For 28-year-old Bernie Carbo, this would be the most memorable game of his Red Sox career.

"It's the most talked-about game I ever played in, and it was in the World Series," he explained. "When I went to bed every night as a kid, I always had my glove with me, and I dreamed of making a big catch or getting a big hit in the World Series."

That dream was about to come true.

✢ ✢ ✢

Nolan retired the first two Red Sox batters in the bottom of the first inning but gave up singles to Carl Yastrzemski and Fisk. Rookie sensation Fred Lynn stepped up and belted a three-run homer into the right-field bleachers, putting the Red Sox ahead 3-0 as the crowd went berserk. Nolan was gone after two innings, and Sparky Anderson marshaled a parade of four relievers over the next five innings. The Red Sox managed just three more hits during that stretch.

Tiant, meanwhile, continued his mastery of the Reds, yielding only two singles over the first four innings. The Reds finally got to him in the fifth. Armbrister pinch hit for reliever Jack Billingham and drew a walk, and Pete Rose singled. Ken Griffey lashed a drive to the 379 mark in left-center, and Lynn crashed into the concrete base of The Wall attempting to make the catch and crumpled to the warning track as Griffey legged out a triple. The game was delayed for several minutes until Lynn felt steady on his feet again, and Bench ripped a two-out single off Tiant that tied the game at 3-3. They were the first earned runs Tiant had surrendered at Fenway Park in 40 innings dating back to mid-September.

Cincinnati picked up two more runs in the seventh. Griffey and Joe Morgan started the inning with singles. Tiant, who had thrown 163 pitches while winning Game 4 in Cincinnati six days earlier and had already authored two complete games in the Series, was just about gassed. He retired Bench and Tony Perez on flyballs, but George Foster slammed a double, and the Reds led 5-3. When light-hitting Cesar Geronimo poled a homer down the right-field line to lead off the eighth, Darrell Johnson could not justify leaving Tiant in the game any longer.

Fenway Park had become a mausoleum as the Red Sox came to bat in the bottom of the eighth. They were losing 6-3 to a team that had rolled up 108 victories during the regular season, and their ace was out of the game. There was little reason for optimism among the fans in the stands, or even among the players in the dugout.

"Everybody was quiet. There was no cheerleading going on," Carbo remembered. "It was not a good situation to be in. We were as quiet and still as the fans were."

But Lynn led off with an infield hit off—literally—Pedro Borbon. Lynn's smash up the middle ricocheted off the reliever's ankle. Rico Petrocelli worked the count full, drew a walk, and all of a sudden the tying run was coming to the plate. Anderson went to his bullpen again, this time for his rookie closer, Rawly Eastwick, who had led the NL with 22 saves and had already won two and saved one of Cincinnati's three wins in the World Series.

---

**BERNIE CARBO**
**Years with Red Sox: 1974-1978**
**Other Major League Teams: Cincinnati,**
   **St. Louis, Milwaukee, Cleveland,**
   **Pittsburgh**
**Position: Outfield**
**Bats: Left**
**Throws: Right**
**Height: 6-0**
**Weight: 175**
**Born: August 5, 1947**
**Birthplace: Detroit, MI**
**Current Residence: Theodore, AL**
**Current Occupation: Manager,**
   **Pensacola Pelicans, Central League;**
   **minister**

---

Eastwick fanned Evans for the first out, and while Burleson was digging in at the plate, Darrell Johnson was looking for a pinch hitter for Roger Moret, who was scheduled to be on deck.

"Darrell came to me on the bench and said: 'Bernie, grab a bat,'" Carbo recalled. "And I said: 'You should tell [Juan] Beniquez to grab a bat, because there's no way I'm hitting.' But he sent me out there anyway. I'm standing in the on-deck circle, and I don't even swing the bat to get loose because I know there's no way I'm hitting. I know as soon as it's my turn, Sparky is going to bring in the lefty, Will McEnaney, and then Beniquez is going to hit for me. Sparky always did things by the book. If he lost, he was going to lose by the book."

Burleson flied out for the second out.

"So now it's my turn to bat, and I'm still standing in the on-deck circle, looking into the Cincinnati dugout, waiting for Sparky to come out," Carbo continued. "The ump says: 'Carbo, get in here!' Now I'm in the batter's box, and I'm still waiting for Sparky to come out. I turned to Johnny Bench, and I said: 'What's he waiting for? Why isn't he coming out?' But he didn't, and now, for the first time, I'm thinking I'd better get prepared to hit!"

Eastwick threw him a cookie with the first pitch, but Carbo wasn't ready and took it for a strike. The next two pitches missed for balls. Carbo always was a patient hitter who had more walks than strikeouts at that juncture of his career, and he wouldn't be tempted by a bad pitch.

Eastwick made another mistake with his next pitch, a fastball, but Carbo swung and missed it. Strike two. Eastwick threw a low fastball on the outside corner with his next pitch, and despite an ugly swing Carbo was able to get a piece of the ball and chop it foul. The next pitch was a slider on the inside corner, and again Carbo barely got a piece of it and fouled it into the ground. Two terrible swings, and it seemed apparent that Carbo was both rusty and overmatched. In the pressbox, the votes for the World Series MVP had already been collected and were in the process of being counted, and Eastwick was the winner.

But his next pitch was a thigh-high fastball, and this time Carbo was ready. He drove the ball to the deepest part of the ballpark, and it easily cleared the 20-foot-high concrete wall at the 420 mark for a three-run homer while the crowd erupted in ecstasy.

"Bernie turned fall into summer with one wave of his magic wand," said pitcher Bill Lee after the game.

It was only the second time in World Series history that a player had clubbed two pinch home runs. Chuck Essegian had been the first to perform the feat for the Los Angeles Dodgers in 1959.

"I knew it was gone as soon as I hit it," Carbo said. And on his animated trot around the bases, his arms thrust into the air and pumping, he passed Pete Rose at third base and cracked: "Don't you wish you were that strong, Pete?"

Cincinnati's three-run lead had just vanished in an instant, but Rose, too, was ensnared in the drama. "Isn't this fun?" he told Carbo. "This is the greatest game I've ever played in."

And the drama was far from over. While the MVP ballots were being torn up in the pressbox, Carbo stayed in the game to play left field. Dick Drago set down the Reds in order in the ninth, and the Sox nearly won it in the bottom of the inning. Eastwick walked Denny Doyle, and Yaz singled him to third. Now Anderson finally went to the bullpen for McEnaney, who walked Fisk intentionally to load the bases with nobody out.

Lynn lofted a shallow fly down the left-field line, not nearly deep enough to score Doyle. But when third base coach Don Zimmer hollered: "No, no, no," Doyle misunderstood him and thought he was yelling: "Go, go, go!" Foster threw him out at the plate for a double play, and Petrocelli grounded out to end the threat.

Carbo was struck out by Pat Darcy to end the 10th, and the Reds threatened in the 11th. Rose was hit by a Drago pitch but was forced out at second on a bad bunt by Griffey. Morgan then launched a ball toward the right-field corner that Evans snared with an over-the-shoulder catch—one of the greatest catches in World Series history—and then wheeled and threw toward first to double up Griffey and end the inning.

Fisk finally won it in the 12th, pulling a Darcy pitch off the foul pole in left for his famous homer that beat the Reds 7-6 and forced a seventh game.

"I went to Cooperstown a few years ago," Carbo said, "and someone at the Hall of Fame recognized me and said: 'You're Bernie Carbo! We have something to show you.' They took me into a room they called the Unsung Home Run Room, and my picture was up there on the wall with Hal Smith, who hit the tying home run before [Bill] Mazeroski's in the 1960 World Series."

Johnson rewarded Carbo with his first start of the World Series in Game 7. Carbo doubled in his first at-bat off lefty Don Gullett, then walked and scored in the third to inaugurate a three-run rally. Carbo grounded out in each of his next two at-bats, and with the Red Sox leading 3-2, Johnson sent Rick Miller out to play left in the seventh. The Reds tied the game that inning and won it in the ninth, 4-3, on Morgan's bloop single.

"We played without Jim Rice, don't forget," Carbo said. "Take Tony Perez, Johnny Bench, Joe Morgan, Pete Rose, or one of those guys out of their lineup, and we beat them. I thought those Red Sox teams were the best teams I ever played on."

✦ ✦ ✦

Carbo played only 17 games for the Red Sox in 1976 before the team, which was off to a dreadful start, dealt him to Milwaukee for outfielder Bobby Darwin and relief pitcher Tom Murphy on June 3. Carbo was so upset he thought about quitting, and Bill Lee staged a one-day walkout in protest. Carbo eventually reported to the Brewers, but he was unhappy in Milwaukee and didn't play well. The Red Sox reacquired him, along with former Sox first baseman George Scott, at the winter meetings in exchange for first baseman Cecil Cooper.

Carbo had a solid year as a role player in 1977, hitting .289 with 15 homers in 86 games while posting a .411 on-base percentage and a .522 slugging percentage. He belted three pinch homers that summer as the Red Sox won 97 games. But longtime owner Tom Yawkey, with whom Carbo had a warm relationship, had passed away in the summer of 1976, and in 1978 the club changed hands with Haywood Sullivan and Buddy LeRoux in control. The new owners of the Red Sox weren't as tolerant of Carbo's substance abuse problems as Yawkey, an alcoholic himself, had been, and shortly after the season began he was sold to the Cleveland Indians.

"If I have a problem—and I did—then help me. Don't trade me," Carbo said, a trace of bitterness evident in his voice more than a quarter of a century after the Red Sox got rid of him.

Two years later, at the age of 33, Bernie Carbo was out of baseball, a .264 lifetime hitter with 96 homers and 358 RBI in 1,010 games.

The transition back into civilian life was a difficult one for Carbo. He returned to Michigan and tended bar while putting himself through cosmetology school. After graduation he opened his own hairdressing salon. But he was still addicted to alcohol and drugs, expensive habits he could no longer afford, even as a small businessman. To feed his habits he began dealing drugs. He sold the salon and soon found himself living on the streets.

"I remember waking up in Chicago one morning, in the rain, in the gutter," Carbo told author Doug Hornig in his book, *The Boys of October.* "I'd fallen asleep there, and during the night someone had parked their car a couple of inches from my head. I don't think he had any idea there was a person sleeping down there. I probably should have died that night. I should have died over and over again. But God had a different plan for me, and He spared my life."

Carbo was contemplating suicide when Bill Lee called him one evening in 1993. Carbo poured out his miseries to his old Red Sox friend, and Lee

Bernie Carbo, whose pinch home run in Game 6 of the 1975 World Series was one of the most dramatic hits in club history, attends a banquet as his achievement is enshrined in the Boston Red Sox Hall of Fame. *(Courtesy of the Boston Red Sox/Cindy Loo)*

contacted another former teammate, Hall of Famer Ferguson Jenkins. The two pitchers put Carbo in touch with BAT, the Baseball Assistance Team that helps former ballplayers in need. Carbo went into rehab, cleaned himself up, and adopted a religious life. He married his psychologist, Tammy, and adopted her 12-year-old son, Chris. Carbo founded the Diamond Ministry, an organization that offers both baseball and life instruction, and he has been clean and sober for over a decade. His natural children from his first marriage have also battled substance abuse problems during their lives, and Bernie and Tammy Carbo are now raising three of his grandchildren at their home outside of Mobile, Alabama.

For the last three years he has also returned to professional baseball, managing the Pensacola Pelicans in the independent Central League. He won't allow his players to bring alcohol on the team bus or into the clubhouse. "Bernie Carbo couldn't play for Bernie Carbo," he laughed.

# Chapter 12

# BUTCH HOBSON

## JULY 13, 1977

There have been a lot of players in Red Sox history who had more talent than Butch Hobson. There have been a lot of players in Red Sox history who had longer careers than Butch Hobson. But none of them played the game harder than Butch Hobson.

Hobson had clouted 25 homers and driven in 72 runs in 90 games for Class AAA Pawtucket when he was called up midway through the 1976 season to replace the immensely popular but aging Rico Petrocelli at third base. While the former University of Alabama quarterback did not have an abundance of natural ability and, as one Boston writer once wrote, went "after every groundball like it was an Auburn fumble," Hobson quickly won over Red Sox fans with his hard-nosed play and hustle. Absolutely fearless, the 25-year-old Hobson could often be seen diving head-first into dugouts while chasing foul pops, and Red Sox fans had to hold their breath until he emerged from his personal mosh pits, always unscathed and almost always clutching the ball. Relieved most of all were the female fans, who swooned over Hobson's Paul Newman-esque good looks and didn't want to see him scarred.

"That's the only way I knew how to play," Hobson explained. "I really never had a fear of getting hurt making a play."

One of his most spectacular death-defying catches came at Fenway Park in a game against the Baltimore Orioles.

"Mike Torrez was pitching; Eddie Murray was the hitter," Hobson remembered. "I always kept my eye on the ball; I'd look down one time, and then I never took my eye off the ball again. So when the ball was hit, I went to it. I looked down and saw how close [to the Baltimore dugout] I was and never looked down again. When I leaped for the ball, Jim Palmer was against the bat rack, which was right next to the steps. He put his right arm out to stop me, and then as I'm going by he pulled it back!"

Palmer's instincts had been obviously trumped by the realization he was extending the arm that had already won three Cy Young Awards and would put him into the Hall of Fame.

"Ellie Hendricks, with all his catching gear on, was down in the runway smoking a cigarette, and I landed on top of him," Hobson continued. "He tried to knock the ball out of my glove, and we almost got in a fistfight down there. And [umpire Nestor] Chylak is following me down there, yelling: 'Show me the ball! Show me the ball!' And Ellie is hollering: 'He didn't catch it! He didn't catch it!'"

But Hobson had, and when he bolted unscathed from the dugout a very long 30 seconds after he had leaped in, he received a thunderous standing ovation from the relieved crowd.

✛ ✛ ✛

Clell Lavern Hobson, Jr., had been born and reared in Alabama, the son of a high school football coach who had played quarterback at Alabama and been the MVP of the 1953 Orange Bowl before signing a contract with the Cleveland Indians and playing minor-league ball for a brief period.

"Until the eighth grade, baseball was my first love," Hobson said. "But when you grow up in Alabama, you're expected to play football."

And if you were any good at football, you were expected to play for the Crimson Tide under legendary coach Paul "Bear" Bryant. Hobson followed in his father's footsteps to Alabama and as a sophomore in the 1972 Orange Bowl was one of the second-ranked Tide's few stars in their 38-6 loss to top-ranked Nebraska for the mythical national championship. But he never completely abandoned baseball, and after being told at a Cincinnati Reds tryout camp that he might have a future in the sport if he committed himself, Hobson returned to Tuscaloosa and informed Bryant he was giving up football.

"Bear Bryant was a huge baseball fan and a real good friend of George Steinbrenner," Hobson remembered. "He smoked these unfiltered Pall Malls, and as I'm sitting in his office, air-conditioned to about 40 degrees

**Boston Red Sox third baseman Butch Hobson unleashes a powerful swing during a game at Fenway Park.** *(Courtesy of the Boston Red Sox)*

in August and filled with smoke, telling him I'm not coming back, he spits out some tobacco and says: 'I've seen you play baseball. You'll be back.'"

Butch Hobson never played another down of football at Alabama. The following spring he set a Southeastern Conference record for home runs and was selected by the Red Sox in the eighth round of the 1973 draft, signing for an $8,000 bonus. He got into a couple of games in 1975 after the Red Sox had clinched the AL East title and picked up his first major-league hit, and by the middle of the 1976 season, he was in the major leagues to stay.

In his very first game after being recalled from Pawtucket and installed in the starting lineup by manager Don Zimmer on June 28, 1976, Hobson hit a double off Baltimore ace Jim Palmer and later in the game blasted a Rudy May pitch off Fenway Park's center-field wall and legged it out for an inside-the-park homer. Hobson hit only .234 with eight homers and 34 RBI in 76 games for the Red Sox as a rookie, but Zimmer loved the way he played the game.

✦✦✦

The Red Sox thought they were building a dynasty after winning the pennant in 1975, and a disappointing 83-79 season in 1976 had been written off as an aberration. They had seven All-Stars on their roster in 1977, and Hobson was another powerful young bat in a lineup that featured future Hall of Famers Carl Yastrzemski and Carlton Fisk, veteran slugger George "Boomer" Scott, and budding young superstars Jim Rice and Fred Lynn. The Red Sox would bash a club-record 213 home runs in 1977, a record that would stand for the next quarter of a century.

After a stuttering start in 1977, by mid-June the Red Sox were again playing like the champions they had been two years earlier. They moved into first place in the AL East on June 13 and 10 days later had built up a five-game lead with a 41-25 record. That lead soon slipped away, but the last three months would feature a taut three-team race between the Red Sox, Yankees, and Orioles. The Red Sox would never lead the division by more than three and a half games the rest of the way, nor would they ever be more than four and a half games behind.

"Every year I played in Boston, up until 1980 towards the end, the whole year was very intense," Hobson said. "Every game was important. Back then it was pretty much Boston, New York, and Baltimore all the way. And then Milwaukee started getting good. That was a tough division."

Hobson was hitting only .236 after 74 games on July 2, 1977, although he had been productive, smashing 13 homers and driving in 51 runs. But on July 3, in a game at Fenway Park against Baltimore, Hobson began a career-best 18-game hitting streak that would include the most memorable game of his Red Sox career.

"Hitters tell you all the time that you get in that zone where the game really slows down, doesn't look as fast as it is," Hobson related. "Except for a few home runs, I had been struggling. I wasn't a rookie anymore, but I was still trying to make my way. Now I was in one of those zones. I was really locked in."

The Red Sox were coming off a doubleheader sweep in Milwaukee in which Hobson had drilled six hits, including an 11th-inning single in the opener that had triggered a four-run, game-winning rally in Boston's 8-5 triumph. The sweep had put the Red Sox back in first place by half a game, and now they were in Cleveland for a four-game series. The Indians had enjoyed only one winning campaign in the previous eight and were destined for another losing season in 1977. But they usually found a way to beat the Red Sox, all too often at times when the Red Sox could least afford a loss.

"We hated playing Cleveland," Hobson admitted. "We played in Cleveland's home opener that year. There was something like 71,000 people, and I'm thinking this is the coolest thing, because I'd played football in front of 72,000. The next day it was empty; there was like 10 people there. It was a dump, and it seemed like the weather was always bad."

But Hobson was looking forward to this series, because 18 of his relatives, including his parents, his maternal grandparents, and an aunt and uncle who lived near Cleveland with their children, would all be attending the four games. He would be staying at his aunt's house in Avon Lake instead of at the team's hotel, and it would be a four-day Hobson family reunion.

"My granddaddy had never seen me play at all," Hobson said. "He got to meet Yaz, but he didn't know who Yaz was. He knew I played football at Alabama, and he knew I played baseball, but he never really knew exactly what or how I did. But every night back at my aunt's house, he'd ask me a lot of questions about the game. So that was a special series for me."

Hobson had a double in the first game of the series on July 11 and scored one of Boston's two runs in a 2-1 victory. He homered the next night off flamboyant young fireballer Dennis Eckersley, but it was the only Red

Sox run in a 7-1 defeat. He also had two singles in the game, his third three-hit game in the last four.

"Eck used to yell at me when he struck me out, because I swung pretty hard. I had the locker next to Yaz, and that's the one thing Yaz told me about hitting: 'Swing hard in case you hit it.' Anyway, when Eck struck me out, he'd yell: 'Why don't you freakin' swing harder!' We gave each other a hard time about that when he came over to play for us. But I didn't hit Eck well."

The next night, July 13, would be the one Hobson would most remember, although initially he wasn't certain if he would be healthy enough to play. He had been hot for 10 days now and had hit safely in eight straight games, but he was almost too hot to play this evening.

"I remember being really sick—I had the flu or something—and not knowing if I'd be able to start the game. My mother was giving me all kinds of remedies at my aunt's house. But if I hadn't played, my dad … well, that wouldn't have been good. He would have dropped one of those 'What would Bear Bryant say?' on me."

Hobson skipped batting practice to conserve his energy, and he threw up in the dugout before the game. But he didn't ask out of the lineup.

> **BUTCH HOBSON**
> **Years with Red Sox: 1975-80**
> **Other Major League Teams: California, New York (AL)**
> **Position: Third Base**
> **Bats: Right**
> **Throws: Right**
> **Height: 6-1**
> **Weight: 193**
> **Born: August 17, 1951**
> **Birthplace: Tuscaloosa, AL**
> **Current Residence: Nashua, NH**
> **Current Occupation: Manager, Nashua Pride, Atlantic League**

"I was really hot, really swinging the bat well, and there was no way I was coming out of the lineup. But the biggest reason was because I had all these people there."

Wayne Garland, a 20-game winner for Baltimore the previous summer who had signed a 10-year contract for $2 million as one of Major League Baseball's first free agents, was on the mound for the Indians in front of 18,524 fans at cavernous Municipal Stadium. A two-run homer by Rice staked Red Sox starter and future Hall of Famer Ferguson Jenkins to a quick lead before he took the mound.

Hobson grounded out to third in his first at-bat, and the Red Sox were leading 3-1 when Hobson singled to left in the fourth to extend his hitting streak to nine games. The Indians tied the game in the bottom of the fourth, but Rice put the Red Sox back in front, 5-3, with his second two-run homer of the game in the fifth, his 23rd homer of the season.

Hobson lashed another single to left off Garland in the sixth but was wiped out in a double play. The Red Sox tacked on another run in the seventh when Rice scored on a passed ball, but Cleveland got that one back in the bottom of the inning off rookie Mike Paxton, who had taken over for Jenkins at the start of the fifth. Hobson collected his third hit of the game with another single to left, this time off lefthanded reliever Sid Monge, in the eighth, but the Red Sox didn't score.

As the Red Sox took a 6-4 lead into the bottom of the ninth with their own high-priced free agent, reliever Bill Campbell, on the mound, it seemed as if the victory was assured and the game would be just another three-hit performance by Hobson, his fourth in five games.

"'Soup' was pretty much automatic," Hobson said. Campbell would set a Red Sox record with 31 saves that season and lead the league.

But Campbell couldn't finish off the Indians. Larvell Blanks coaxed a one-out walk, and Jim Norris singled him to third. An infield hit by Duane Kuiper scored Blanks, and a walk to Buddy Bell loaded the bases. Campbell fanned John Lowenstein for the second out but then hit Andre Thornton with a pitch, forcing home Norris with the tying run. That brought up 6-3, 220-pound righthanded-hitting Charlie Spikes with a chance to win it for the Indians right there.

"I was thinking: 'We gotta make a play here. We've gotta get an out to keep this game going," Hobson recalled.

The thought had barely crossed Hobson's mind when the ball came screaming at him.

"Charlie Spikes was a pull hitter, and it was a rocket. Zim had just moved me over a step toward the line, and I had thought I was already on the line. If he hadn't moved me that step, that ball would have got by. It was one of those that took a hop high in the air and caught me in the gut."

Hobson ran to third with the ball and stepped on the bag to force Bell for the third out and send the game into extra innings.

Righthander Jim Kern, who had entered the game in the eighth, went back out for the Indians in the top of the 10th. The 6-5, 185-pound Kern was one of the hardest throwers in the game. He had posted a 10-7 record with 15 saves and a 2.36 ERA while striking out 111 batters in 118 innings for the Indians in 1976, and he had been just as dominant in 1977. Kern, who would be pitching in the All-Star Game the following week, had recorded 12 saves and struck out 49 batters in 53 innings coming into this game. He had allowed just one home run all season.

"Kern was an intimidating guy," Hobson said. "He was a fastball-slider guy who threw 97, and he was big."

Kern blew a third strike past Yastrzemski, one of the best fastball hitters in the game, to start the 10th.

"Yaz didn't miss too many fastballs," Hobson said.

Kern then retired Fisk for the second out. But Scott ripped a single to center and shocked everyone in the ballpark by stealing second. Rick Miller beat out a single to shortstop, bringing Hobson to the plate.

"I was a low-ball hitter," Hobson said. "Zim would say: 'You like the low hard one, Hobson. Don't let it get by.'"

And that's what Kern threw him.

"I don't remember what the count was. I just remember it was a fastball down and in," Hobson recollected. "I saw it real good, just like I was seeing every pitch at that time. I remember hitting it, and it was so close to the foul pole. It went in the upper deck, and, of course, there was nobody up there."

The three-run homer, Hobson's 16th of the season, put the Red Sox ahead 9-6. Hobson said it was the longest ball he ever hit.

"I used to watch Jimmy and Boomer and those guys hit those long home runs, and I would admire the distance they'd get. And when I hit that one, I said to myself: 'I'm up there with the big boys now.'"

It was also the only four-hit game Hobson ever had for the Red Sox. He would have another one with the California Angels near the end of his career.

"Any time you get four hits in a game, the kind of hitter I was, you gotta remember those," he chuckled.

The Indians pushed across a harmless run off Bill Lee in the bottom of the 10th, and the Red Sox won 9-7 to hold onto their half-game lead.

"Those were all big games for us to win. Being a young guy and winning a game like that and everybody getting excited, that was really exciting for me," Hobson reflected. "My dad was pumped up, too, and that just made it that much more of a pleasure."

Hobson homered for the third straight game in the final game of the series, and his sixth-inning RBI single off Al Fitzmorris broke a 4-4 stalemate and propelled the Red Sox to a 7-4 triumph. He had put on quite a show for his family, going 9-for-16 in the series with three homers and a

Butch Hobson, whose reckless style of play made him immensely popular with Boston Red Sox fans, is now the manager and part-owner of the Nashua Pride of the independent Atlantic League. *(Courtesy of Chaz Scoggins)*

double, scoring four runs, and driving in six while stroking the game-winning hit in each of the last two games.

Hobson's 18-game hitting streak would come to an end on July 25, but he would hit .349 for the month with nine doubles, seven homers, and 22 RBI in 27 games.

"This was one of those spots in my career where I was locked in, where I was seeing the ball come out of the pitcher's hand," he reminisced. "It can be done. It's just a matter of consistency, and I just wasn't consistent enough to be a better hitter."

✦ ✦ ✦

The Red Sox would go on to win 97 games in 1977 but finished in a tie with Baltimore for second place, two and a half games behind the Yankees. Hobson would set Red Sox records for third basemen with 30 homers and 112 RBI that still stand.

He was off to a strong start in 1978 when his right elbow began unraveling. Those years of being tackled on the artificial turf in Tuscaloosa and diving for groundballs in ballparks finally caught up to him.

"That's why he could throw around corners but could never throw straight to first base," quipped Bill Lee.

Hobson committed a staggering 43 errors that summer, and his elbow was so sore he would often run the ball halfway across the infield before throwing it. Between pitches he would be seen trying to move the floating bone chips in his elbow to a less intrusive spot.

"Doc [Arthur] Pappas said he could operate and take those things out," Hobson related. "But back then they didn't scope. They had to cut, and I would have missed the rest of the year. We were ahead by 13 games, and I couldn't see myself not being a part of it.

"But in September I went into Zim and said: 'I can't do it anymore.' I couldn't throw the ball to the mound. When you reach the point where you can't throw the ball, you don't want the ball hit to you anymore, because you don't want to screw the game up."

Hobson was relegated to designated hitting duties the rest of the year. The Red Sox finished with 99 wins, but their 14-game lead over the Yankees vanished and they lost a one-game playoff for the division title.

Hobson bounced back to hit 28 homers and drive in 93 runs for the Red Sox in 1979. But when the club, never having won another pennant, was broken up after the 1980 season, Hobson was among the players traded.

After his playing career ended, he managed in the New York Mets system before returning to the Red Sox organization. He managed the Red Sox in 1993 and 1994, and is currently the manager and a minority owner of the Nashua Pride in the independent Atlantic League. He lives in Nashua, New Hampshire, with his second wife, Krys, and their four children.

# Chapter 13

# JIM RICE

## MAY 9, 1978

Midway through the 1946 season, Cleveland Indians manager Lou Boudreau began employing a novel defensive shift every time Red Sox slugger and notorious pull hitter Ted Williams came to bat with the bases empty. Such a strategy had been used—very briefly—once before against Williams. Five years earlier, in 1941, Chicago White Sox manager Jimmy Dykes had placed three of his infielders and all three outfielders to the right of second base one afternoon only to see Williams poke the ball to left field and waltz into second base with an uncontested double. Dykes never did it again.

After Williams blasted three homers and knocked in eight runs to beat the Indians 11-10 in the first game of a doubleheader on July 14, 1946, a frustrated Boudreau resurrected the shift that came to bear his name in the second game, exaggerating the Dykes shift even more by putting all four of his infielders on the right side and leaving only his leftfielder to defend the entire left side of the diamond.

"I wanted to hit a homer more than ever," the ever-cocky Williams admitted at the time, "so I could tell Boudreau: 'You put them in the right position all right, Lou, but you should have had taller men.'"

The Boudreau Shift became a common defense by all opponents against Williams and cost the stubborn slugger several hits a year over the remainder of his career. But Williams did beat it from time to time by hitting the ball to left, most notably on September 13, 1946. That was the night he got that home run he wanted against the Boudreau Shift by lobbing a ball into left field and legging it out for an inside-the-park homer, the only one of his career. That homer in Cleveland beat the Indians 1-0 and clinched the pennant for the Red Sox.

Almost 32 years later, on the night of May 8, 1978, slugger Jim Rice, one of Williams's worthy successors in left field for the Red Sox, stood at the plate in wonderment as the Kansas City Royals went into a unique shift designed to thwart him. Plate umpire Mike Reilly was so bewildered by seeing four outfielders playing as deep as they could at Fenway Park, he actually delayed the game for a few moments while he counted the number of Royals on the field and made certain Kansas City manager Whitey Herzog had not sneaked an extra defender out there.

What made the shift so surprising was that, unlike Ted Williams, the righthanded-hitting Jim Rice was not a dead-pull hitter. Many of his homers cleared the fences from left-center to right-center, and Rice even drove the ball a long way to right field for homers and triples. He had lashed 15 triples in 1977 and would do so again in 1978 by whacking 15 more to lead the league in that department.

So why did Whitey Herzog think a shift—any shift—would be able to contain Rice?

+ + +

James Edward Rice was born on March 8, 1953, in Anderson, South Carolina. He was one of nine children born to Roger, a supervisor in a company that manufactured radio antennae, and Julia Mae Rice. Jim grew up at a time when the Old South was evolving, however reluctantly, into the New South. By the mid-1960s the civil rights movement had taken hold, but there was still resistance. The hard-line segregationists were more than happy to put their old prejudices aside, though, and turn the new laws to their advantage when it suited them. Jim Rice provided one of those advantages in Anderson.

Rice became such a standout athlete in football, basketball, track, and baseball at Westside High School, which was predominantly black, that the town's high school desegregation line was cleverly redrawn before his senior year in 1970. Rice attended Hanna High that year, and major-league scouts flocked to watch his games.

"There's a good chance no one would have ever known about him before integration. The scouts never went to black baseball games. The results weren't in the papers," Olin Saylor, Rice's American Legion coach,

**Boston Red Sox leftfielder Jim Rice goes all out to snare a flyball in the gap during a game at Fenway Park. Centerfielder David Henderson backs up Rice on the play.** *(Courtesy of the Boston Red Sox)*

said a few years later. "There wasn't any black Legion. I'll say for certain that Jim Rice never would have been a number-one draft choice were it not for integration."

But some scouts wrote him off as a high pick anyway after watching him arrive late for a Legion game one night and then take a nap on the bench instead of taking infield with his teammates. What Red Sox scout Mace Brown knew that many of the other scouts did not was that Rice was not pampered by his parents. While they encouraged his athletic endeavors, he had to work for his spending money. Rice was late that night because he had been loading boxes at a produce company, and his relief worker hadn't shown up on time.

"Mace knew the family and the kid," Sam Mele, another Red Sox scout, said several years later. "He knew that Jim Ed Rice was anything but lazy. We all know who's right now, don't we?"

The Red Sox picked him in the first round of the 1971 draft. He hit a modest .256 with five homers that summer for Williamsport in the short-season New York-Penn League and then began to display his prodigious power at Winter Haven in the Class A Florida State League the following year. Rice hit .292 with 20 doubles, 13 triples, and 17 homers while knocking in 87 runs and leading the league with 80 runs and 143 hits. He was named to the FSL All-Star Team.

Rice won the Class AA Eastern League batting crown in 1973 with a .317 average for Bristol while belting 27 homers and driving in 93 runs. He again made the All-Star Team, and before the end of the season Rice and fellow Bristol hotshot Fred Lynn were both elevated to Class AAA Pawtucket. Rice, only 20 years old, hit .378 with four homers and 10 RBI in 10 playoff games for the Pawtucket Red Sox, including a three-run homer against Tulsa that clinched the Little World Series.

Rice was slated for a full season at Pawtucket in 1974 and won the International League's Triple Crown, hitting .337 with 25 homers and 93 RBI. *The Sporting News* named him its Minor League Player of the Year, and in August the Red Sox called up their prodigy. Rice got into 24 games for the Red Sox, hitting .269 with one homer and 13 RBI.

> ## JIM RICE
> **Years with Red Sox: 1974-89**
> **Other Major League Teams: None**
> **Position: Outfield**
> **Bats: Right**
> **Throws: Right**
> **Height: 6-2**
> **Weight: 205**
> **Born: March 8, 1953**
> **Birthplace: Anderson, SC**
> **Current Residence: North Andover, MA**
> **Current Occupation: Red Sox TV analyst and special assignment instructor**

The 21-year-old Rice didn't show much in spring training in 1975, hitting only .161 without a home run in 17 exhibition games. But Red Sox manager Darrell Johnson wasn't concerned; he knew the kid was ready. Rice and Lynn would form a devastating rookie combo that would spark the Red Sox to the pennant.

The 6-2, 200-pound Rice began the 1975 season as the designated hitter while old pro and six-time Gold Glover Carl Yastrzemski played left. When Yaz separated a shoulder at mid-season and had to move to first base, Rice took over in left field for the remainder of the season.

Rice was hitting .309 with 22 homers and 102 RBI when his hand was broken by a pitch thrown by Detroit's Vern Ruhle on September 21. That put him out of the playoffs and World Series, and his bat was sorely missed when the Cincinnati Reds outlasted the Red Sox in seven dramatic games. Three of the four Red Sox losses in the World Series were by one run, and Rice's replacement, Cecil Cooper, hit only .105 with one RBI.

In almost any other year but 1975, Jim Rice would have been the American League's Rookie of the Year. But Lynn, who hit .331 with 47 doubles, 21 homers, and 105 RBI, not only won that award but the league's MVP award as well.

The following year was a disappointment for the Red Sox, and Rice was not immune. The Red Sox played sub.-500 ball for most of the season, and only by winning 15 of their last 18 games were they able to finish the year in third place with an 83-79 record. Rice hit 25 homers, but his batting average dipped to .282 while his RBI total fell to 85, and he led the league in strikeouts with 123.

Rice and the Red Sox were both back with a vengeance in 1977. Rice had a monster campaign, hitting .320 while leading the league with 39 homers and driving in 114 runs. He also led the league in slugging at .593 and in total bases with 382, the most by an AL player in 37 years. With 29 doubles and 15 triples to go along with his 39 homers, Rice became the first AL player to reach double digits in all three of those categories since Mickey Mantle in 1955. He also had a three-homer game against Oakland. The Red Sox won 97 games and weren't eliminated from the AL East race until the next-to-last day of the season.

Rice was destined for an even greater season in 1978, prompting Whitey Herzog's desperate measures to try to hold him in check.

The Red Sox began the season rather modestly, going 11-9 in the month of April while Rice hit .303 with five homers and 17 RBI in the 20 games, including a streak of driving in runs in eight consecutive games. And when Rice got scorching hot in May, so did the Red Sox.

Rice clubbed two homers and had four RBI in a 9-6 win over the Baltimore Orioles on May 1. That began a string of nine consecutive multiple-hit games for the 25-year-old slugger.

When the Kansas City Royals, the two-time defending AL West champions, arrived in Boston for a brief two-game series on Monday, May 8, Rice was hitting .364 with a .703 slugging percentage, nine homers, and 32 RBI in 27 games. He had just been named the American League's Player of the Week after going 16-for-29 for a .552 average with two doubles, two triples, and four homers for a 1.172 slugging percentage, and knocking in 15 runs while scoring eight times in a 6-1 week that had brought the Red Sox within two games of first-place Detroit in the AL East.

Rice's fourth-inning, two-run homer on Saturday had ignited a 3-0 win over the Chicago White Sox in the second game of a doubleheader, and his two-run homer in the first inning on Sunday had propelled them to a 5-0 whitewash of the White Sox. Those two homers were the first two in an incredible 18-day run for Rice during which he would blast 11 homers, every one of which either tied the score or put the Red Sox ahead. There has been no comparable stretch of clutch slugging by any Red Sox player in the last quarter of a century—and perhaps ever—than Rice's streak from May 6-23, 1978.

But Herzog could not know that then, although he might have sensed it. All he knew was that Jim Rice was on a formidable tear with nine hits—six of them for extra bases—and 10 RBI in the last four games alone. Herzog had to try to design a way to stop him, even if the strategy he employed would have to be more psychological than practical against a powerful hitter with a short, compact swing who hit the ball where it was pitched and didn't try to pull everything. He had to create a weakness, even if it was an artificial one, where there was none.

Said Kansas City infielder Jerry Terrell at the time: "How do you pitch to Jim Rice? Well, he has a 35-inch bat. You pitch him 40 inches away and hope he can't reach it."

Echoed Royals catcher Darrell Porter: "I would rather see [seven-time AL batting champion] Rod Carew 10 times a day than Jim Rice one time with three on."

Herzog did nothing unusual with his defense in the first inning, and Rice cracked a double during a four-run rally. But after the Royals came up with three runs in the third and cut the Red Sox lead to 4-3, Herzog scrambled his fielders when Rice led off the bottom of the inning.

Terrell moved from third base to left field, and leftfielder Tom Poquette positioned himself in left-center. Second baseman Frank White moved over to third base, and first baseman Clint Hurdle stationed himself midway between first and second. It was an alignment Herzog had used once before, against Minnesota slugger Harmon Killebrew in 1973.

"I thought somebody had come out of the bullpen, and that stopped the game," Rice recalled some 27 years later.

Mike Reilly, the plate umpire, was more confused by the defense than Rice, and he counted the number of Royals on the field before letting Dennis Leonard throw a pitch. Rice remained unruffled.

"Why should I find it distracting?" he said after the game. "There are still only nine men out there."

Rice flied out to center in that at-bat. But when he batted again in the fifth, he hit a pop-up in the vicinity of third base that White, unaccustomed to playing on that side of the infield, couldn't track, and it landed untouched on the skin of the infield for a single.

With the Red Sox clinging to a 5-4 lead in the seventh and Bernie Carbo at second with two outs, Herzog didn't fool around with Rice and ordered Leonard to walk him intentionally. The strategy backfired when lefthander Al "The Mad Hungarian" Hrabosky was brought in to face Yastrzemski, and he belted a three-run homer to put the game out of reach. The Red Sox won 8-4.

Herzog was asked after the game if he thought the defense was effective, especially in light of Rice's pop-fly single. "To be honest, I don't mind if he hits a single, especially here," the manager replied.

Red Sox manager Don Zimmer thought the defense was worthless. "They can't place them over the fence," he noted, "and he will hit some there, too."

Herzog didn't disagree. "What I'd really like to do is put two guys on top of the Citgo sign (in Kenmore Square) and two in the net. Heck, I might put five outfielders out there sometime."

Jim Rice hit one out the very next night. It would be the most memorable game of his career, and it would be the last time any team would ever overshift against him when he batted.

"I wasn't around when they put a shift on Williams, and I had never seen one against anyone else before," Rice said, explaining why he selected this game above all others. "So I guess that put me in an elite category, although now you see them against a lot of pull hitters. But I never considered myself a pull hitter, and I wasn't going to change anything because they put a shift on me. Pitch me inside, I pull the ball. Pitch me outside, I hit it where it's pitched. To me, it was a sign of respect."

✤ ✤ ✤

A Tuesday night crowd of 22,369 was in the stands at Fenway on May 9, eager to see if the Royals would use the shift on Rice again. They did, and Rice drilled a single up the middle in the first inning off veteran righthander Jim Colborn, a one-time 20-game winner for Milwaukee who was pitching his last season in the majors.

RBI singles by Rick Burleson and Jerry Remy put the Red Sox ahead 2-0 in the second inning, but Rice, with the defense playing him normally, dribbled a ball in front of the plate and was thrown out to end the inning with two on.

Then in the fifth, with the Red Sox still leading 2-0 with one out and the bases empty, Rice batted again, and the Royals went into their four-outfielder, three-infielder defense. Rice belted a long foul to left on the first pitch, and the next one came sailing at his head. Rice ducked, and the ball hit him in the shoulder blade.

Rice never reacted when he was plunked, always dropping his bat and calmly taking first base. But this time he was irked. He didn't charge the mound like a raging bull like so many other hitters do. One of the strongest men in baseball—at least twice in his career he snapped bats in half while checking his swing—Rice just walked slowly out there, wagging a finger at Colborn while an anxious hush fell over the crowd. Plate umpire Bill Haller and Porter, the catcher, rushed out to try to intervene, but the determined Rice brushed them off. Players on both teams left their benches and milled around in front of their dugouts, preparing to brawl but waited to see exactly what the mild-mannered Rice was going to do. Colborn, his arms dangling submissively at his sides, waited patiently for him to arrive.

"I thought I was going to be Rice-A-Roni," Colborn quipped afterward, referring to a popular supermarket product.

"I didn't know what to think," Zimmer said after the game. "The ball almost hit him in the face. Jimmy is a pretty easygoing guy. I've seen him knocked down. I've seen him with a broken wrist. And he's always taken it in stride. If he wanted to flatten him, he would have."

That wasn't Rice's intention. "I'm not going to go out there and start something," he said at the time. "I don't think he was throwing at me. I think the pitch slipped, because it didn't have much velocity. I told him: 'If you're going to hit me, don't hit me in the hands, arms, or eyes, or somewhere it would put me out of the lineup.'"

"When he came out there, I thought it was serious. He is extremely awesome," Colborn said. "I asked him if he was all right, knowing full well my fastball can't hurt anybody. But, to be honest, the ball wasn't that far inside. He was leaning out over the plate, like most of the hitters do on that team."

Twenty-seven years later, Rice altered his original version of the incident.

"I think they wanted to hit me," he said. "They knew I was on a hot streak, and pitchers know what kind of numbers you have against them. Sometimes they try to intimidate you.

"Also," Rice added, "Porter thought I was peeking at pitches. The whole night he kept saying: 'You're looking back here. Don't do it.' I told him I didn't have to look back there. I never liked to know what was coming. Sometimes someone on second base tried to give you the signs, but I never wanted to know. I just hit the ball. But maybe that's why they hit me."

Having said his piece to Colborn, Rice went to first base, and the game resumed. The only disappointed person in the ballpark was Herzog.

"I wish Rice would have slugged him, because then he would have been out of the game and never would have hit that home run," the Kansas City manager joked.

But that was still in the future. Rice was left stranded, and the Royals tied the game in the seventh when Dennis Eckersley hit Hurdle with a pitch and Amos Otis clubbed a two-run homer.

Remy started the bottom of the inning by belting a triple, and with the go-ahead run on third base that late in the game the Royals couldn't risk putting one of their infielders into the outfield for Rice. They had to play it by the book and even bring the infield in to try to cut down Remy if he tried to score on a groundball. But there was no defensive strategy for what happened next, other than walking Rice intentionally and taking their chances with two future Hall of Famers in Yastrzemski—who had hit the three-run homer the night before when Rice was passed—and Carlton Fisk and three-time All-Star Fred Lynn.

"With Yaz hitting behind me, maybe they thought giving up two runs was better than maybe giving up three," Rice suggested more than a quarter of a century later.

So the Royals pitched to him, and Rice blasted a Colborn pitch far over the screen in left and deep into the night for a two-run homer, putting the Red Sox back in front 4-2.

"There was no revenge motive at all. I wasn't anxious to hit a home run the next time," Rice insisted after the game. "You can't be anxious; you gotta be relaxed. We had a man on third in a tie game. I'm just up there to make contact and get the run in."

As much as the fans and the media wanted to regard the home run as a response to the shift, a loud "Take that!" to Herzog, Rice said the homer, while satisfying, was nothing more than capitalizing on a bad Colborn pitch.

"When a guy hits a home run, it's usually off a mistake. How many times do you ever hear a pitcher say somebody hit a good pitch?" Rice said in 2005. "But any time you can hit a home run to win a ball game, it's a good feeling. My only goal every year was to get 100 RBI. And to me that home run just got me two RBI closer."

The Red Sox won the game 4-3 for their seventh straight win and closed within a half-game of first place. Herzog never used a shift on Rice again, and neither did any other manager.

"He hits the ball too hard to too many areas of the field. The fact that he hit 15 triples two years in a row tells you that," Herzog said in retrospect, and with respect.

"The next time I saw a shift like that," Rice said, "I was the hitting coach [in Boston] and we were doing it against Ken Griffey."

✦ ✦ ✦

Rice went on to win the MVP Award in 1978, leading the league with 46 homers and 139 RBI while batting .315. An incredible 30 of his 46 homers were struck in clutch situations, either tying the score or putting the Red Sox ahead. With 406 total bases, he became the first American Leaguer to reach 400 since Joe DiMaggio in 1937. He also led the league in hits with 213, triples with 15, and in slugging at .600 while scoring 121 runs. The only disappointment was that the Red Sox, after winning 99 games, lost a one-game playoff to the New York Yankees for the AL East crown. Rice had an RBI single in that 5-4 defeat.

In 1979 Rice became the first player in major-league history to have three straight years with 35 homers and 200 hits, and he led the AL in total bases for the third straight season, a feat accomplished previously in league history only by Hall of Famers Ty Cobb and Ted Williams. He hit .325 with 39 homers and 130 RBI.

Rice missed a month in 1980 when his wrist was broken by a pitch thrown by Chicago's Chris Knapp, but he forged a 21-game hitting streak in September and finished the year at .294 with 24 homers and 86 RBI in 124 games. Following the strike-torn 1981 season, Rice hit .309 with 24 homers and 97 RBI. He led the AL in homers with 39 and tied for the lead in RBI with 126 in 1983 while hitting .305 and logging 21 assists in left field, the most by a Red Sox outfielder since 1944.

And pitchers were reminded that it was never wise to try to intimidate Rice after Matt Keough hit him with a pitch in the first inning on July 2 that year at Yankee Stadium. In Rice's second-most memorable game, revenge was a motive. Too late, Don Zimmer, by then a coach with the Yankees, issued a warning to Keough.

"He used to throw at me a lot when he was with Oakland," Rice said of Keough. "He pitched me up and in the first time, hit me, and Zimmer

Jim Rice, one of the most prolific sluggers in Red Sox history, now works as an analyst on the team's television broadcasts.
*(Courtesy of the Boston Red Sox)*

got up on the top step of their dugout and yelled at him: 'You leave that man alone!'"

Rice followed with two-run homers in the third and fourth innings off Keough, and the Red Sox routed the Yankees 10-4.

"The second one went into the third tier in left field. I watched that one," remembered Rice, who never stood at the plate to admire his home runs. "I never tried to show up anybody. But that was payback. And Zimmer yelled at him again: 'What did I tell you? Leave that man alone!' He never threw at me again."

Rice also had his second three-homer game on August 29—six years to the day after his first—and drove in six runs in an 8-7 win at Toronto.

Rice had 28 homers and 122 RBI in 1984 and had 27 homers and 103 RBI in 1985 as he battled some nagging injuries. His last big year for the Red Sox came in 1986, when he hit .324 with 39 doubles, 20 homers, and 110 RBI while collecting 200 hits. The Red Sox won the pennant, and Rice hit .333 in the World Series against the New York Mets and scored six runs.

But at the age of 35, Rice's reflexes were prematurely slowing. His production nose-dived over the next two and a half years, and the Red Sox released him during the 1989 season. He finished his 16-year career with a .298 average, 382 homers, and 1,451 RBI in 2,089 games. Eight times he drove in more than 100 runs, he hit over .300 seven times, and he hit more than 30 homers in four seasons. He also played in eight All-Star Games.

Rice was inducted into the Red Sox Hall of Fame in 1995. He ranks third on the club's all-time lists in home runs, RBI, total bases, at-bats, and hits with 2,452. He is fourth in games, runs with 1,249, and extra-base hits with 834. Rice also ranks sixth with 373 doubles and 79 triples, and seventh with a .502 slugging percentage.

Rice, who is also an outstanding golfer, spent three years as a roving hitting instructor in the Red Sox' minor-league system before serving as the hitting coach with the major-league team from 1995-2000. He is currently a special assignment instructor and an analyst on Red Sox telecasts. Rice and his wife, Corine, have two grown children and reside in North Andover, Massachusetts.

# Chapter 14

# DENNIS ECKERSLEY

## SEPTEMBER 17, 1978

Dennis Eckersley arrived in Winter Haven, Florida, just a few days before the end of spring training in 1978, armed with a blazing fastball, a cocky attitude, and his own argot. What no one could be sure about when the Red Sox traded four players to the Cleveland Indians to get the flamboyant 23-year-old righthander was whether he had the fortitude to pitch under pressure in a pennant race. He talked a good game—if you could find someone to translate his vocabulary—but was he a gamer? Eckersley had enjoyed three brilliant seasons in Cleveland, including a no-hitter. But there was never any pressure in Cleveland, pitching for bad teams in front of 75,000 empty seats at Municipal Stadium.

Dennis Eckersley would answer that question about pressure with an exclamation point less than six months later, and he would do it under the pressure of unbearable personal circumstances that had little to do with baseball.

✦✦✦

Dennis Lee Eckersley was born on October 3, 1954, in Oakland, California. The middle of three children of a sailor in the U.S. Navy, Eckersley was a multisport star at Washington High School in Fremont, California, starring in football, basketball, and baseball. After Cleveland drafted him in the third round in 1972, the 18-year-old Eckersley signed and pitched a shutout for Class A Reno in his professional debut. Despite that auspicious beginning, his first year in pro ball was undistinguished, and Eckersley found himself back in Reno again the following year. This time he excelled, going 12-8 with a 3.65 ERA and 218 strikeouts in 202 innings. That earned him a promotion to Class AA San Antonio in 1974, where Eckersley went 14-3 with a 3.40 ERA, led the league in wins and strikeouts, and was named the Texas League's Righthanded Pitcher of the Year.

Cleveland, which had not had a winning record since 1968, had a new manager in future Hall of Famer Frank Robinson in 1975. Although the 20-year-old Eckersley had not yet pitched an inning of Triple-A ball, Robinson liked what he saw of the 6-2, 190-pound fireballer in spring training and kept him on the roster.

"I was surprised," Eckersley said. "Cleveland probably didn't want to rush me. But they gave Frank the power, and he took a shot with me."

After 10 scoreless relief outings to start his major-league career, Eckersley was inserted into the rotation, shut out Oakland 6-0 in his first start, and finished the year with a 13-7 record, a 2.60 ERA, and Rookie Pitcher of the Year laurels from *The Sporting News*.

Eckersley fanned 200 batters in 199 innings in 1976 while posting a 13-12 record with a 3.44 ERA and earning the lasting enmity of hitters for taunting them. The Indians were 81-78, their first winning season in eight years, although they finished fourth, 16 games behind the New York Yankees.

"You know what it was?" Eckersley said, addressing his reputation for cockiness. "It's because you're scared. That's the psychology of it. When you're acting angry and demonstrative, it's really to hide that fear. And it worked for me. It comes across as cocky, but it's that protection from fear."

On May 30, 1977, Eckersley pitched a no-hitter, outdueling California Angels flamethrower Frank Tanana to win 1-0 with 12 strikeouts. That performance was part of a hitless string of 22 1/3 innings over three games, the second-longest such streak in major-league history behind Cy Young's 23-inning stretch in 1904. Eckersley also threw a one-hitter at the Milwaukee Brewers on August 12, allowing only a first-inning triple by Cecil Cooper. He pitched two scoreless innings in the All-Star Game and led the Cleveland staff in wins, ending up at 14-13 with a 3.53 ERA for a team that reversed direction again and lost 90 games.

The Red Sox, who had won 97 games in 1977 but finished in a tie for second, were looking for a potential ace. They had already signed free agent

Flamboyant Boston Red Sox righthander Dennis Eckersley gets ready to deliver a pitch during a spring training game in Winter Haven, Florida. *(Courtesy of the Boston Red Sox)*

World Series hero Mike Torrez away from the Yankees, but longtime ace Luis Tiant was aging, broke a finger in spring training, and the Red Sox desired a younger one-two punch. The Indians saw an opportunity to bolster themselves in several areas by accepting Boston's offer of Rick Wise, a 19-game winner in 1975, young righthander Mike Paxton, and a pair of highly promising rookies in third baseman Ted Cox and catcher Bo Diaz. So on March 30, 1978, the deal was made with backup catcher Fred Kendall accompanying a reluctant Eckersley to Boston.

"You'd think nobody was going to trade me, because I was so valuable. People were talking about it, but I was saying no way," Eckersley remembered. "I didn't want to leave all my friends, guys I had grown up with. It was a security thing. What an idiot! I'm going to Boston, and I don't want to leave Cleveland. What are you? Crazy? But I really didn't."

Eckersley, with his matinee-idol looks, collar-length black hair, electric personality, and unique vernacular acquired from veteran pitcher Pat Dobson in Cleveland, was an immediate hit with Red Sox fans. This was how Eckersley once described a contentious contract negotiation: "Yeah, I wore a three-piece for the occasion, and they chilled me. It was bogus, man. A real turnoff. I didn't want the Bogart without the iron up front. I wanted to psych in on the game."

In Eckersley's vocabulary, iron was money, grease was food, oil was liquor, cheese was a fastball, a yakker was a curveball, a Bogart was a big game, and being bridged was giving up a home run. A granny was a grand slam. Because his control was so extraordinary and he always gave up a lot of home runs (most of them solo), Eckersley was a self-described "bridgemaster."

"Pat Dobson had this vernacular, a name for everything," Eckersley explained. "I just picked it up. I didn't invent anything. Maybe I embellished it. But I used it constantly, and nobody knew what the hell I was talking about."

While Eckersley's colorful public persona was that of a brash, loose, fun-loving guy without a care in the world, the reality was very much different. Away from the ballpark, his personal life was a wreck. His wife of five years had just left him for his best friend, Cleveland centerfielder Rick Manning, and they were battling for custody of their two-year-old daughter, Mandy. During the next few years Eckersley would battle with alcohol as well, an addiction he would not conquer until the mid-1980s with his baseball career at the crossroads.

But in 1978 Dennis Eckersley hid his personal crises extremely well, and they did not materially affect his performances on the diamond for the Red

Sox. The year would be his best ever as a starting pitcher and include the most memorable game of his Red Sox career.

"I was totally focused, and you would think it would be the opposite," Eckersley recalled. "When things happen to you off the field, there are two ways you can go about it. You can take gas, or you can look at it as things are tough at home, and here at the ballpark is the only place it's good. So I put everything into the game. I had a chip on my shoulder whenever I took the mound—as if I needed another one—and it was life or death for me."

✛ ✛ ✛

Eckersley went winless in five April starts, getting four no-decisions. But the Red Sox went 11-9 during the month, and in May Eckersley began winning with regularity. He was 5-0 that month, including a 4-0 shutout against the Toronto Blue Jays, and by the end of May the Red Sox were in first place with a 34-16 record and a three-and-a-half-game lead in the AL East standings. At the All-Star break Eckersley was 10-2 with a 3.33 ERA, and the Red Sox were ahead by nine games over second-place Milwaukee and threatening to turn the division race into a runaway.

On August 25 he blanked the Angels 6-0 at Fenway Park for his 15th victory, and five days later he beat the Blue Jays 2-1 in the first game of a doubleheader with a five-hit, nine-strikeout performance to hike his record to 16-5. The Red Sox were riding a six-game winning streak and held a seven-and-a-half-game lead over the Yankees.

And then things began to unravel in a hurry. The Blue Jays won the second game 7-6, and the Red Sox lost five of six, cutting their lead to four games over the onrushing Yankees, who had been 14 games back in mid-July. Tiant halted the skid by shutting out the Orioles 2-0 in Baltimore, and the lead was still four games when the Red Sox and Yankees clashed in a four-game weekend series at Fenway Park September 7-10.

"I never thought it was slipping away until that series," Eckersley remembered. "Then it was like: 'Here they come!' And we couldn't beat them. That's when panic set in."

The Yankees blasted Mike Torrez 15-3 in the first game and beat up on rookie Jim Wright in the second, winning 13-2. The lead was down to two games when Eckersley took his 16-6 record—including a 3-0 mark against New York—and 3.15 ERA to the mound against Yankees ace Ron Guidry, who was 20-2 with a 1.84 ERA, on Saturday afternoon. The Yankees had scored a total of 15 runs in the first three innings of the previous two games, so the sellout crowd of 33,611 at Fenway relaxed a little when Eckersley blanked the Yankees on one hit over the first three innings.

With the game still scoreless, the Yankees had runners on first and second with two outs in the fourth when Lou Piniella hit a pop-up behind second base. The wind took it "like a Frisbee," Eckersley said at the time, and the ball fell untouched between five Red Sox defenders for a double. Before the Red Sox could get the third out, Eckersley was gone and the Yankees had poured across seven runs. That's all they got, and that was more than they needed in a 7-0 victory that shaved the Red Sox lead to a single game. Although the Red Sox managed just two hits off Guidry, who held them hitless over the last eight and two-thirds innings, seldom-used second baseman Frank Duffy, who was filling in for injured Jerry Remy at second base, was singled out as the villain for not catching Piniella's pop-up. Eckersley had played with Duffy in Cleveland, and when he saw the grilling Duffy was enduring at the hands of the media after the game, he tried to break up the interrogation.

| DENNIS ECKERSLEY |
|---|
| **Years with Red Sox:** 1978-84, 1998 |
| **Other Major League Teams:** Cleveland, Chicago (NL), Oakland, St. Louis |
| **Position:** Pitcher |
| **Bats:** Right |
| **Throws:** Right |
| **Height:** 6-2 |
| **Weight:** 190 |
| **Born:** October 3, 1954 |
| **Birthplace:** Oakland, CA |
| **Current Residence:** Hopkinton, MA |
| **Current Occupation:** Red Sox TV analyst |

"Frank Duffy's not the reason we lost this game. Leave him alone," Eckersley demanded. "I pitched horseshit, and we didn't hit Guidry. I'm the one who should face the music, not him. The 'L' goes next to my name."

The Yankees knocked out raw rookie Bobby Sprowl in the first inning the next day and won the game 7-4 to sweep the series. In what came to be known as the "Boston Massacre," the Yankees outhit the Red Sox 67-21 and outscored them 41-9. The 14-game lead the Red Sox had was now gone, and the two teams were tied for first place with 86-56 records.

The Red Sox continued to stumble during the next week, splitting a pair of games with the Orioles at Fenway and then dropping two games in Cleveland. Eckersley lost one of those games 2-1, and early the next morning he was in a courtroom finalizing his divorce.

The Red Sox were only one and a half games behind the Yankees when they flew into New York for a three-game rematch. But the Yankees won the first two games 4-0 and 3-2, and now the Red Sox were behind by three and a half games with only 14 left to play. They had lost 14 of 17 games since Eckersley's 2-1 victory over Toronto back on August 30, and they were in danger of falling completely out of the race. The consensus was that if Eckersley did not beat the Yankees in the last game of the series on September 17, the Red Sox were finished and would be remembered as the biggest chokers in baseball history.

"The abuse we have taken, and the abuse we must be prepared to take for the entire winter, we richly deserve," shortstop Rick Burleson admitted.

"There are no words to describe this," acknowledged 39-year-old Carl Yastrzemski, who had played in two World Series for the Red Sox. "I can't ever remember feeling so humiliated. It just doesn't make sense: When has this good a team ever been so badly whipped?"

"This game, after all the years when you look back, there was not a more important game that I pitched for the Red Sox. Ever! Because we never got that close again," Eckersley cited as the reason for choosing this one game from among the 241 he pitched in a Boston uniform as his most memorable. "This was the season, that game, the stop-the-bleeding game."

✦ ✦ ✦

Eckersley did not sleep well the night before that start. "I never slept well back then. Anytime!" he said. "I ripped hard then; I really did. I was really carefree back then, and I think that helped me. I was never uptight about anything."

A sellout crowd of 55,088, sensing the kill, filled Yankee Stadium on that Sunday afternoon.

"I felt more pressure than I ever felt in my entire life in that game. Ever!" Eckersley said. "Yankee Stadium, to me, is pressurized more than any other stadium. I never liked how I felt there. You know when you feel like you've got it, and I never really felt like I had it anytime I pitched in Yankee Stadium. There was a mystique about the Yankees, and it was real. They were a tough team for me with all those lefthanded hitters."

So how can he explain beating them four times in five decisions in 1978?

"They scored me some runs," Eckersley stated simply. "That's the way to explain everything, because I had gotten beaten up by them when I was in Cleveland. I don't remember pitching them any differently with the Red Sox."

At the same time he was feeling skittish about facing the Yankees, the adrenaline was flowing.

"The biggest stage I ever had with Cleveland was Opening Day and the Game of the Week … and in Cleveland we were never the Game of the Week," Eckersley said. "When I came here, it was like a big deal every time I started, and that helped. Then the stage got bigger playing the Yankees. Until I came here I never knew what that was all about. They hated the Yankees in Cleveland, too, but not like here! I said: 'My God! This is intense!'"

Eckersley's mound opponent on this memorable afternoon would not be the invincible Guidry this time. The Yankees countered with rookie righthander Jim Beattie, who had a 5-7 record with a 3.65 ERA.

"It was helpful to think that you don't have to be perfect, and as a starting pitcher, that's huge. If you're going against Guidry, you can't make a mistake, because he won't make a mistake. You've got no chance," Eckersley related. "But I don't remember going into it thinking: 'Well, Beattie's pitching. I'll be all right.' Everybody was counting on me, and I had never been in that situation before."

As pumped as he was when he took the Yankee Stadium mound in the bottom of the first inning after Beattie had retired the Red Sox, Eckersley felt drained. There was the emotional trauma of his divorce only three days earlier coupled with the emotion of pitching this particular game.

"I remember it being hot as hell. I didn't feel like I had good stuff. I was just trying to get by," said Eckersley, the author of 13 complete games in 31 starts to that point of the season. "I remember thinking I wasn't going to be able to complete this thing."

Nevertheless, as he had done the previous week in Boston, Eckersley allowed the Yankees just one hit over the first three innings. This time, however, the Red Sox staked him to a 1-0 lead in the third when Burleson led off with a single, stole second, and scored on a two-out single by Yaz.

"It was a relief to go ahead," he said.

The Yankees mounted their first threat in the bottom of the inning when Eckersley walked the ninth hitter, Bucky Dent, and Willie Randolph drilled a two-out single for the first New York hit. Dent sped around to third, and Randolph alertly took second on the throw. That brought up Thurman Munson, a .298 hitter and the league's MVP in 1976, with the tying and go-ahead runs in scoring position.

"He was one of the toughest righthanded hitters, a really tough out, because he never tried to pull the ball," Eckersley remembered. "I had a hard time with him because he always stayed on my slider and tried to flip it the other way."

Munson had reached on an error by third baseman Butch Hobson in the first inning. Every ball hit to Hobson had become an adventure by then. He had floating bone chips in his right elbow and couldn't throw with any strength or accuracy, but he kept playing through the pain as his error total spiraled. The error had been his 41st of the season. Munson grounded another ball to Hobson, but this time he threw the Yankees catcher out to end the inning.

The Red Sox picked up another run in the fifth. Dwight Evans led off with a single, and Burleson sacrificed him to second, from where Jerry Remy singled him home. It was still 2-0 after six, and Eckersley, despite lacking his best stuff, was working on a one-hitter.

The Red Sox chipped away at Beattie and scored another run in the seventh when Evans walked, went to third on a hit-and-run double by Burleson, and scored on a sacrifice fly by Remy. The Yankees finally nicked Eckersley for a run in the bottom of the seventh. Chris Chambliss singled for only the second New York hit, Roy White drew a two-out walk, and Gary Thomasson ripped an RBI single that cut the Red Sox lead to 3-1. Lefthanded-hitting Jim Spencer was on deck to bat for Dent.

"I had a tough time with Jim Spencer," Eckersley said. "I knew I was gone as soon as he pinch hit."

Manager Don Zimmer summoned sinkerballing righthander Bob Stanley, and Eckersley, who had pitched six and two-thirds innings of three-hit ball, went into the clubhouse to watch the rest of the game on television.

The Red Sox salted the game away with three runs in the eighth off relievers Sparky Lyle and Ken Clay. Lyle, the league's reigning Cy Young Award winner, couldn't retire any of the three batters he faced. Carlton Fisk led off the inning with a walk, Duffy pinch hit for Jack Brohamer and singled, and George Scott pounded an RBI double. Hobson greeted Clay with a two-run double, and the Red Sox now led 6-1.

The Yankees made a bid to get back into it in the bottom of the inning as another Hobson error and one by Remy let two unearned runs cross the plate.

"I was just begging at that point," Eckersley said. "When we started making errors—which is how we'd been playing—I'm thinking: 'How are we going to give this thing back?' After losing that many games, we were ready to give it back. That team was so vulnerable at that point, and that's why that game was so huge. I was thinking: 'Just get through this game, and let's get the hell out of here!'"

Eckersley received his alms when Reggie Jackson, who had reached on Remy's error, foolishly tried for second and was cut down by rightfielder Dwight Evans for the second out. Stanley caught Chambliss looking at a third strike, and the Red Sox were out of the jam. Yaz added the coup de grace with a homer in the ninth, and the Red Sox won 7-3 to end their slide and inch back within two and a half games of first place. Eckersley, with Stanley finishing up the combined four-hitter for his ninth save, was now 17-6 and 4-1 against the Yankees. And the Red Sox were back in the race.

✢ ✢ ✢

The Red Sox would lose only two games during the final two weeks of the season, rolling up a 12-2 record in that stretch and pushing the Yankees down to the wire.

"Every day, every day was intense," Eckersley remembered.

Eckersley recorded his 18th win in a 5-1 complete-game victory over the Tigers in Detroit and notched his 19th with a 6-0 shutout over the Tigers at Fenway on September 26. Four days later Eckersley became a 20-game winner for the only time in his career, beating the Blue Jays 5-1 with a five-hitter and nine strikeouts at Fenway Park.

"That meant a lot," Eckersley said, reflecting on his 20th victory. "I didn't think I was going to get it after losing to Cleveland. That game was intense, too. I gave up a homer to Roy Howell in the first inning, but that was it. I punched out Howell and [John]Mayberry to end the game."

It was also the Red Sox' seventh straight victory and it kept them within one game of the Yankees, who were riding a six-game winning streak with one game left on the schedule.

Tiant's 5-0 win the next day, coupled with a stunning 9-2 loss by the Yankees to the lowly Indians, set up a one-game playoff at Fenway to decide the division title. The Red Sox lost it 5-4, and there was no denying they had let a race they had won at midseason get away from them. But at least they lost with dignity, having staged a furious rush during the last two weeks when everybody was expecting them to roll over and pack it in for the season. Eckersley's victory in front of a hostile crowd at Yankee Stadium had convinced them they could still win, and they nearly did.

"I remember Yaz was upset after we lost that game. A lot of people were upset," Eckersley recalled. "But I looked around, and we were such a great team, and I'm thinking we're going to be doing this every year. This is the best team I've ever played for. I couldn't imagine not being back."

Eckersley finished that year with a 20-8 record and a 2.99 ERA. He had another strong season the following summer, going 17-10 with a 2.99 ERA. But seven consecutive complete games, five of them pitching on short rest when Zimmer decided to go to a four-man rotation in a bid to stay close in the pennant race, took its toll on his arm.

"I don't think I ever really recovered from that," Eckersley said. "Things were never quite the same."

The last of those seven complete games was a memorable one, however. On July 28, 1979, in a match-up of future Hall of Fame pitchers, Eckersley outdueled Ferguson Jenkins in Texas to win 1-0.

He had a few other outstanding games for the Red Sox, just not enough of them. He threw a one-hitter in Toronto on September 26, 1980, and on May 21, 1981, he tossed a two-hit shutout against Oakland and fanned 12 batters. On April 10, 1982, he became the first Red Sox pitcher in 30 years to hurl a shutout on Opening Day when he whitewashed the Orioles 2-0 in Baltimore. Eckersley also started the All-Star Game in Montreal that summer but took the loss in a 4-1 defeat.

After Eckersley posted a 9-13 record with just two complete games and a 5.61 ERA in 1983, it was clear he was mentally beaten in Boston. He badly needed a change of scenery, and the Red Sox traded him, along with infielder Mike Brumley, to the Chicago Cubs the following May in exchange for first baseman Bill Buckner. The rejuvenated Eckersley went 10-8 with a 3.03 ERA in 24 starts to help the Cubs win the NL East Division title and had another good year in 1985, going 11-7 with a 3.08 ERA. But after going 6-11 with a 4.57 ERA in 1986, Eckersley looked washed up at 32.

After the season he checked himself into a rehab clinic in Rhode Island and stopped drinking. Just before the start of the 1987 season, the Cubs traded him to his hometown team, the Oakland Athletics.

"No one knew I was this clean guy yet," Eckersley said. "I don't blame them for trading me. But when Dallas Green told me I was going to Oakland, I remember telling him: 'I ain't done yet.'"

Oakland manager Tony La Russa planned to use Eckersley as a set-up reliever for closer Jay Howell. But when Howell went down with an injury, Eckersley inherited the closer's role and instantly became one of the top saviors in baseball.

Eckersley would lead the AL in saves twice during the next six seasons, and in 1990 he would post a 4-2 record with 48 saves and a microscopic

Hall of Famer Dennis Eckersley, a 20-game winner for the Boston Red Sox and the only pitcher in major-league history to win 150 games and save 300, now works as a studio analyst on Red Sox telecasts. *(Courtesy of Chaz Scoggins)*

0.61 ERA. In 1992, when he went 7-1 with a league-leading 51 saves and a 1.91 ERA and fanned 93 batters in 80 innings, he won both the Most Valuable Player and Cy Young Awards. Eckersley finished his career by returning to the Red Sox for his last season in 1998. At the time of his retirement at the age of 44, he had pitched in 1,071 games, more than any pitcher in major-league history.

"The fact that I was a sidearmer, about whom people said: 'How's he gonna last?' was what made that special," he said. "Knowing me, how it all began, it's amazing that it happened."

Dennis Eckersley is the only pitcher in major-league history with 150 victories and 300 saves, finishing with a 197-171 record and 390 saves to go along with a 3.50 ERA. He was elected to the National Baseball Hall of Fame in 2004 and enshrined in the Red Sox Hall of Fame the same year. He was 88-71 during his Red Sox years.

Since his retirement Eckersley has worked as a postgame analyst on Red Sox telecasts. Recently remarried, Dennis Eckersley and his wife, Jennifer, reside in Hopkinton, Massachusetts.

# Chapter 15

# JERRY REMY

## OCTOBER 2, 1978

O n September 30, 1967, 14-year-old Jerry Remy and his dad, Joe, were among the 32,909 fans crammed inside venerable Fenway Park to watch Carl Yastrzemski clout a three-run homer, powering the "Impossible Dream" Red Sox to a 6-4 victory over Minnesota that pulled them into a first-place tie with the Twins on the next-to-last day of the season.

"I got hooked with that team. That was the year that made me a loyal follower of the Red Sox," Remy remembered. He and his father would get tickets for three or four games a year, but 1967, he said, "was a special year. You never left the radio or the TV. I remember that year better than some of the years when I was playing."

Exactly 11 years and two days later, Remy, now 25 years old, was again inside Fenway Park, this time playing second base in front of another SRO crowd of 32,925 and trying to help the Red Sox win their 100th game of the season and the American League East Division championship.

✦✦✦

Gerald Peter Remy was born on November 8, 1952, in the southeastern Massachusetts city of Fall River. His father was a furniture salesman, and his mother, Connie, was a dance instructor. He also had a younger sister, Judy. Remy grew up in the town of Somerset, not far from the Rhode

Island border, and in his senior year at Somerset High School he earned All-State honors as a second baseman. At 5-9 and 165 pounds, the lefthanded-hitting Remy wasn't physically imposing, and it was unusual for pro scouts to pay much attention to someone who played strictly second base. Second baseman in the majors were usually converted shortstops who lacked the range or arm necessary to play that position at the highest level of baseball. But the Washington Senators chose him anyway in the 1970 June draft, the 453rd player taken.

"I didn't know what to do. Some people said I should sign, and other people said I should go to college," Remy remembered. "I wasn't a good student, but I decided to go to St. Leo's in Florida."

He stayed only two weeks, returned home, and enrolled at Roger Williams College. When he was chosen by the California Angels in the winter draft a few months later, this time he knew what to do. But he didn't impress many people in the organization when he reported in the spring of 1971.

"I had heard the Angels were going to release me after my first spring training," Remy said back in 1976. But he had an angel of his own in Kenny Myers, the scout who had signed him and doubled as the organization's minor-league hitting instructor. "Kenny told them to keep me because of my speed. He said he could teach me how to play. I owe him a lot and only wish he could have been here to see me make it."

Myers died less than 18 months later. But the Angels heeded Myers's advice, kept Remy, and assigned him to Magic Valley, a co-op team in the rookie short-season Pioneer League. Co-op teams are generally made up of an organization's least-promising prospects. But Remy played well for the Idaho club, hitting .308 with 16 stolen bases and 25 runs scored in 32 games.

The Angels sent him to Stockton in the Class A California League in 1972, where he hit .262 with 32 stolen bases. Playing for Quad Cities in the Class A Midwest League the following year, Remy had a breakout season. He won the league's batting crown with a .335 average, legged out 10 triples, and made the All-Star team. Now Remy was a prospect, and the Angels promoted him to Class AA El Paso in 1974.

Remy spent little more than half a season in the Texas League. After hitting .338 with 34 doubles, 21 stolen bases, and 74 runs in 91 games, he was advanced to Class AAA Salt Lake City, where he hit .292 in 48 games.

Remy made a favorable impression on Angels manager Dick Williams during spring training in 1975, and despite his limited experience in Triple-A beat out veteran Denny Doyle to become the regular second baseman.

**Boston Red Sox second baseman Jerry Remy gets rid of the ball quickly to turn a double play as Harold Baines of the Chicago White Sox arrives too late to break it up.** *(Courtesy of the Boston Red Sox)*

The Angels had not had a winning season since 1970, and they had little power in their lineup. Williams, who had taken over as manager midway through the 1974 season, decided to rebuild the club around speed and a pair of young fireballers named Nolan Ryan and Frank Tanana. The Angels may have been a little more exciting to watch in 1975, but they weren't any more successful. They scored the fewest runs in the league and finished last in the AL West with a 72-89 record.

Remy, however, had a solid rookie year, hitting .258 and scoring 82 runs in 147 games. Teammate Mickey Rivers led the league in stolen bases with 70, and Remy finished fifth with 34 and made the Topps All-Rookie team.

Remy followed up his freshman season by hitting .263 with 35 stolen bases and 63 runs in 143 games for the Angels in 1976. Again the Angels were the lowest-scoring team in the league, but after Williams was fired in mid-season, Norm Sherry guided them to a winning record the rest of the way. California finished fourth with a 76-86 record, and Remy received the team's Owner's Trophy from owner and retired actor/singer Gene Autry as "the Angel who most truly exemplified the qualities of inspirational leadership, sportsmanship, and professional ability."

Remy's leadership qualities were so admired he was named the team captain at the tender age of 24 in 1977. The Angels were no longer the lowest-scoring team in the league, but they still couldn't win and ended in fifth place with a 74-88 record, their seventh straight losing campaign. Remy turned in another good season, finishing tied for third in the league with 41 stolen bases while scoring 74 runs in 154 games and hitting .252. He also drilled 10 triples and hit a career-high four homers. It seemed like he would be a fixture in Anaheim for years to come. Remy, however, knew different.

The Angels had used some of Autry's riches to sign free agent Bobby Grich to play shortstop in 1977. But Grich had injured his back lifting an air conditioner and appeared in only 52 games, and he could no longer play shortstop. Grich had been a Gold Glove second baseman with the Baltimore Orioles before signing with the Angels, so Remy didn't need a crystal ball to tell him he was going to be the odd man out.

"Harry Dalton was the GM, and I told him: 'If you can get me back to Boston again, that would be great,'" Remy said. "It was the team I grew up with, and it was a good team. I was afraid I would get traded to San Diego or somewhere like that."

So the Angels traded Remy to the Red Sox for righthanded pitcher Don Aase, who had enjoyed an impressive rookie half-season in Boston. Remy was coming home, and he was coming home to one of the most talented teams in the majors.

The Red Sox had won a pennant in 1975 and won 97 games in 1977, when they finished in a tie for second in the AL East and placed seven players on the All-Star team. They were expected to contend again in 1978. In a weird coincidence, the second baseman Remy would be replacing in Boston was Denny Doyle, who had been sold to the Red Sox in 1975 after

Remy beat him out and had been a catalyst in the team's pennant drive that summer.

"It was strange, but Denny was a good guy, and he understood the way baseball worked," Remy said. "The first time it happened, it worked out great for both of us. I got to play in the big leagues, and he got to play in the World Series."

Remy did everything that was expected of him in 1978, hitting .278 with 30 stolen bases, 87 runs, and 24 doubles in 148 games. He even made the All-Star team for the only time in his major-league career, although he didn't get to appear in the game.

The Red Sox got off to a torrid start in 1978. Jim Rice was having his MVP year, and newcomer Dennis Eckersley was on his way to becoming a 20-game winner. The Red Sox moved into first place on May 13 with a 21-11 record. By July 5 they were 54-24, on a pace to win 112 games, and had a 10-game lead over the second-place Milwaukee Brewers. The race, such as it was, looked like a runaway. The New York Yankees, who had won the East Division title and the pennant in each of the previous two years, were a distant 14 games behind and in turmoil. Yankees manager Billy Martin could not get along with superstar outfielder Reggie Jackson or owner George Steinbrenner. "One's a born liar, and the other's convicted," Martin said. Steinbrenner had been convicted in 1974 of making illegal campaign contributions to Richard Nixon and given a suspended sentence. Steinbrenner fired Martin and replaced him with low-key Bob Lemon.

**JERRY REMY**
**Years with Red Sox: 1978-84**
**Other Major League Teams: California**
**Position: Second Base**
**Bats: Left**
**Throws: Right**
**Height: 5-9**
**Weight: 165**
**Born: November 8, 1952**
**Birthplace: Fall River, MA**
**Current Residence: Weston, MA**
**Current Occupation: Red Sox TV**
  **analyst**

But the Red Sox began to slip after the All-Star break. An ankle injury sidelined All-Star shortstop Rick Burleson, Remy's double-play partner, for 17 games, 10 of them losses, and the Red Sox' thin bench was exposed. The Yankees began playing well under Lemon, and by the beginning of August the Red Sox lead had been shaved to four and a half games. They built it back to nine games by the middle of the month, however, and the team seemed to be back on track again.

Remy went on a tear, forging a 19-game hitting streak. On August 20 Remy, never renowned for his power, hit the seventh and last homer of his major-league career by virtue of getting a fourth strike during a game in Oakland. Remy swung at and missed a nasty spitball from Matt Keough for what should have been strike three. But the ball dropped so sharply, plate umpire Durwood Merrill was deceived into thinking the ball had been foul-tipped. Over the protests of Keough, catcher Bruce Robinson, and Oakland manager Jack McKeon, Merrill kept Remy at the plate, and he slammed Keough's next pitch over the right-field fence for a three-run homer that beat the Athletics 4-2 and boosted the Red Sox' lead to eight and a half games.

Five days later Remy, who had hit safely in 26 of 27 games, chipped a bone in his wrist while making a tag at second base. The Red Sox did not disable him because he could still be useful as a pinch runner, and he did help them win an extra-inning game against the Angels at Fenway Park on August 27. The Angels had just taken a 3-2 lead in the top of the 12th when Carl Yastrzemski led off the bottom of the inning with a single. Remy pinch ran and scored the tying run from second on a two-out error by third baseman Carney Lansford, and moments later Butch Hobson singled home the winning run.

But Remy did not bat for 15 games, eight of them Red Sox losses. The last three of those games he missed were part of the infamous "Boston Massacre."

The red-hot Yankees, who had pulled back within four games of the Red Sox, arrived at Fenway for a four-game series on September 7. They crushed the Red Sox 15-3 in the first game and routed them 13-2 in the second. Eckersley took his 16-6 record to the mound in Game 3 in a bid to stem the tide. But Remy could only watch helplessly from the bench while his replacement at second base, a rusty Frank Duffy who had rarely played during the summer, misplayed a pop-up that led to seven two-out runs in the fourth inning. The Yankees won 7-0, and the Red Sox lead was down to a single game.

Remy was rushed back into the lineup for the final game on September 10.

"I wasn't 100 percent," Remy said about his wrist, "but I could play. I had no choice, really, but to play. [Carlton] Fisk was playing hurt in the second half, and so was Hobson."

Remy played six and a half innings, but his presence was inconsequential. The Yankees won 7-4 to sweep the series and pull into a first-place tie with the Red Sox. And when the Yankees won the first two games of a three-game set between the two rivals at Yankee Stadium the following weekend, the Red Sox were three and a half games back with just 14 left and in danger of plunging out of the race that they seemingly had locked up back in July.

For more than a quarter of a century the 1978 season has been regarded as a colossal Red Sox choke by their fans. The Yankees have never received due credit from most New Englanders for battling their way back into the race by playing .716 ball after July 18, rolling up a 53-21 record from that date on. The Red Sox did play some bad baseball during the second half but overall played well enough to win 99 games. Only three Red Sox teams have ever won more. And the 1978 Red Sox have never received enough credit for the way they played during the last two weeks of the regular season when they won 12 of 14 to force a one-game playoff for the division title.

The Red Sox, behind Eckersley, salvaged the final game of the series in Yankee Stadium on September 17, winning 7-3. Remy knocked in a pair of runs with a single and a sacrifice fly. When veteran Luis Tiant beat the Blue Jays 3-1 in Toronto on September 23, the Red Sox were back within one game of the Yankees.

"I don't even remember how I did that last week," Remy recalled. "But we were winning. The games weren't even close, and we were just hoping the Yankees would lose one."

For the next seven days, neither team would lose, setting up one of the most tense and dramatic finishes in baseball history. After Eckersley beat Toronto 5-1 on September 30 for his 20th victory, there was only one game left on the schedule, the Red Sox were still a game behind, and the Yankees were finishing up with the weak Cleveland Indians, losers of 90 games, including nine of 14 against the Yankees. The outlook wasn't good, especially with future Hall of Famer Catfish Hunter, considered one of the best "money" pitchers of his generation, starting the final game in New York. It looked as if the Red Sox were going to come up just short.

But while Tiant was shutting out the Blue Jays 5-0 on two hits, the Indians, behind lefthander Rick Waits, were clobbering Hunter. Cleveland won 9-2, and for only the second time in American League history and the first time since 1948, there would be a one-game playoff for a title.

For Jerry Remy, who had hit .354 after returning to the lineup following his wrist injury, this was the opportunity to experience what he had only witnessed as an ordinary fan 11 years earlier. The playoff game with the Yankees at Fenway Park on October 2, 1978, would be the most memorable game of his Red Sox career.

"I would never play in any other playoff game except this one," Remy explained. "I never got to the playoffs or the World Series, and it was a great one. The whole world was watching because it was the only game that day, and they still show it on *ESPN Classic*.

"Because of the magnitude of that game, I felt very much like I did in my first game in the big leagues," Remy continued. "I didn't want to do something to lose the game and become one of the Boston goats, and at the same time I was having good thoughts about being one of the heroes. But once the game started, I settled down."

✚ ✚ ✚

The Yankees had held back their ace, lefthander Ron Guidry, just in case the race came down to a one-game playoff and keeping him fresh for the first game of the ALCS against the Kansas City Royals if it didn't. Guidry had been virtually unbeatable all year, posting a 24-3 record with a 1.72 ERA. Interestingly, all three of his defeats had been to pitchers named Mike: Milwaukee's Mike Caldwell, Baltimore's Mike Flanagan, and Toronto's Mike Willis. The Red Sox would be sending another Mike, Mike Torrez, to the mound. A year earlier Torrez had been pitching for the World Champion Yankees, winning 17 games during the regular season and two more in the World Series against the Los Angeles Dodgers after being dealt by Oakland in April when it became obvious to Athletics owner Charles O. Finley that the righthander was headed for free agency after the season. The Red Sox had outbid everyone else for Torrez, who signed a seven-year deal worth $2.65 million. Torrez had posted a 16-12 record with a 3.92 ERA for the Red Sox in 1978, but he hadn't been quite as good as they had expected, yielding 267 hits in 243 1/3 innings. By the time the Red Sox gave up on him five years later, Torrez was considered a bust in Boston.

But Torrez seemed to be on his game on this early autumn afternoon. He gave up only two hits over the first six innings, a two-out double to Mickey Rivers in the third and an infield hit to Lou Piniella in the fourth. The Red Sox took a 2-0 lead against Guidry during that time.

"I don't think we got him with his best stuff," Remy remembered. "His best stuff was unbelievable. But even with a little less he was still great."

Guidry struck out Rick Burleson and Jim Rice in the first inning, sandwiched around a fly to left by Remy. But 39-year-old Carl Yastrzemski, playing like it was 1967 and he was 28 years old again, yanked a homer down the right-field line to open the second.

"It had to be Yaz. Who else?" Remy asked rhetorically. "It was like he was expected to do that. That got everything going in the right direction, and Torrez was pitching real good for us."

George Scott led off the third with a double and was sacrificed to third by Jack Brohamer. But Burleson bounced to third with the infield in, and Remy again flied to left to end the inning.

The Red Sox didn't threaten again until the sixth, when they scored their second run. Burleson led off with a double, and Remy sacrificed him to third.

"I would have been surprised if I was asked to do anything else in that situation," Remy said.

Rice singled, picking up his 139th RBI of the season, and the Red Sox led 2-0. Rice took second when Yaz grounded to first, and Guidry walked Carlton Fisk intentionally to get to the lefthanded-hitting Fred Lynn. Few lefthanded hitters, outside of the ageless Yastrzemski, were capable of pulling one of Guidry's fastballs or wicked sliders. But for some reason Piniella, the Yankees rightfielder, decided to play Lynn closer to the line. Lynn pulled a Guidry pitch toward the right-field corner that ordinarily would have been for extra bases and probably scored two more runs, but Piniella got to the ball in time to snare it for the final out.

"That was a big, big play," Remy recalled. "No one expected him to be able to pull Guidry. I guess Piniella said later he knew Guidry didn't have his best stuff, and that's why he was playing there."

"I did have a good reason for being out of position," Piniella explained later. "[Catcher Thurman] Munson and I talked about it between innings, and we agreed that Guidry's slider was more the speed of a curveball, far slower [than usual], and that Lynn was apt to pull him."

Still, the way Torrez was pitching, it looked like the Red Sox might have enough runs.

"Every inning we were getting closer and closer to moving on," Remy said. "Now we were only three innings away, and you start thinking about the finish line."

Torrez gave up a pair of one-out singles in the seventh to Chris Chambliss and Roy White, and then retired pinch hitter Jim Spencer on a fly to Yaz in left. Now all Torrez had to do was dispense with light-hitting Yankees shortstop Bucky Dent.

Dent's batting average had declined in every season since hitting .274 as a rookie for the Chicago White Sox in 1974. He was hitting .242 with only four homers and 37 RBI in 377 at-bats as he stepped into the batter's box. Torrez quickly got ahead of him with two strikes, and Dent fouled the next nasty sinker off his instep and collapsed at the plate in pain. While Dent was being attended to, Mickey Rivers, the on-deck hitter, picked up Dent's bat and noticed it was cracked. He took it back to the dugout and replaced it with one of his own—one he later claimed was corked.

When the pain had subsided enough, Dent stepped back into the batter's box, swung at the next pitch, and lofted a soft, high fly to left that settled into the net just inside the foul pole, 315 feet away. Yaz's knees buckled as he watched the ball barely clear the lip of the 37-foot Green Monster for an improbable three-run homer that wiped out the Red Sox lead and put the Yankees ahead 3-2. The sellout crowd at Fenway was equally stunned, and for the first time that afternoon was silenced.

"It was one of those Fenway drop-into-the-net kind of things," Remy said. "I sometimes had trouble figuring if a ball was going out or not, so I would watch Yaz. He seemed to be getting himself into position to play the ball off The Wall, and then I saw him almost collapse.

"It was crushing because it was the first time they had scored and the lead was gone, but that only made the score 3-2," Remy continued. "We still had three more innings to come back."

Torrez walked the next batter, Rivers, and manager Don Zimmer brought in Bob Stanley to face Munson. Rivers stole second, and Munson cracked a double off The Wall to make it 4-2.

George Scott chased Guidry with a one-out single in the bottom of the inning, and when Zimmer used washed-up righthanded-hitting Bob Bailey to pinch hit for Brohamer, Yankees manager Bob Lemon countered with fireballing righthander Goose Gossage, whose 26 saves led the league. Bailey feebly struck out in his last at-bat in the major leagues, and Burleson grounded out.

"No one was anxious to see Gossage," Remy said. "But he was in there early enough that we were thinking he might not be able to finish the game."

The Red Sox fell further behind in the eighth when Reggie Jackson slammed a Stanley pitch into the center-field bleachers for his 27th homer, putting the Yankees ahead 5-2.

"That one killed me! I felt worse about that home run than Dent's," Remy related. "Now we were three runs down against Gossage."

But the Red Sox, who had come back from the dead once already during the last two weeks, began to resurrect themselves in the bottom of the inning. Remy started the rally with a double.

"I never pulled Gossage," Remy said. "But he threw me a slider, the adrenaline was flowing, and I pulled it down the first-base line. I couldn't do that once in a hundred at-bats against him."

One out later Yaz singled Remy home. Fisk and Lynn followed with singles, and suddenly the Yankees' lead had been chopped to 5-4. Gossage got out the eighth without further damage, but the Red Sox had the top of the order coming up again in the ninth.

"We're back in the game now," Remy said, "and with our offense, I'm thinking we can win this game."

Burleson coaxed a one-out walk from Gossage, and Remy turned on a fastball this time and lined a single to right that Piniella lost in the late afternoon sun. Piniella put on the brakes and waited for the ball to reappear. When it did, bouncing to his left, he flashed out his glove and snagged it before it could get past him.

"I remember going to the plate thinking the one thing I don't want to do is hit into a double play. I had to get the ball in the air," Remy said. "Gossage was pretty much on fumes by then. I knew it was going to be a basehit, so I was watching Burleson and didn't know Piniella lost it in the sun. He stuck out his glove, and, like magic, the ball bounced into it. If that ball gets by him, I get a triple and the game is tied. I probably score, we win the game, and I'm a hero."

But the hero was the sun-blinded Lou Piniella.

"It was pure luck," Piniella admitted afterward. "Pure luck that I was in the right place and could get my glove out there in time."

Burleson, unsure if Piniella might catch the ball on the fly, could only get as far as second base on Remy's hit.

"Burleson did the right thing by stopping at second," Remy said. "What else could he do? He couldn't let himself get thrown out at third."

Had Burleson been on third, he would have scored the tying run easily on Rice's subsequent flyball to right. He went to third on that ball. But when Yaz fouled to third baseman Graig Nettles, the Yankees were the East Division champions.

The Yankees cruised through the remainder of the postseason, beating the Royals 4-2 in the ALCS and sweeping the Dodgers in the World Series. There can be little doubt that the Red Sox would have done the same. Yankees owner George Steinbrenner expressed that sentiment when he paid a consoling visit to Zimmer in the Red Sox clubhouse after the game and told him: "The World Series was decided out there today."

"Losing that game was a tremendous disappointment," Remy said more than a quarter of a century later. "But at the same time, I felt we would be

Jerry Remy, whose career was cut short by a series of knee injuries, is now a highly popular color commentator on Boston Red Sox telecasts. *(Courtesy of the Boston Red Sox)*

together for four or five more years, and we'd win it at least one of those years, maybe even the next year."

Remy couldn't know then how quickly the fortunes of the Red Sox and his own career would unravel.

✦✦✦

Remy was hitting .304 after 73 games in 1979 when he tore up his left knee while sliding into home at Yankee Stadium on July 1. He avoided surgery but played only seven games the rest of the year.

"It was never quite right after that," Remy said. "I lost my first-step quickness at second base, and balls I used to beat out for hits, now I was out by half a step. Almost every winter they went back in there to try and fix things until finally there was nothing left to fix."

Remy was off to a .313 start after 63 games in 1980 when he tore cartilage in the same knee. This time he submitted to surgery and missed the rest of the season.

Remy was free of injuries in 1981, but the players shut down the game for seven weeks in mid-season with a strike. He hit .307 in 88 games and had six hits to tie a club record in a 20-inning loss to Seattle on September 3-4. Remy scored a career-best 89 runs in 1982 while hitting .280. But by 1984 his left knee was bothering him again. Three more surgeries failed to repair the damage, and at the age of 33 he retired during spring training of 1986, only six months before the Red Sox finally made it back to the World Series.

Remy finished his career with a .275 average in 1,154 games with 208 stolen bases and 605 runs.

Since his retirement Remy has worked as a color analyst on Red Sox telecasts and has remained immensely popular with the fans. He has started his own website and founded a hot dog stand outside of Fenway Park. Jerry and his wife, Phoebe, have three grown children and live in the Boston suburb of Weston.

# Chapter 16

# RICH GEDMAN

## SEPTEMBER 18, 1985

A player hitting for the cycle—a single, double, triple, and home run in the same game—is just about as common as a pitcher throwing a no-hitter. Since the beginning of the Twentieth Century and the advent of major-league baseball's modern era, and through the 2005 season, there had been fewer than 200 cycles, or less than two per year on average.

As unusual as that feat is, it's an even rarer occurrence for catchers. Catchers—at least since the end of World War II—are generally players who are too slow to play any other position. And because triples are hard enough to get even for the swiftest of ballplayers in modern baseball, a slow-footed catcher has almost no chance of hitting one in any game, much less in a game where he also singles, doubles, and homers.

Since the dawning of baseball's modern era, only 11 catchers have hit for the cycle. Hall of Famer Mickey Cochrane is the only one to do it twice, in 1932 and 1933. Entering the 2006 season, only five catchers had hit for the cycle in the previous 60 years. Rich Gedman was one of them.

"At face value, it's a pretty extraordinary feat. Rich Gedman hitting for the cycle. What? Are you kidding me?" the former Red Sox catcher reflected 20 years after the event. "Individually, that's the best thing in baseball I've ever done. The incredible part is how it happened."

✦✦✦

Richard Leo Gedman, Jr., was born on September 26, 1959, in Worcester, Massachusetts. He was the middle of five children. His father, Richard, Sr., was a truck driver who had to retire at an early age because of a medical disability. Richard and Martha Gedman raised their family in a tough working-class neighborhood in New England's second-largest city. Rich never liked to fight, but he did when he had to.

"I was a city kid, and it was the Law of the Neighborhood," he remembered. "Survival of the fittest. And stay away from the toughest guys."

Rich Gedman starred in baseball at St. Peter's of Worcester as a pitcher and first baseman, and his school won the Massachusetts state title in 1977. But the six-foot, lefthanded-hitting Gedman weighed well over 200 pounds, didn't look athletic, and so most scouts didn't give him much of a look. Bill Enos, a scout for the Red Sox, was the exception. He saw Gedman's raw potential, and the Red Sox signed him as a free agent in the late summer of 1977. Because of his size and lack of speed, there was only one position for which he was professionally suited: catcher.

"Bill Enos went through every other position with me, and it was very difficult to take. But he was probably right," Gedman recalled. "I could play the outfield, but I wasn't fast enough to do that. Third base, first base … I didn't have the power to play there; I was a line-drive hitter then. Shortstop and second base, it's obvious why I couldn't play there. He said: 'You're a five-inning pitcher, at best. And that's the way I see it. You have a chance to blossom as a catcher.' So I said: 'Okay, let's try it. But I don't have a mitt. Can you get me a mitt?' And I got a new mitt, which was great."

The Red Sox worked him out several times in the bullpen at their Class AAA farm team in Pawtucket, Rhode Island, which was just a short drive from Worcester, and then sent him to the Fall Instructional League. Gedman progressed rapidly and began his pro career in 1978 at Class A Winter Haven, where he hit .300 and made the Florida State League All-Star Team.

Gedman started to show flashes of power at Class AA Bristol the following summer, hitting .274 with 25 doubles, 12 homers, and 63 RBI in 130 games. He was already playing Triple-A ball in his third season, leading International League catchers in assists and double plays, and the Red Sox brought him up to the majors in September. Gedman, not quite yet 21 years old, caught a one-hitter by Dennis Eckersley in his first start for the Red Sox.

Boston Red Sox catcher Rich Gedman gets set to receive a throw as Tony Fernandez of the Toronto Blue Jays starts his slide toward the plate in a game at Fenway Park. *(Courtesy of the Boston Red Sox)*

Gedman started the 1981 season at Pawtucket but was called up in mid-May after hitting .296 in 25 games. Playing 62 games for the Red Sox during the strike-shortened season, Gedman hit .288 with 15 doubles and five homers in 62 games and finished second in the American League Rookie of the Year balloting behind New York Yankees pitcher Dave Righetti. *The Sporting News* named him the league's Rookie Player of the Year.

But his playing time dwindled under manager Ralph Houk, a former catcher himself, during the next two years. He started only two games during the final two months of the 1983 season.

"I was still a kid," Gedman said, "and Ralph was a veteran player's guy."

But Gedman put his idle time to good use during the second half of 1983 when Red Sox coach Walt Hriniak took him under his wing.

"I learned how to be a professional during the second half of '83," Gedman related. "I'd been showing up for work every day, but I didn't know what to do. At home you'd get plenty of swings in your 15 minutes of batting practice. But on the road you might get eight or 12 swings a day. So Walter told me: 'You've got to change some things. If you get 12 swings and have to face LaMarr Hoyt or Richard Dotson the next day, what chance are you going to have? Now imagine if it goes on for two weeks like that. How are you going to be prepared? Show up tomorrow at three o'clock, and I'll make sure you have enough swings that if you get up there, you'll have a chance.'"

Gedman hit .294 in limited duty that year and then went off to play winter ball in Venezuela.

"I was supposed to play 30, 35 games," Gedman said. "One of their catchers got hurt, and I played 60 out of 65. When I went to spring training, I was ready to play. And in '84, Ralph said I was the most improved player he'd ever seen."

Gedman became the regular Red Sox catcher and hit .269 with 26 doubles, 24 homers, and 72 RBI. He followed that up with an All-Star season in 1985, hitting .295 with 30 doubles, five triples, 18 homers, and 80 RBI. Ten of his 18 homers were clutch ones, either tying the score or putting the Red Sox ahead. He also led AL catchers in assists and gunned down 47 of 104 base stealers.

And on September 18, 1985, less than a week shy of his 26th birthday, Rich Gedman enjoyed the most memorable game of his Red Sox career. The incredible thing, as he alluded to, was that he was dreading going to Fenway Park that day.

Three months earlier, on June 23, a nasty brawl had broken out in Toronto after Red Sox pitcher Bruce Kison hit Blue Jays slugger George Bell with a pitch in the fourth inning. An enraged Bell had charged the mound and delivered a karate kick to Kison's midsection, and players from both benches emptied onto the field.

"When I ran out to the mound, he had already kicked Kison. And he turned around and hit me twice," Gedman remembered. "So I'm not looking to fight with anybody except him. And then I'm getting banged around all over the place. I'm like a freakin' weeble, just getting banged around by everybody. After that I learned to keep my mask on."

The previous night the Red Sox and Blue Jays had played each other for the first time since that June afternoon. The Red Sox had edged the Blue Jays 6-5 at Fenway Park, and no one had been hit by a pitch, nor had there been any incidents. But there was still a lot of bad blood boiling between the teams, and Gedman had a premonition it might spill over in this game, especially since Al Nipper was scheduled to pitch. If anybody on the Red Sox staff was determined to get retribution on Bell, it would be Roger Clemens or the feisty Nipper. Gedman was so worried, he literally prayed before the game that there would be only baseball.

✦ ✦ ✦

"We'd had the fight in Toronto. There was a lot of anger, a lot of edginess," Gedman related. "You didn't know if there might be a fight, or something else. And if there is, you wonder how you're going to handle yourself. If I was confronted by George again, would I try to do something? Yeah. But I wasn't going to cold-cock him from behind. I was just going to make sure I was bigger than him, to try and make peace, not fight the fight. I don't know why I thought that way, because my instincts, from where I grew up as a kid, were to knock his lights out. But I was a kid then.

"Dealing with the uncertainty of what might happen, it wasn't like you were going there to play the game. Who's going to do something? Is somebody going to drill him, and here we go again?

"I don't want to sound holier than thou, but that day I prayed," Gedman admitted. "I prayed that I wouldn't do anything wrong that day. But if I had to fight, I was going to protect myself. I wasn't going to get blindsided again."

As it turned out, nothing went wrong for Rich Gedman that night. In fact, everything went right.

Gedman, who had taken a .300 batting average into the game, grounded out to shortstop in the first inning, and Bell led off for the Blue Jays in the second.

"Sure enough, Nip throws a fastball inside to George, and I can see he's thinking about going out to the mound," Gedman recalled. "I said—and I wasn't even mad: 'George, let's just play the game, will ya?' Nip didn't care; he'd just as soon drill you as look at you."

Bell kept his temper in check, perhaps because the Blue Jays were involved in a taut race with the New York Yankees for the AL East title and he couldn't afford to get suspended again. Bell had already been suspended by the league for two games after the Kison incident. So Bell stayed at the plate, and Nipper struck him out. The Red Sox then scored three runs off Jim Clancy in the bottom of the inning on a sacrifice fly by Glenn Hoffman, an RBI double by Dwight Evans, and a single by Wade Boggs.

Gedman came to the plate again in the third and lashed a homer, his 18th of the season, into the screen to put the Red Sox ahead 4-0.

"I hadn't had a lot of success against Clancy, and to hit a home run to left-center off him, it was like: 'Holy Cow! Where did that come from?,'" Gedman remembered.

Dennis Lamp relieved the ineffective Clancy in the fourth. Hoffman walked and Evans fouled to third. Boggs and Bill Buckner singled, scoring Hoffman, and on the throw to the plate Buckner hobbled down to second. Jim Rice was walked intentionally, loading the bases, and Toronto manager Bobby Cox went to the bullpen again, bringing in lefthander John Cerutti to pitch to Gedman.

Gedman wasn't annoyed by the maneuver. "It's strategy. What are the percentages that work best for them? I would have walked Rice to get to me, too. He was much more dangerous than I would have been. I just wanted to put on a good at-bat in that situation."

He cleared the bases with an opposite-field triple to left, making the score 8-0. Despite his lack of speed, the triple was the 12th of Gedman's five-year major-league career. But it would also be his last.

"I hit a line drive right at George," Gedman recalled. "The ball was cutting away from him, he dived or slipped, the ball went into the corner, and nobody was backing him up. Who gets a triple to left field at Fenway Park?"

After Tony Armas grounded out and Mike Easler walked, Marty Barrett singled home Gedman.

Nipper took a one-hitter into the fifth inning. With one out, Cliff Johnson grounded a single to right and took a wide turn at first base. By the time he started retreating toward the bag, Gedman was waiting there with the ball and tagged him out.

"We were just trolling," Gedman explained. "It didn't happen often, but we did get guys sometimes. Any time there was nobody on and a ball is hit on the ground to the right side, the catcher automatically starts to break to back up the play at first. On basehits to right field when the first baseman has come off the bag, he knows he can stay out there because I'll be trailing the play and be on the bag. It wasn't designed to get anybody; it was designed so that runners knew you were behind them and had to slow down, and it afforded your team a slight mistake so that if somebody bobbled the ball, the runner wouldn't take an extra base. Anyway, Evans threw it to Marty, and Marty threw it to me. Cliff being Cliff, he was happy about getting a hit and took too wide a turn. Nowadays guys usually don't take a big turn; they just stand on first admiring their hit."

> **RICH GEDMAN**
> **Years with Red Sox: 1980-90**
> **Other Major League Teams: Houston, St. Louis**
> **Position: Catcher**
> **Bats: Left**
> **Throws: Right**
> **Height: 6-2**
> **Weight: 215**
> **Born: September 26, 1959**
> **Birthplace: Worcester, MA**
> **Current Residence: Framingham, MA**
> **Current Occupation: Manager, Worcester Tornadoes, Can-Am League**

The Red Sox added to their lead in the bottom of the fifth. Buckner singled, and Rice doubled him to third. Gedman came up, facing the lefthanded Cerutti again.

"I hit a ball right off the plate, straight up in the air but high enough that everybody's safe," Gedman remembered. "How do I get an infield hit? I think I probably had ten in my career."

Buckner came home on the single, making the score 10-0, and Gedman had his fifth RBI of the game.

The Blue Jays, having cleared their bench by this time, spoiled Nipper's bid for a shutout in the seventh when Ron Shepherd doubled and Lou Thornton singled him home. In the bottom of the inning, 28-year-old rookie righthander Tom Filer came on to mop up the game for Toronto.

Boggs singled for his fourth hit of the game, and Eddie Jurak pinch ran for him. Buckner singled, and Rice doubled, scoring Jurak. That brought Gedman to the plate, blissfully unaware that he needed a double to complete his cycle. All he was thinking about was Filer, who had owned him in the minor leagues.

"I had played against Tom Filer a lot when he was in the Yankees organization, and I was just an out to him," Gedman related. "But I remembered how he got me out, with sliders, and I said: 'I'm going to look for it.' He throws me a slider on the first pitch, and I hook a line drive to the right of the first baseman. But if that ball doesn't bounce into the stands for a ground-rule double, if it only hits the railing, I might have only gotten a single.

"That's what I mean about it being such an incredible night. I was worried about a fight, and then I get four hits I wouldn't ordinarily get: a home run to left-center, a triple into the left-field corner, a chopped ball off the plate for an infield hit, and a ball that bounces into the stands for a ground-rule double."

Buckner and Rice were awarded home on the double, giving Gedman seven RBI in the game. He knew he was having a good night at the plate, but when the crowd of 17,985 rose to give him a standing ovation, he had no idea why. Behind him, on the center-field scoreboard, a message was informing the fans that he had just hit for the cycle.

"So here I am, standing out at second base, and people are clapping for me, and I'm so unaware," he recalled. "That wasn't what I was in tune with during a game. I really wasn't paying attention. I never really thought about how I'm doing, only how the team is doing. Most of the time I was only focused on getting more runs than the other team or keeping the other team from scoring."

The Red Sox won 13-1. Al Nipper pitched a complete-game six-hitter, there were no ugly incidents, and Rich Gedman became the 16th player—and probably the unlikeliest—in the 85-year history of the Red Sox to hit for the cycle.

"It's the only thing I can say I've done in baseball that most guys haven't done," Gedman said proudly, 20 years later.

✦✦✦

The Red Sox finished the 1985 season in fifth place with an 81-81 record. They won the pennant in 1986. Gedman's batting average slipped to .258, but he rapped 29 doubles and 16 homers and drove in 65 runs in 135 games. He hit two grand slams, including a pinch shot off lefthanded relief ace Willie Hernandez—the AL's MVP two years earlier—to beat the Tigers 9-6 in Detroit on August 10. He also caught Roger Clemens's first

20-strikeout game on April 29, tying a major-league record for catchers with 20 putouts, and played in his second straight All-Star Game. He also threw out 44 of 88 base stealers that year.

Gedman hit .357 in the American League Championship Series against the California Angels. In the memorable fifth game, when the Red Sox were one strike away from elimination, Gedman went 4-for-4 and was hit by a Gary Lucas pitch with two outs in the top of the ninth, allowing Dave Henderson to bat and hit his famous two-run homer that kept the game going. In the 11th inning of that game, Gedman reached on a bunt single, moving Don Baylor to third base, from where he scored the winning run on Henderson's sacrifice fly in the Red Sox' 7-6 victory. Gedman also hit a home run in the World Series against the New York Mets and was selected as the catcher on *The Sporting News* All-Star Team.

Gedman became a free agent after the season. At the age of 27 and a two-time All-Star, a lefthanded-hitting catcher who could hit with power, he should have been in high demand on the open market. But his timing was unfortunate. Baseball owners had illegally colluded to restrict the movement of free agents, and Gedman found no suitable offers except the one from the Red Sox. For the first time since the advent of free agency a decade earlier, salaries declined in 1987-88. Several years later the owners would be found guilty of collusion and forced to pay $280 million in penalties. As a victim of the scheme, Gedman received a high six-figure settlement. But the collusion wrecked his career.

Under the rules, Gedman could not re-sign with the Red Sox until May 1, 1987. When he did, he went right into the lineup the next day without any formal workouts. He went hitless in his first 20 at-bats and had just one hit in his first 31, then suffered a groin injury in July and a broken thumb later that month that required surgery. Gedman hit just .205 with one homer in 52 games, and the remainder of his career was marred by injuries.

He broke his foot six games into the 1988 season and played only 95 games, hitting .230 with nine homers, although he did hit .357 with a homer against Oakland in the ALCS. The 1989 season was even worse as Gedman hit .212 with only 13 extra-base hits and 16 RBI in 93 games. After playing only 10 games during the first two months of 1990, he was traded to Houston for a minor-leaguer. Gedman played 40 games for Houston, then became a free agent again and signed with the St. Louis Cardinals. After spending two years in a backup role, Gedman left St. Louis, played one year in the minors for Columbus in 1993, and then retired at the age of 34.

Rich Gedman, a two-time All-Star catcher for the Boston Red Sox, currently manages the Worcester Tornadoes in the independent Can-Am League. *(Courtesy of Chaz Scoggins)*

"I played mad," Gedman said of those years following collusion. "I was made to believe I had done something wrong, which I hadn't. I was a bitter man. How does someone go from playing in the All-Star Game two years in a row to looking like he doesn't know how to play? I take the blame for failing. I let the game beat me up, I let my surroundings beat me up, and I couldn't pull myself out.

"I was crushed … devastated. I don't mean to sound like a weak guy, but I felt like Boston turned on me, not only the team but the fans. I had friends who wanted to talk to me and help me, but I wasn't ready to hear it. I played with a boulder on my shoulder, and it hurt. I had never played ticked off. I loved the game of baseball; I love it to this day. But what I went through was not a whole lot of fun. I was at my lowest low, and I couldn't do anything about it."

Rich Gedman played 906 games for the Red Sox from 1980-90, hitting .259 with 83 homers and 356 RBI.

Gedman spent the next few years running baseball camps and clinics while also helping to coach a prep school team outside of Boston. He coached his own two sons in Little League and Babe Ruth, then coached for two years in the independent Northeast League before taking the job as manager of the Worcester Tornadoes in the independent Can-Am League in 2005. He led the Tornadoes to the pennant in their first year of existence.

Rich Gedman and his wife Sherry, a former professional softball player, have three children and reside in Framingham, Massachusetts.

# Chapter 17

# BRUCE HURST

## OCTOBER 23, 1986

A s a Mormon boy growing up in Utah, a state that has produced very few major-league baseball players, Bruce Vee Hurst never realized how feral this superficially genteel game could be. Drafted in the first round in 1976 and signed by the Red Sox, the 18-year-old lefthander with the sweeping curveball was immediately overwhelmed by the ferocity of the competition. On at least two occasions early in his career he had to be talked out of quitting, and not until 1986—his 11th year in pro ball and his fifth full season in the majors—had he finally put everything together.

Now, on a pleasant 64-degree October evening, he was standing on the familiar mound at Fenway Park. Game 5 of the 1986 World Series against the New York Mets was about to begin, and 28-year-old Bruce Hurst was ready to throw the first pitch of the most memorable game of his Red Sox career. Somewhere out there were scores—perhaps even hundreds—of former coaches and managers, former teammates and opponents, who never could have conceived of Hurst pitching a game of this magnitude.

✛ ✛ ✛

"I wanted it faster than it happened," Hurst acknowledged almost 20 years later. "You have to consider where I came from and the quality of the competition I played against. But eventually I got there.

"Baseball is such a fragile mental game," Hurst explained. "You take your eyes off the ball, and the game comes up and bites you so fast. When athletes sense weakness, they will get you—the good ones, anyway—and I had gotten bitten so many times by then, I had learned how to stay focused on the task at hand."

Born on March 24, 1958, in St. George, Utah, Bruce Hurst starred in both basketball and baseball at Dixie High School in St. George. He was an all-state player in basketball, but with a lively fastball and a nasty, biting curveball, the Red Sox envisioned him as a top-of-the-rotation pitcher and made him the 22nd overall selection in the 1976 draft.

Befitting his status as a first-round draft pick, Hurst was put on the fast track to the majors. He went 3-2 with a 3.00 ERA at Elmira in the short-season New York-Penn League in 1976, then went 5-4 with a 2.08 ERA at Winter Haven in the Class A Florida State League the following year.

Elbow and shoulder problems limited Hurt to just six games at Bristol in the Class AA Eastern League in 1978. Starting at Winter Haven in 1979 to take advantage of the warm weather, Hurst rolled up an 8-2 record with a 1.93 ERA and was promoted to Bristol at mid-season. He went 9-4 with a 3.58 there, and his combined record for the year was 17-6 with a 2.88 ERA.

On Opening Day in 1980, the 22-year-old Hurst found himself with the Red Sox. He still hadn't pitched at Triple-A, and it became apparent quickly that he still wasn't quite ready for the major leagues. After a rocky start, Hurst was sent down to Pawtucket, where he spent three months and posted an 8-6 record with a 3.94 ERA. The Red Sox recalled him later in the season, but his ERA in 12 games for the major-league team that season was 9.10.

Hurst spent most of the 1981 campaign pitching in Pawtucket, where he was 12-7 with a 2.87 ERA. The Red Sox brought him up in September, and he went 2-0 with a 4.30 ERA in five starts. The 6-3, 207-pound lefthander spent all of 1982 in Boston but pitched much of the year with bone chips in his elbow and was ineffective, going 3-7 with a 5.77 ERA. Off-season surgery removed the chips, and in 1983 he finally began to live up to his promise, going 12-12 with a 4.09 ERA. Hurst had another 12-12 record in 1984, but his ERA improved to 3.92. Although he began striking out hitters with more frequency in 1985, the year was a setback for the 27-year-old pitcher as he went 11-13 and posted a 4.51 ERA.

Heading into the 1986 season, Hurst's Red Sox record was only 42-46 with a 4.59 ERA. But it was a breakthrough year for Hurst, who posted a 13-8 record with a 2.99 ERA and 167 strikeouts in 174 innings. Five times

**Boston Red Sox lefthander Bruce Hurst displays his high leg kick before delivering a pitch during a game.**
*(Courtesy of the Boston Red Sox)*

that year he fanned 11 or more batters in a game, including a 14-strikeout effort against the Texas Rangers. He had two memorable duels a week apart with future Hall of Famer Tom Seaver, who was pitching for the Chicago White Sox, that season. He pitched a five-hitter with 11 strikeouts on April 12 but lost to Seaver 3-1. Six days later Hurst faced Seaver again and this time threw a three-hitter with 11 strikeouts and beat him 2-1.

Hurst was leading the league in strikeouts when he pulled a groin muscle in a game against Minnesota on May 31. He missed a month and a half. But he was unbeatable down the stretch as the Red Sox pulled away in the American League East race, earning AL Pitcher of the Month honors after going 5-0 with two shutouts and a 1.07 ERA in September. Hurst provided the Red Sox with a lefthanded complement for young righthanded ace Roger Clemens, who went 24-4 with a 2.48 ERA and led the league in both wins and ERA. Hurst finished second in the league in shutouts with four and was fourth in ERA.

Hurst beat the California Angels 9-2 in the second game of the American League Championship Series, then pitched the first six innings in the famous Game 5 that unlikely hero Dave Henderson had been compelled to win twice: once with a two-out, two-strike home run off Donnie Moore in the top of the ninth inning that had put the Red Sox ahead 6-5, and again with a sacrifice fly in the 11th after the Angels had tied the game in the bottom of the ninth. The Red Sox had gone on to win the ALCS in seven games, with Clemens pitching the clincher.

Hurst had five days' rest when he started Game 1 of the World Series against the New York Mets' Ron Darling in front of 55,076 fans at Shea Stadium on October 18. The Mets had experienced an ordeal of their own in the NLCS before getting past the Houston Astros in six games. But they had won 108 games during the regular season and were heavily favored to win the World Series.

"I was a little nervous," Hurst remembered. "But once I got on the mound and looked around and saw Wade [Boggs] and Marty [Barrett] and Geddy [Rich Gedman], everything seemed so familiar. I threw my first warm-up pitch, and the nervousness was gone."

Hurst struck out the first two batters he faced, Mookie Wilson and Lenny Dykstra, retired the first five, and gave up only three singles through the first six innings. The Mets had put the first two runners aboard in the sixth, but Hurst had fanned Darryl Strawberry and induced Ray Knight to bounce into a double play to end that threat. The Red Sox, however, had managed only two singles off Darling, and the game was scoreless going into the seventh.

The Red Sox then manufactured a run without benefit of a hit. Jim Rice led off with a walk and took second on a wild pitch. After Dwight Evans was retired on a comebacker, Mets second baseman Tim Teufel let Gedman's grounder roll through his legs for an error, and Rice scampered home from second.

It would turn out to be the only run of the game. Having given up four hits and four walks while striking out eight batters in eight innings, Hurst turned the game over to Calvin Schiraldi, who polished off the 1-0 shutout and picked up a save.

The Red Sox mounted an 18-hit attack against ace Dwight Gooden and four relievers and routed the Mets 9-3 the next night to take a stunning 2-0 edge, and the World Series moved to Boston for the next three games. Giddy Red Sox fans, anticipating a long-awaited end to the club's 67-year championship drought, were confident the Sox could wrap up the Series at Fenway. But former Sox lefthander Bobby Ojeda beat them 7-1 in Game 3, and two Gary Carter homers powered the Mets to a 6-2 triumph the following night to even the World Series at two wins apiece.

Al Nipper, who had compiled a 10-12 record with a 5.38 ERA during the regular season, had been a somewhat controversial choice by Red Sox manager John McNamara to pitch Game 4. But McNamara knew he could start Hurst on his normal four days' rest and Clemens on five days' rest in the next two games, which he concluded was a huge advantage. But to make the strategy work, Hurst knew winning Game 5 was an absolute must.

"It was the last game at Fenway, and going back to New York down 3-2 would have been tough. And," he added, "I thought it would be my last chance to pitch in the World Series."

✛ ✛ ✛

Hurst's opponent, Doc Gooden, just 21 years old and already a three-year major-league veteran, could be a formidable adversary. He had been the NL Rookie of the Year in 1984 after winning 17 games and leading the league with 276 strikeouts in just 218 innings, and his second year had been even better. Gooden had won the NL's pitching Triple Crown, going 24-4 with a 1.53 ERA, eight shutouts, and 268 strikeouts. But he had looked mortal in 1986, going 17-6 with a 2.84 ERA and 200 strikeouts in 250 innings, and the Red Sox had pounded him in Game 2. He would be pitching on just three days' rest against Hurst.

"I never got intimidated pitching against anyone," Hurst said. "Gooden had phenomenal stuff, but I was used to seeing Roger Clemens pitch every five days. It's exciting to watch guys with great stuff; but guys with command, guys who can change speeds, can pitch well, too, and I felt like I could compete with guys like that."

An SRO crowd of 34,010 at Fenway Park greeted Hurst vociferously as he took the mound. He gave up a one-out double to Teufel, whose error had presented him with the victory in Game 1, but retired the other three Mets on grounders to second baseman Marty Barrett.

The Red Sox left the bases loaded in the first inning but staked Hurst to a 1-0 lead in the second when Dave Henderson tripled and coasted home on a sacrifice fly by Spike Owen. The Mets put two runners on in the third but couldn't score, and the Red Sox picked up an unearned run in the bottom of the inning when Bill Buckner reached on an error by shortstop Rafael Santana and came around to score on a single by Dwight Evans.

Hurst faced his first serious jam in the fifth.

**BRUCE HURST**
**Years with Red Sox: 1980-88**
**Other Major League Teams: San Diego, Colorado, Texas**
**Position: Pitcher**
**Bats: Left**
**Throws: Left**
**Height: 6-3**
**Weight: 215**
**Born: March 24, 1958**
**Birthplace: St. George, UT**
**Current Residence: Gilbert, AZ**
**Current Occupation: Pitching consultant, Major League Baseball**

Kevin Mitchell and Mookie Wilson led off with singles, and Santana bunted them both into scoring position with the top of the order coming up. The Mets were a basehit away from tying the game.

"That inning was very critical," Hurst remembered. "There are always three to five outs you have to get in a game if you're going to win, and you don't know ahead of time which ones they are. When the Mets gave me an out by bunting, and I could face Dykstra—a lefthander—I felt I had a good chance to get out of it."

Hurst fanned Dykstra and retired Teufel on a groundball to third.

The Red Sox chased Gooden in the fifth and gave Hurst a four-run cushion. Rice led off with a triple, and Don Baylor singled him home. Evans sent Baylor to third with another single that finished Gooden, and lefthander Sid Fernandez came on to fan Gedman for the first out of the inning. Henderson, beginning to forge a reputation for post-season heroics, followed with an RBI double to make the score 4-0 before Fernandez could put down the uprising.

"One thing Roger and I always talked about was when your team scored, you really want to go out and put up a zero," Hurst related. "That's how you keep momentum on your side."

Hurst retired the Mets in order in the sixth, then in the seventh gave up a leadoff single to Ray Knight, who was left stranded there. Not until the eighth did the Mets, who had been shut out by Hurst for 15 innings, finally break through and score.

Teufel sliced a solo homer down the right-field line with one out to break Hurst's hex, and Keith Hernandez followed with a single. But Hurst retired Carter and Strawberry and took a 4-1 lead into the ninth. He got Knight on a grounder to third and Mitchell on a pop to first, then was tagged for another run when Wilson doubled and scored on a Santana single, the Mets' 10th hit of the game. Dykstra, a .295 hitter representing the tying run, was at the plate, but McNamara left Hurst in.

"I hadn't labored in the middle innings, and I had pitched Dykstra tough," Hurst replied when asked if he was surprised to be left in the game. "Mac had gotten confidence in me during the season. But I knew if I didn't get him out, I'm out of there."

Hurst set up Dykstra perfectly and struck him out on the pitch he planned to, a high and inside fastball that the Mets outfielder waved at feebly.

"I threw it as hard as I can—which probably wasn't very hard," Hurst said, recalling the final pitch. "But it was all I had."

The Red Sox were 4-2 winners and had a 3-2 edge in the Series heading back to New York.

The 10-hit complete game was not a masterpiece for Bruce Hurst. But it would be the last World Series game the Red Sox would win for 18 years, and he had walked just one batter while striking out six. Twenty-three of his 27 outs were recorded on groundballs, pop-ups, or strikeouts, including 17 of the last 18.

+ + +

A home run by Henderson and an RBI single by Barrett had put the Red Sox ahead 5-3 in the 10th inning in Game 6 at Shea Stadium, and they were one strike away from winning the World Series for the first time since 1918 when everything suddenly unraveled.

"If you had the luxury of taking a knee in baseball, we would have been World Champs," Hurst reflected two decades later. "But you have to put the ball in play. You have to play all the outs."

Three straight two-strike singles by Carter, Mitchell, and Knight produced a run, and a wild pitch by reliever Bob Stanley scored Mitchell with the tying run. When first baseman Bill Buckner let Mookie Wilson's bounding ball slip between his legs, Knight raced home from second with the winning run. Had the Red Sox won that night, the likely MVP of the World Series would have been Hurst.

A rainout the next day enabled McNamara to bypass Oil Can Boyd and come back with Hurst on three days' rest in Game 7 on October 27.

"I had been prepared for the probability, and I felt like I had earned it," Hurst recounted. "Oil Can was a good pitcher; don't get me wrong. But I had pitched well all through September and the playoffs and now in the World Series. I felt as comfortable as I had ever felt in the major leagues."

The Red Sox staked Hurst to a 3-0 lead in the second against Ron Darling on back-to-back homers by Evans and Gedman and an RBI single by Wade Boggs.

Hurst retired 16 of the first 17 Mets he faced, allowing only a two-out single by Knight in the second inning. But the Mets had fouled off a lot of pitches and run up his pitch count to nearly 100, and Hurst finally lost his edge in the sixth.

"It wasn't like I was getting pounded. I felt like I was still strong," Hurst remembered. "The only pitch I would have liked back was the 3-1 pitch to Hernandez."

The Mets loaded the bases with one out, and Keith Hernandez ripped a two-run single. Carter blooped a ball in front of right-fielder Evans, and while Hernandez was forced at second, Wally Backman scored the tying run. Rice made a circus catch in left field off Strawberry to end the rally, but Hurst was finished for the evening. The Mets tattooed the Red Sox bullpen for five runs in the next two innings and won 8-5 to win the World Series.

✦ ✦ ✦

Bruce Hurst pitched two more seasons for the Red Sox, compiling an 18-6 record in 1988 when they made the playoffs again only to be swept by the Oakland Athletics in the ALCS. Hurst then became a free agent and pitched four years for the San Diego Padres before finishing his career in 1994 with the Colorado Rockies and Texas Rangers.

Bruce Hurst, who won two games in the 1986 World Series, acknowledges the cheers of the crowd as he is inducted into the Boston Red Sox Hall of Fame.
*(Courtesy of the Boston Red Sox/Julie Cordeiro)*

His 88 wins for the Red Sox rank sixth on the club's list for lefthanders. He was inducted into the Red Sox Hall of Fame in 2004.

Bruce Hurst, his wife Holly, and their children presently live in Gilbert, Arizona, where he helps with a family hardware business. Hurst also works as a consultant for Major League Baseball, teaching the art of pitching to international baseball programs.

# Chapter 18

# DAVID HENDERSON

## OCTOBER 25, 1986

D avid Henderson's ultra-dramatic two-out, two-strike home run in the ninth inning of Game 5 of the 1986 American League Championship Series ranks right up there with the most famous home runs in Red Sox history. Indeed, it has been enshrined in the Red Sox Hall of Fame as one of the franchise's most memorable moments. You can rank Henderson's ALCS homer, Carlton Fisk's Game 6-winning homer in the 1975 World Series, Bernie Carbo's game-tying three-run pinch homer in the same game, David Ortiz's 14th-inning homer in Game 4 of the 2004 ALCS that ignited the incredible Red Sox run to a World Series Championship, and Ted Williams's farewell homer in the final at-bat of his career in 1960, in any order you choose. Henderson, however, will rank them differently.

Henderson's career with the Red Sox was brief, lasting only 54 weeks and 123 games, so his Boston highlights are few but indelible. While Henderson will not deny the impact his homer against the California Angels had on Red Sox history, his most memorable game—and home run—came two weeks later that same season. And although much of his 14-year major-league career was relatively undistinguished from the months of April through September, Henderson's postseason heroics in 1986 served as a springboard to a national reputation as one of the great October clutch hitters in baseball history.

+ + +

David Lee Henderson was born into a large family of six children in the central California town of Dos Palos on July 21, 1958. His father, Odell, worked for the California state highway department. He already had good baseball bloodlines while growing up. His uncle, Joe Henderson, pitched three years in the major leagues from 1974-77 with the Chicago White Sox and Cincinnati Reds. David Henderson was an outstanding athlete in both football and baseball, a high school All-American as a running back at Dos Palos High while attracting the notice of scouts as a baseball player. When the first-year Seattle Mariners picked him in the first round of the 1977 draft, making him the 26th choice overall, Henderson passed up a multitude of college scholarship offers, including offers from USC and Nebraska, to play football and signed with Seattle.

It seemed like a good decision. By signing with an expansion team, he would automatically be on the fast track to the major leagues, and the 19-year-old outfielder's first year in pro ball was outstanding. Playing for Bellingham in the short-season Class A Northwest League, Henderson hit .315 and drove in 63 runs in 65 games while bashing 16 home runs to share the league title. He was named to the league's All-Star team and was also picked for the Topps Class A Rookie All-Star team.

Dogged by a nagging Achilles tendon injury, Henderson struggled in his second year at Class A Stockton, hitting only .232 with seven homers and 63 RBI in 117 games. Back in A ball for another year at San Jose in 1979, Henderson regained his All-Star status by hitting .300 with 27 homers, 99 RBI, and 103 runs and helped the Missions win the California League pennant. The Mariners bumped Henderson to Triple-A in 1980, and a knee injury that necessitated arthroscopic surgery limited him to 109 games, during which he hit a modest .279 with only seven homers and 50 RBI for Spokane.

But the wretched Mariners, coming off a 103-loss season and averaging barely 10,000 fans a game, were impatient for a star from their farm system. On Opening Night in 1981, 22-year-old David Henderson was their starting centerfielder. He wasn't ready for the big time yet. He hit only .167 in 59 games for the Mariners and spent half the season back in Spokane.

"You never know when you're ready for major-league pitching," Henderson reflected a quarter of a century later. "I could do everything except hit a slider on the black. But nobody can hit a slider on the black. The difference for me, as a young kid, was that I couldn't stop swinging at it."

**Boston Red Sox centerfielder David Henderson fouls off a pitch during a game at Fenway Park.** *(Courtesy of the Boston Red Sox)*

By 1982, ready or not, Henderson was in the major leagues to stay. His statistics for a weak Seattle team from 1982-86 were decent but not spectacular, and certainly not what the Mariners expected from a first-round draft choice. Henderson's batting average ranged from .241 to .280, and he consistently hit 14 home runs every summer except for 1983, when he cracked 17. His RBI totals varied from a low of 44 to a high of 68.

"We were losing 95, 100 games every year, and half the roster would turn over," Henderson remembered. "I also played for six managers in Seattle who all wanted to do things their way, and every year I felt like I had to win my job all over again."

By the middle of the 1986 season, the Mariners concluded the 28-year-old Henderson was never going to become a superstar. He was looking at impending free agency, so the Mariners were looking to deal. The Red Sox were in a pennant race and looking for a reliable, veteran shortstop and an outfielder to back up rapidly aging Tony Armas, who had led the AL with 43 homers only two years earlier, in center field. On August 19 the Red Sox and Mariners swung a six-player trade. The Red Sox sent rookie shortstop Rey Quinones, pitchers Mike Brown and Mike Trujillo, and minor-league outfielder John Christensen to Seattle in exchange for shortstop Spike Owen and Henderson.

Owen, who was hitting .246 at the time of the trade, stepped right into the Red Sox lineup and played regularly the rest of the way despite batting a meager .183 in 42 games. Henderson, who had been having another decent year in Seattle with a .276 average, 19 doubles, 14 homers, and 44 RBI in 103 games, mostly sat on the bench. He had just 51 at-bats over the final six weeks of the season, hitting .196 with one homer and three RBI.

"I'd get into games in the late innings when they took Tony Armas out," Henderson said. "I'd get four at-bats a week, and they'd all be against the other team's closer."

Henderson was still sitting when the East Division champion Red Sox met the West Division champion Angels in the ALCS. He appeared in only two of the first four games, both times as a late-inning caddy for Armas. His role changed forever after the fifth inning of Game 5 on October 12 when Armas twisted his ankle while fielding a double by Doug DeCinces in the second inning and had to leave the game after five.

Henderson wasn't much healthier than Armas at that time. He was playing with torn cartilage in his right knee that would require off-season surgery.

"I could barely move," he remembered. "But there was no one else."

Henderson took over in center field in the bottom of the sixth and immediately looked like a goat when he misplayed a soft flyball by Doug DeCinces into a double and then leaped for Bobby Grich's long fly, snagged it as he crashed into the fence … and then dropped it behind the fence for a two-run homer that put the Angels ahead 3-2. The Angels added two more runs in the seventh, and as the Red Sox came to bat in the ninth, the festive crowd of 64,223 was preparing to celebrate the first pennant in the club's 26-year history. Mike Witt had allowed only six hits over the first eight innings and hadn't walked a batter. But Bill Buckner started the inning with a single, and one out later Don Baylor belted a homer into the left-field stands, cutting California's lead to 5-4. Witt got Dwight Evans to pop up for the second out, and the Angels were now one out away from eliminating the Red Sox.

But California manager Gene Mauch didn't want Witt to face lefthanded-hitting Rich Gedman, who was 3-for-3 against the righthander with a single, double, and two-run homer in the game. Mauch went to the bullpen for veteran lefthander Gary Lucas, who hadn't hit a batter in 322 innings of pitching dating back to May of 1982. But he hit Gedman with his first pitch, and the tying run was aboard. With the righthanded-hitting Henderson, who had struck out against Witt in the seventh, due up, Mauch went to the bullpen again, this time for his closer, Donnie Moore. The righthanded Moore had ranked fifth in the league in saves with 21 during the regular season and posted a rocky save in Game 3 of the ALCS, allowing two runs in two innings of work in the Angels' 5-3 win. But Moore versus a rusty Henderson seemed like a classic mismatch, and Red Sox manager John McNamara had no one else.

"We were beat, man. It was over," Red Sox second baseman Marty Barrett said afterward.

Henderson worked the count to 2-and-2, and on the top step of the Angels dugout Mauch was accepting a congratulatory hug from Reggie Jackson. Henderson desperately fouled off two nasty forkballs from Moore to stay alive, then caught the next one on the fat of the bat and sent it deep to left field. Henderson, like Carlton Fisk 11 years earlier, took a couple of steps out of the batter's box and stopped to watch the flight of the ball, and when it went into the stands he leaped high into the air, pirouetted, and landed awkwardly on his balky right knee. The Angels and their fans were in total shock as Henderson gleefully trotted around the bases. The Red Sox now led 6-5.

"We were on our deathbeds. The heartbeat meter was a straight line," said Red Sox ace Roger Clemens after the game. "Then Hendu goes deep, and it starts beeping again."

"We are ballplayers, so we fail most of the time," Henderson reflected honestly later that afternoon. "But you don't think about failure; you just go for it."

Donnie Moore never got over his failure. Less than three years later the despondent pitcher shot himself to death.

Henderson's homer, as dramatic as it was, didn't win that game for the Red Sox. The Angels recovered long enough to tie the game up in the bottom of the ninth. But the Red Sox won it in the 11th on Henderson's bases-loaded sacrifice fly off Chuck Finley.

"Everybody I talk to from Boston thinks that homer in Game 5 was my highlight. It wasn't," Henderson said frankly. "That at-bat wasn't much more than a pinch-hitting role, and anybody can get lucky and hit a home run as a pinch hitter. I was just trying to survive, man. I really had no business hitting that home run. It never should have happened."

But Henderson started every game for the Red Sox during the remainder of the 1986 postseason, and before long he was in a groove. The Red Sox pummeled the demoralized Angels 10-4 and 8-1 in the final two games at Fenway Park to win the pennant and then went to New York to play the heavily favored Mets in the World Series.

"Tony was ready to come back by the start of the World Series, but anybody will tell you that when a player is hot, you don't take him out of the lineup," Henderson said. "So Mac kept playing me."

> **DAVID HENDERSON**
> **Years with Red Sox: 1986-87**
> **Other Major League Teams: Seattle, San Francisco, Oakland, Kansas City**
> **Position: Outfield**
> **Bats: Right**
> **Throws: Right**
> **Height: 6-2**
> **Weight: 220**
> **Born: July 21, 1958**
> **Birthplace: Merced, CA**
> **Current Residence: Bellevue, WA**
> **Current Occupation: Seattle Mariners TV analyst**

The Mets had won 108 games during the regular season, 13 more than the Red Sox. But the Red Sox surprised the Mets by winning the first two games at Shea Stadium. Henderson had two of Boston's five hits in Game 1, won by the Red Sox 1-0. He had three more hits in Game 2, including a homer off Mets phenom Dwight Gooden, as the Red Sox throttled the Mets 9-3.

"I think the pitch I hit for the home run off Gooden was 97 miles an hour, and I still got him," Henderson said with pride. "I read in the papers before the World Series that Gooden said American Leaguers couldn't hit fastballs. Yeah? Well, in the two games I faced him in the World Series, I hit for the cycle. I could always hit a fastball."

Back at Fenway for Game 3, Henderson had one of the five hits off Bobby Ojeda and scored the only Red Sox run in a 7-1 loss. He hit a sacrifice fly in Game 4, a 6-2 setback as the Mets evened the Series. Henderson was instrumental in a 4-2 victory for Bruce Hurst in Game 5. He tripled off Gooden and scored the first run in the second inning on a sacrifice fly by Spike Owen, then climaxed the Red Sox scoring with an RBI double in the fifth off Sid Fernandez.

Henderson was already having a magnificent World Series, hitting .444 with a double, triple, homer, four RBI, and four runs scored in the first five games as the two teams shuttled back to New York with the Red Sox one win away from capturing their first World Championship since 1918. While Game 6 on October 25 was destined to become one Red Sox fans can never forget, this would be the game Henderson will always remember.

✦ ✦ ✦

"I'd gotten a lot of hits and some big RBIs in the World Series, and now I'm feeling like I'm Jim Rice or Dwight Evans," Henderson recalled. "I'm not the guy at the bottom of the lineup anymore, the guy they talk about in the pregame meetings between the pitchers and the catchers and say: 'Just don't walk him.'"

At Shea Stadium in front of a crowd of 55,078 on an overcast, 53-degree Saturday night, the Red Sox quickly nicked Ojeda, a former teammate who had won 18 games for the Mets and led the NL in winning percentage, for a run in the first inning. Wade Boggs beat out an infield hit and scored on a double by Evans. Henderson, batting seventh in the order that night, flied to deep left in the second.

"I just missed it," Henderson said ruefully. "I'd known Ojeda for years—we grew up in the same part of California—and I knew he'd throw me a changeup. I hit it to the warning track."

The Red Sox picked up another run in the inning anyway on singles by Owen, Boggs, and Marty Barrett. Henderson flied out to center in the fourth, but the Red Sox still led 2-0.

Roger Clemens, who had posted a 24-4 record during the regular season and was soon to be named the AL's Most Valuable Player and Cy Young Award winner, held the Mets without a hit over the first four innings, walking one and striking out six. New York finally broke through for a pair of runs in the fifth, one of them unearned, to tie the game. Darryl Strawberry walked, stole second, and raced home on a single by Ray Knight. Mookie Wilson followed with a single, and Knight took third when Evans misplayed the ball in right field, from where he scored on a double-play ball.

Henderson grounded out to short in the sixth, and the game was still deadlocked heading into the seventh. New York manager Davey Johnson decided Ojeda was cooked after giving up eight hits and two walks in six innings and went to the bullpen for righthander Roger McDowell. The Red Sox touched him for an unearned run.

McDowell walked Barrett to start the inning, and he moved up on a hit-and-run grounder by Buckner. A throwing error by third baseman Knight on Jim Rice's grounder allowed Barrett to take third, and with Rice moving on the pitch to Evans, preventing an inning-ending double play, Barrett scored on an unusual 4-6-3 groundout by Evans that put the Red Sox ahead 3-2. The Red Sox almost had another run in the inning when Rich Gedman singled, but leftfielder Wilson threw out Rice trying to score from second, leaving Henderson on deck for the fourth time in the game. Henderson led off the eighth with a single off McDowell.

"McDowell was a sinkerball pitcher," he remembered. "I just wanted to take the ball the other way, and that's what I did, a ball just out of the reach of their second baseman, Tim Teufel."

Owen sacrificed Henderson to second. In a controversial move that has never been satisfactorily explained, McNamara took Clemens, who had allowed only four hits and one earned run with eight strikeouts, out of the game and sent up rookie Mike Greenwell to pinch hit. McNamara claimed Clemens had a blister and asked out. Clemens insisted he wanted to stay in and could have pitched with the blister. Henderson watched McNamara, pitching coach Bill Fischer, Clemens, and Don Baylor huddle before going up to hit.

"I saw blood, but I thought for sure he'd go another inning. He'd have all winter to heal," Henderson recalled. "I don't know what was said because Clemens, Baylor—who wasn't playing that night and was like an assistant manager—McNamara, and Fischer were off by themselves. But whatever was said, apparently Clemens didn't say the right thing."

Greenwell struck out, and McDowell walked Boggs intentionally and Barrett unintentionally to fill the bases. Jesse Orosco relieved McDowell and got Buckner to fly out to center and end the threat. With Clemens out of the game, the Mets rallied quickly to tie it in the bottom of the eighth off Calvin Schiraldi when pinch hitter Lee Mazzilli singled and scored on a sacrifice fly by Gary Carter. The game went into extra innings tied at 3-3.

Henderson might have won it for the Red Sox in regulation had he not been left standing in the on-deck circle for the fifth time when Gedman bounced into a double play to end the ninth. Henderson instead led off the

10th against righthander Rick Aguilera. It was the fifth time in the game he was leading off an inning.

"I don't think anybody knows this story," Henderson related with a chuckle, "but I was more worried about Mel Stottlemyre before that at-bat than I was about Rick Aguilera. Stottlemyre was the Mets pitching coach, but he had been the minor-league pitching coach with the Mariners when I first started with them, and he knew my weaknesses just about as well as anybody. Right before Aguilera faced me in the 10th, Stottlemyre went to the mound and had a long conversation with him. That led me to believe he knew how to get me out, and that worried me. Now I'm sure all he said was: 'Don't give this guy anything good to hit.' But I still hit the home run that put us ahead and almost ended the 85-year curse of the Red Sox.

"It was a one-oh pitch that ran in on me, but I got the head of the bat out on it," Henderson remembered. "I was backpedaling toward first base—almost a moonwalk—and when it hit off the Newsday sign [on the facing of the first deck], I went into my home run trot. I thought we had it won right there, and then we added an insurance run."

Before the inning was over, Boggs had doubled and scored on a single by Barrett, staking the Red Sox to a 5-3 lead.

Schiraldi, the hard-throwing rookie who had saved nine games for the Red Sox while posting a 4-2 record and 1.41 ERA after being called up in midseason, began his third inning of relief work and quickly retired the first two batters in the bottom of the 10th. The second out was a flyball that Keith Hernandez lofted to Henderson in center field. With the Red Sox one out away from ultimate victory, the loosey-goosey Henderson couldn't resist sticking it to Mets fans.

"I threw the ball into the bleachers out there and said: 'Na-na-na-na-na!' They started throwing beer and stuff at me," he said with a laugh.

The Mets thought it was all over, too. Shea Stadium's message board in left field was flashing congratulations to the Red Sox for winning the World Series. But it was far from over.

Gary Carter singled. Kevin Mitchell pinch hit for Aguilera, took a strike, and singled. Schiraldi, who had averaged more than a strikeout per inning during the regular season, got ahead of Ray Knight 0-and-2 but couldn't finish him off. Knight singled, scoring Carter, and the Mets had closed the gap to 5-4. McNamara went to the bullpen for Bob Stanley, who uncorked a wild pitch as Mitchell sprinted home with the tying run and Knight grabbed second.

"Even though they were hitting the ball, you thought they had to hit one right at somebody sooner or later," Henderson recalled. "When Knight got to second, I was worried something bad was about to happen. I was hoping the next ball would be hit to me. Because I was the anointed hero, I'd either make a diving catch or throw the runner out at the plate."

The next ball wasn't hit anywhere close to Henderson. Dave Stapleton had replaced the veteran Buckner, who had played on a gimpy ankle since tearing it up in the 1974 World Series with the Los Angeles Dodgers, at first base in every postseason game that the Red Sox had led in the late innings. But McNamara had left Buckner in this time, presumably because he wanted his regulars on the field to celebrate when the Red Sox won. And now the Red Sox paid the price for that folly when Mookie Wilson's bouncing ball slipped between Buckner's legs for an error as a jubilant Knight dashed home with the run that beat the Red Sox 6-5.

David Henderson's home run, which only minutes before would have been classified as one of the greatest moments in Red Sox history, was now merely a footnote and all but forgotten … except by Henderson.

"To me, it is still one of the greatest World Series games ever played," he said.

✦✦✦

Two days later the dejected Red Sox lost Game 7 by an 8-5 score, and the New York Mets were World Series champions. Henderson walked, was hit by a pitch, and scored one of the Red Sox runs. He finished the World Series with a .400 average, going 10-for-25 with two homers, five RBI, and six runs scored.

Expecting to be the everyday centerfielder for the Red Sox in 1987, Henderson played only 75 games and batted just 184 times, hitting .234 with eight homers and 25 RBI. When the aging Red Sox got off to a slow start, the club embarked on a youth movement, and many of the veterans were either jettisoned or relegated to backup roles. On September 1 the Red Sox traded Henderson to the San Francisco Giants for reserve outfielder Randy Kutcher.

Henderson became a free agent after the 1987 season and signed with the Oakland Athletics. Henderson enjoyed the best years of his career with the Athletics, and they won three straight pennants and a World Series. In the biggest of games, he had a knack for rising to the occasion, the same way he had in Boston.

"I went to three more World Series and won one," Henderson said. "The guys I feel sorriest for were Rice and Evans, because those guys never got another chance to go back."

David Henderson is beaming as his dramatic two-out, two-strike pinch homer in the ninth inning of Game 5 of the 1986 ALCS is enshrined in the Boston Red Sox Hall of Fame.
*(Courtesy of the Boston Red Sox)*

Henderson's best major-league season was 1988, when he batted .304 with 38 doubles, 24 homers, 94 RBI, and scored 100 runs for the Athletics. He hit .375 with a homer and four RBI as the Athletics beat the Red Sox in the ALCS, then hit .300 with a pair of doubles in the World Series, which the Dodgers won in five games.

Henderson hit three homers and a double as Oakland beat Toronto in five games in the ALCS in 1989, then hit .308 with two doubles, two homers, and four RBI as Oakland swept the earthquake-interrupted World Series from the Giants in four straight games. On October 27 he matched a World Series record by homering in consecutive innings in Oakland's 13-7 Game 3 victory.

The Athletics were back in the World Series in 1990 but were swept by the Cincinnati Reds. Henderson had only three hits in the Series, his last. But in 20 World Series games during his career, Henderson hit .324 with six doubles, a triple, four homers, 10 RBI and 15 runs. His World Series slugging percentage was .606, 170 points higher than his career regular-season slugging percentage of .436.

David Henderson played for Oakland for three more seasons, then played with the Kansas City Royals in 1994 before retiring with a lifetime average of .258 with 197 homers and 708 RBI in 1,538 games. In 36 postseason games with the Red Sox and Athletics, he hit .297 with 10 doubles, a triple, seven homers, and 20 RBI while scoring 24 runs and slugging .570.

How can he explain the chasm between his regular-season and postseason performances?

"Teams spend a whole lot of money preparing scouting reports on teams they might play in the postseason, so they're going to stick by them," Henderson explained. "No pitcher or catcher is going to go away from those and have to go back to the dugout after giving up a home run and say: 'I thought we'd try something different.' So I always knew from the very first at-bat how they were going to pitch me during the whole series. I thought postseason play was easy. And I was never nervous."

After his retirement from baseball, Henderson operated a combination batting cage and restaurant in the Seattle area for a while. Divorced and the father of two sons whom he enjoys spending as much time with as possible, Henderson, who lives in Bellevue, Washington, is now semi-retired. He works as a part-time broadcaster on Seattle Mariners telecasts.

# Chapter 19

# MIKE GREENWELL

## SEPTEMBER 2, 1996

For much of his career, Mike Greenwell had some tough acts to follow. But he made certain that one of the last games of his Red Sox career would be an almost impossible act to top.

In New York center field has always been the glamorous position, Joe DiMaggio started the legacy, and Mickey Mantle was his worthy successor. Not everyone who has followed them has always measured up, however. In Boston the glamorous position has been left field, where for a period of nearly 60 years it was patrolled almost exclusively by just four players: Ted Williams, Carl Yastrzemski, Jim Rice, and Mike Greenwell. Those four outfielders were named to the All-Star Team 48 times, posted 27 seasons with .300 batting averages, 25 years with 25 homers, 23 seasons with 100 RBI, won nine batting titles, eight home run titles, seven RBI crowns, four MVP awards, and three Triple Crowns. Left field is a Boston legacy that has been revived by Manny Ramirez, who has added to those numbers.

"I loved being a part of that history," Greenwell said a decade after his retirement. "Someone once told me there were 12 U.S. presidents while there were only four Red Sox leftfielders. I thought that was all pretty neat … and funny. Balls would hit halfway up The Wall, and fans would yell at me: 'Yaz would have had that,' or 'Ted would have had that,' or 'Rice would have had that.' And any year I didn't hit .300, I got hammered by the fans. Even .297 wasn't good enough for them. But I loved it because they cared. I thought it was special to put on a Red Sox uniform."

Both Williams and Yaz have been elected to the Hall of Fame, and Rice may yet get to Cooperstown himself. Greenwell's career wasn't as long or as distinguished as his three predecessors in left field, but he was a career .303 hitter who early on had the responsibility of batting cleanup for the Red Sox. And on September 2, 1996, as his career was winding down, Greenwell performed a feat that not only had never been done by any of the other leftfielders, it had never been done by anyone in major-league history.

+++

Michael Lewis Greenwell was born on July 18, 1963 in Louisville, Kentucky, the youngest of Leonard and Martha Greenwell's seven children. When Mike was five, the family moved to Florida, where Leonard found work in construction.

"We were your typical hillbilly family. I grew up in a trailer, and we didn't have a lot," Greenwell recalled. "But the word failure wasn't in my vocabulary. I had tremendous drive, and from the time I was eight or nine I would tell people I was going to be a major-league baseball player someday. I remember telling my wife, Tracy, when she was 16 and I was 13 that I didn't know how deeply we should become involved because I'd be leaving someday to play in the majors. She laughed. We still laugh about that."

Mike was a star quarterback on the Fort Myers High School team as well as a standout third baseman on the baseball team. George Digby, the legendary Red Sox scout, always had a keen eye for hitters. He had signed five-time American League batting king Wade Boggs in 1976, and in 1982 he strongly recommended the lefthanded-hitting Greenwell to the Red Sox, who drafted him in the third round.

Greenwell hit .269 with six homers and 36 RBI in 72 games for Elmira in the short-season New York-Penn League that summer but also committed 31 errors at third base. A knee injury in 1983 limited him to 48 games at Class A Winston-Salem, and he was returned to Carolina League club in 1984, where he hit .306 with 16 homers and 84 RBI but again had defensive problems, making 30 errors.

The Red Sox moved Greenwell to the outfield in 1985 and also bumped him all the way to Triple-A ball at Pawtucket. He was still only 22 and hit a modest .256 with 13 homers and 52 RBI, but the Red Sox brought him up in September anyway.

Jubilant Boston Red Sox leftfielder Mike Greenwell is greeted at home plate after hitting a home run at Fenway Park.
*(Courtesy of the Boston Red Sox)*

The 6-0, 200-pound outfielder made an instant splash in the big leagues. His first three hits were home runs, including a two-run shot in the 13th inning that beat Toronto 4-2. His fourth homer of the month was a 12th-inning blast in an 8-7 loss to Milwaukee. He hit .323 in 31 at-bats for the Red Sox.

Greenwell began the 1986 season at Pawtucket and hit .300 with 18 homers and 59 RBI in 89 games before being recalled by the Red Sox in late July. The Red Sox were on their way to winning the division title and the pennant, and Greenwell played sparingly. But he hit .314 in 34 at-bats and was placed on the postseason roster. He went 1-for-2 in the American League Championship Series against the California Angels and was hitless in three World Series at-bats against the New York Mets.

The Red Sox began breaking up their aging team in 1987, and Greenwell, still classified as a rookie, got an opportunity to play regularly. Although it was a painful rebuilding year for the club, which plunged to fifth place with a 78-84 record, Greenwell stood out with his .328 average, 19 homers, 31 doubles, and 89 RBI. He finished a distant fourth behind Oakland's Mark McGwire in the balloting for AL Rookie of the Year but was named to the Topps and Baseball Digest All-Rookie Teams.

Fielding an entirely home-grown lineup in 1988, the Red Sox rebounded and won the AL East title with an 89-73 record. Greenwell emerged as a full-fledged star, hitting .325 with 22 homers and 119 RBI while also belting 39 doubles and eight triples and stealing 16 bases. He finished third in the AL in hitting behind teammate Wade Boggs, was second to Boggs in on-base percentage at .420, third in RBI, hits, and total bases, fourth in triples, and fifth in slugging percentage at .531. When the votes were counted for the Most Valuable Player at the end of the season, Greenwell was second to Oakland's Jose Canseco, who had just become the first player in baseball history to hit 40 homers and steal 40 bases in the same season. Greenwell was also named to the Silver Slugger Team.

Greenwell hit .404 with eight homers and 31 RBI in June that year and was named the league's Player of the Month. He also fashioned a 19-game hitting streak, played in the All-Star Game, and hit for the cycle in a 4-3 win over the Baltimore Orioles on September 14. He homered against Oakland in the ALCS, but the young Red Sox were swept in four straight games.

If Red Sox fans were expecting Mike Greenwell to evolve into the next Jim Rice, however, they were going to be disappointed. Greenwell would never develop into a classic power hitter in the mold of the three previous leftfielders. But he would be a consistent hitter and run producer when he wasn't being hindered by injuries, which took a toll on him over his career.

"The bar was set high because of what was going on in baseball," Greenwell said. "The year I hit 20 homers, it was a legitimate 20 homers. But guys were starting to hit 40, 50 homers, and now we know why. I lost the Rookie of the Year to Mark McGwire, and we know he was taking supplements. I lost the MVP to Jose Canseco, and he's admitted to using steroids. Later on I kept hearing from ownership that if I could hit 30 or 35 homers, it would put me on a different level. I knew what it would take, and I wasn't willing to do that. I'll admit I thought about it, and it was a tough decision. But I didn't want to put the rest of my life in danger. I'm proud that what I achieved in the game came through hard work, not something I stuck in my body."

Greenwell hit .308 with 14 homers, 36 doubles, and 95 RBI while stealing 13 bases in 1989. He put together a 21-game hitting streak, played in the All-Star Game again, and hit an inside-the-park homer off Yankees lefthander Greg Cadaret on July 7. His ankle began bothering him during the second half of the season, however, and he spent two weeks on the disabled list.

The ankle continued to be a nagging problem in 1990, and he started wearing a portable protective cast. He hit .297 with 14 homers, 30 doubles, and 73 RBI. On September 1 he legged out another inside-the-park homer against Cadaret at Fenway Park, and this time it was a grand slam. Greenwell also doubled twice, singled, and had five RBI in that 15-1 rout. The Red Sox captured their third AL East title in five years with an 88-74 record but were swept by the Athletics again in the ALCS as Greenwell was hitless in all four games.

The Red Sox then lapsed into mediocrity, and worse, during the early 1990s. The club finished second with an 84-78 record in 1991, and Greenwell hit .300 with 83 RBI and 15 stolen bases. But his home runs dwindled to nine, and he played the final weeks with a sore right knee and groin.

It was a lost year for both Greenwell and the Red Sox in 1992. Greenwell played only 49 games, hitting .233, before submitting to surgeries on his right elbow and right knee. The team finished last in the AL East with a 73-89 record, the first of three consecutive losing seasons for the Red Sox, who had not endured a dismal stretch like that in 30 years.

Greenwell bounced back in 1993 to hit .315 with 13 homers, 38 doubles, six triples, and 72 RBI. But now his left knee was bothering him, and he underwent arthroscopic surgery after the season. On Opening Day in 1994, Greenwell hurt his left shoulder crashing into The Wall while trying to make a catch, and he was never healthy that season. He slumped to .269 with 11 homers and 45 RBI in 95 games before undergoing surgery again.

"That was the way I played. I'd run through walls, slide head-first into first base, and I suffered a lot of injuries because of that," he said.

The Red Sox turned their fortunes around in 1995 and won another division title with an 86-58 record in a strike-delayed season. Mo Vaughn won the MVP Award, but Greenwell contributed by hitting .297 with 15 homers and 76 RBI in 120 games.

Greenwell would play just one more injury-plagued season in the majors. But he would leave the game with one very big bang.

Greenwell was hitting only .222 on May 3, 1996, when the bat slipped awkwardly out of his hands. The knob caught his ring finger and tore a ligament that required surgery to repair. He didn't return to the Red Sox lineup until late July. But he began hitting immediately and had his average up to .285 on August 8.

> **MIKE GREENWELL**
> **Years with Red Sox: 1985-96**
> **Other Major League Teams: None**
> **Position: Outfield**
> **Bats: Left**
> **Throws: Right**
> **Height: 6-0**
> **Weight: 200**
> **Born: July 18, 1963**
> **Birthplace: Louisville, KY**
> **Current Residence: Alva, FL**
> **Current Occupation: Amusement park operator, high school coach**

"That was like my spring training," he remembered. "I was healthy, feeling good, had my timing back, and was just starting to get in a groove."

Then he tweaked a hamstring and played only twice in a 12-day stretch. Back in the lineup on August 24, Greenwell belted a pair of doubles in a 9-5 victory over the Seattle Mariners at Fenway Park. Four days later he went 2-for-4 with a homer and two RBI in a 7-4 win over the Angels in Anaheim. After going hitless in a 7-0 loss at Oakland on August 30, he sat out the next day while the Red Sox were shut out again, 8-0. Greenwell played the final game of the series and went 2-for-3 with a double and two RBI in an 8-3 Red Sox victory, and the team flew to Seattle for a Labor Day game. Greenwell wasn't particularly looking forward to it. He never liked playing in the gloomy Kingdome.

"It was always a tough atmosphere. I had trouble seeing the ball on defense," he explained. "It wasn't like going into Yankee Stadium. The

Mariners didn't have much history. It was just another game to me at that point."

That viewpoint was about to change radically during the next few hours. This would be the most memorable game of Mike Greenwell's career and one of the greatest hitting days in major-league history.

"It was a dream day, and it felt like I was in a dream," he said, looking back nine years later. "That day was unbelievable."

✦✦✦

Greenwell, whose average was .264 with just four homers and 25 RBI in 53 games, wasn't the only Red Sox player battling through a difficult season in 1996. The club's longtime ace and three-time Cy Young Award winner, Roger Clemens, was on his way to winning his third strikeout crown and owned a 3.68 ERA. But his record was only 8-11 when he went to the mound that evening in front of 24,470 fans at the Kingdome. Clemens, like Greenwell, was playing his last season with the Red Sox. Both were at constant odds with third-year general manager Dan Duquette, who had little interest in keeping veteran players around, especially those who spoke their minds and criticized his policies.

Despite their struggles, the defending AL East champions were still on the fringes of the pennant race. Although their record was 70-67, they were only six and a half games behind the Yankees and Orioles with four weeks left in the season.

The Mariners, who had won their first AL West title the previous year, were also trying to stay in their division race. With a 71-65 record, they were six games behind the Texas Rangers. So there was a lot at stake for both teams.

Bob Wolcott, a 22-year-old righthander with a 7-10 record and a 5.65 ERA, started for the Mariners and retired Greenwell the first time he faced him.

"After he got me out, I remember switching from my 34-inch bat to a 35-inch bat. I remember that because after the game the Hall of Fame asked for my bat, and it was the only 35-inch bat I had on the trip, and I didn't want to give it up," he related. "I did, though.

"If I felt I was too strong or overly aggressive and was getting too far out in front of pitches, I'd use the longer bat to slow me down a little bit," Greenwell explained. "I also used a 33-inch bat sometimes against soft-throwing lefthanders because it would shorten my swing and force me to keep my front shoulder in."

The Mariners nicked Clemens for a run in the third on singles by Dave Hollins and Joey Cora and a sacrifice fly by Alex Rodriguez, then quickly made it 5-0 in the fourth.

Ken Griffey Jr. singled, Jay Buhner walked, and Paul Sorrento singled home Griffey. Mark Whiten hit a comebacker that Clemens threw away trying to start a double play at second, and Buhner scored. Dan Wilson hit another ball back to the mound that Clemens also threw away while trying for a double play. Sorrento scored, and Whiten ended up on third, from where he scored on a sacrifice fly by Hollins.

And then Greenwell went to work, turning Labor Day into his personal holiday.

Wolcott was working on a one-hitter and easily retired the first two Red Sox batters in the fifth, striking out Reggie Jefferson and getting Troy O'Leary on a flyball. But Tim Naehring drew a walk, and Greenwell drilled a homer into the right-field stands.

"It was pretty much down the line, and I knew it was gone as soon as I hit it," Greenwell said. "I remember getting back to the dugout and telling people that I had this feeling they weren't going to get me out again that night. Sometimes, as an athlete, you get that feeling it's going to be your night, and I had that feeling."

The Mariners were still leading 5-2 when the Red Sox batted in the seventh. Righthander Bobby Ayala had relieved Wolcott by this time, and Jefferson stroked a double to left-center. O'Leary and Naehring both walked, loading the bases for Greenwell.

"Ayala was a tough pitcher for me. I hated to face him," Greenwell said. "He had a nasty little sinker and a herky-jerky motion, and I didn't have a lot of success against him. But, like I said, I was having one of those nights."

Greenwell blasted the ball into the right-field stands for a grand slam, putting the Red Sox ahead 6-5. It was the second time Greenwell had driven in six runs in a game during his major-league career, having previously accomplished the feat in a 15-2 rout of the Texas Rangers on April 14, 1988. But he wasn't finished yet.

"I remember running around the bases thinking they were going to hit me the next time," he recalled. "You hit back-to-back homers, one of them a grand slam, and you know they're going to knock you down. I knew I was going to get dropped the next time up."

Reggie Harris took over for Clemens in the bottom of the seventh but couldn't protect the lead. Cora doubled with one out, and A-Rod, who would be the league's batting champ at year's end, belted his 35th homer of the season into the left-field stands, putting Seattle back in front 7-6. Red Sox manager Kevin Kennedy yanked Harris after he walked Griffey, but Kerry Lacy wasn't any sharper. He walked Edgar Martinez and Buhner to load the bases.

Kennedy went right back to the bullpen and brought in rookie lefthander Vaughn Eshelman to pitch to the lefthanded-hitting Sorrento, but Seattle manager Lou Piniella sent up Brian Hunter to pinch hit, and he drew another walk, forcing in Griffey and upping the Mariners' lead to 8-6.

Veteran lefthander Norm Charlton, the Mariners' closer with 14 saves, took over in the eighth and started the inning by walking Mo Vaughn. Wil Cordero pinch hit for Jefferson and struck out, and Kennedy sent up rookie Rudy Pemberton to hit for O'Leary. Pemberton would have a phenomenal September for the Red Sox, collecting 21 hits in 41 at-bats for a .512 batting average, but Charlton got him to bounce back to the mound as Vaughn took second.

Naehring kept the inning alive by drawing his third walk of the game, and speedy Lee Tinsley pinch ran. Greenwell stepped in. With the tying runs on base, now he knew he'd get a pitch to hit instead of being hit. It wasn't the proper time to send a message; the two defending division champions both desperately needed to win this game.

"I never had much trouble with Charlton," he said. "But he threw me a nasty pitch down and away, and I hit it right down the third-base line, right over the bag."

Greenwell coasted into second with a two-run double, and the game was tied. It was still tied after nine innings, and Greenwell was scheduled to bat fifth in the top of the tenth.

"Early in that inning, I said to Tim Naehring in the dugout: 'Let me get up, and I'll win this game.' I was just hoping no one else would drive in a run before me," he admitted. "I already knew I had tied the record. Someone had been in the clubhouse watching the game on TV and told me the announcers had said I had just tied a major-league record by driving in all eight runs. Sometimes players don't like to be aware of those things. But I just saw it as an opportunity to do something no one had ever done before."

Piniella brought in lefthander Rafael Carmona, who had a 6-2 record, to pitch. Vaughn flied out to center, and Cordero walked. Pemberton lined to right for the second out, but Jeff Manto, who had taken over for Naehring at third, drew yet another walk. Again Greenwell came through for the Red Sox.

"It was pretty ugly, a bloop single into right," he remembered. "And there was a play at the plate, but it wasn't close."

Heathcliff Slocumb retired the Mariners in the bottom of the tenth, and the Red Sox held on to win 9-8. Mike Greenwell had four of the seven Red Sox hits in the game and had driven in all nine of their runs. It was the first time in major-league history anyone had driven in that many runs while accounting for all his team's runs. George Kelly of the New York Giants had knocked in all the runs in an 8-1 victory over the Boston Braves on June 26, 1924, and Bob Johnson had accounted for all the Philadelphia Athletics' scoring in an 8-3 win over the St. Louis Browns on June 12, 1938.

"After the game we went to a place across the street, F.X. McCrory's, to celebrate," Greenwell said. "And just as we walked in the door, Chris Berman is on TV saying: 'This just in from Seattle ... Mike Greenwell nine and the Mariners eight.' Who couldn't get a charge from hearing that? There were more Mariners fans in there than Red Sox fans, but they all turned around and applauded."

Vladimir Guerrero of the Anaheim Angels nearly matched Greenwell's feat in a game against the Red Sox in 2004, finishing with nine RBI in a game the Angels won 10-7. But to date, no one has duplicated or surpassed Greenwell's solo performance against the Mariners that night.

✦✦✦

Greenwell finished the 1996 season with a flourish. He had three more hits, including a double and two RBI, in an 11-9 loss to the Mariners the next day. He hit safely in 21 of his last 25 games, including six straight multiple-hit games, while driving in 21 runs. But by the time the team returned to Boston, he knew his Red Sox career was over.

"When we got back, I found a note on my chair in the clubhouse from Duquette, congratulating me on that day," Greenwell said. "I thought it was so impersonal. Why couldn't he stop by the cage during batting practice and shake my hand? But he never did.

"I was making $3.2 or $3.4 million my last year, and my contract was up. I had never taken the club to arbitration or filed for free agency," he continued. "The last conversation I ever had with Duquette, I told him I didn't care how much he paid me, or if I even had a regular job anymore, but that I wanted to come back and play another year for the Red Sox. I knew if I came back, I could earn a job. He told me he didn't think they'd be interested. That shocked me, and that's when I knew I was done."

Mike Greenwell, a lifetime .303 hitter for the Red Sox, keeps himself busy with several ventures in Southwest Florida.
(Courtesy of Mike Greenwell)

Going into the last game of the season—his last game in a Red Sox uniform—Greenwell was riding a 12-game hitting streak and had his average up to .299. The Red Sox beat the Yankees 6-5 to end the year at 85-77 and in third place, but Greenwell was held hitless. He finished at .295 with 20 doubles, seven homers, and 44 RBI in 77 games.

Over his career Mike Greenwell hit .303 with 1,400 hits in 1,269 games for the Red Sox, including 275 doubles, 130 homers, and 726 RBI. He also drew 460 walks and struck out only 364 times in 4,623 at-bats. He currently ranks ninth on the club's all-time list in doubles and tenth in hits.

Greenwell was only 33, but he didn't want to play in the majors anymore and instead signed a contract to play in Japan with the Hanshin Tigers.

"Having played in New England, I never wanted to play anywhere else," he explained. "I had 20 offers to play for other major-league teams. The reason I went to Japan was because I didn't want to put on another major-league team's uniform. And I've never set foot inside Fenway Park since the day I left."

His career in Japan was brief. He fouled a ball off his foot, broke it, and decided to retire.

Near the end of his Red Sox career, Greenwell had started his own business, a family-style amusement park in Cape Coral, Florida. He's also involved in real estate development now and coaches baseball and football at Riverdale High School in East Fort Myers. Mike, Tracy, and their two sons live in Alva.

# Chapter 20

# JOHN VALENTIN

## OCTOBER 10, 1999

The vast majority of athletes, in any sport, learn that the game gets progressively difficult as the level of competition intensifies. That is why so very few of them ever make it to the top of their game. John Valentin, however, was one of those extremely rare athletes who enjoyed an inverse career; that is, the stiffer the competition became, the better his statistics became.

John William Valentin was born February 18, 1967, in Mineola, New York, just a few weeks before the Red Sox began their "Impossible Dream" season that culminated in a pennant. His father, Arnold, was a long-haul truck driver who had moved to New Jersey from Puerto Rico at the age of 16. Arnold and Divina Valentin had another son, also named Arnold, who was two years older than John. Playing sports with his older brother and his friends enabled John to develop his skills at a faster pace. But for the first quarter-century of John Valentin's life, any thoughts of a major-league career in baseball would have seemed also to be an impossible dream.

Valentin starred in both baseball and basketball at St. Anthony in Jersey City, New Jersey, where his partner in the back court was David Rivers, who later went on to star at Notre Dame and in the NBA with the Los Angeles Clippers. But athletes didn't enroll at St. Anthony in hopes of furthering their baseball careers.

"Once I started playing baseball, it became my first love. But I never thought seriously about a major-league career," Valentin said. "St. Anthony had a reputation as a basketball school. The baseball team was probably below average, and I didn't get recruited by any colleges for baseball because of my size. I was five-eight and about 120 pounds when I graduated from high school. I had an offer to play basketball for a Division III school, but I decided if I wasn't good enough to play baseball, I'd just go to Seton Hall because my brother was already there, and it was a good school."

Valentin, having grown a couple of inches and gained about 20 pounds, batted ninth in the Pirates' batting order as a freshman walk-on. No one could foresee then that he was destined to become one of the best postseason clutch hitters in Red Sox history. In his sophomore year he was joined by another future Red Sox star, slugging first baseman Mo Vaughn. Valentin, now standing six feet even but still weighing only 170 pounds, had a breakout year as a junior in 1988, hitting .392 with a school-record 21 doubles and earning third-team All-America honors. All of a sudden he was a prospect. The Red Sox drafted him in the fifth round and signed him for a $42,000 bonus.

The 21-year-old Valentin began his pro career in the Class A short-season New York-Penn League, and, as expected, did not hit much. He batted only .217 with eight extra-base hits in 60 games for Elmira but did lead the league's shortstops in fielding. Assigned to Winter Haven in the Class A Florida State League in 1989, Valentin hit a decent .270 in 55 games before being promoted to Lynchburg in the Class A Carolina League, where he batted only .246. The Red Sox promoted Valentin to New Britain in the Class AA Eastern League in 1990, where he hit just .218 in 94 games.

Valentin dedicated himself to getting stronger over the winter. He lifted weights and bulked up to a solid 190 pounds. Back at New Britain in 1991, Valentin was batting just .198 after 23 games when he caught a break. Pawtucket shortstop Luis Aguayo, a former major-leaguer, went on the disabled list, and Valentin was summoned to fill in. Now just one step below the major leagues, Valentin, reunited with former Seton Hall teammate Vaughn—the Red Sox' first-round pick in 1989—showed he could swing a potent bat. In 100 games for Pawtucket, Valentin hit a solid .264 with 22 doubles, nine homers, and 49 RBI while drawing 60 walks and striking out only 42 times.

Valentin went to spring training with the major-league club for the first time in 1992 and was the last cut. Manager Butch Hobson elected to start the year with 28-year-old veteran Luis Rivera, who was coming off a decent .258-8-40 campaign with 22 doubles for the Red Sox.

**Boston Red Sox shortstop John Valentin pulls another pitch during a game at Fenway Park.** *(Courtesy of the Boston Red Sox)*

Valentin put together a solid first half in the Class AAA International League, hitting .260 with 18 doubles and nine homers in 97 games. Meanwhile, a punchless Red Sox team was facing its first losing season in a decade, and Rivera was hitting .220 with no homers and 24 RBI. The Red Sox were in fifth place with a 45-51 record when Valentin was called up on July 27 and inserted immediately into the lineup. His eighth-inning RBI single helped wrap up a 7-5 victory over the Texas Rangers at Fenway Park that night, and he played shortstop regularly for the Red Sox for the remainder of the season.

Valentin's first major-league homer was a grand slam off Seattle's Mike Schooler on August 22, a blow that tied the game at 6-6 and propelled the Red Sox to a 10-8 win. On September 30 Valentin's fourth-inning homer off Toronto's David Cone provided Frank Viola with the only run he needed in a 1-0, one-hit victory over the Blue Jays. Valentin finished his rookie season with a .276 average, 13 doubles, five homers, and 25 RBI in 58 games.

In subsequent seasons John Valentin's bat would just get stronger and stronger. Beginning in 1993, Valentin and Vaughn, the two Seton Hall alumni, would forge a strong one-two punch for the Red Sox.

Valentin's 1993 season was delayed when he broke his ring finger while fielding a ground ball near the end of spring training. Returning to the lineup on April 20 in Seattle, Valentin belted a solo homer in the seventh that put the Red Sox ahead 2-1 and sparked them to a 5-2 win. Ten days later he walloped a pair of homers and drove in five runs in a 6-1 win over the California Angels. Valentin hit .313 after the All-Star break, finishing the year at .278 with 40 doubles—tied for third most in the American League—11 homers, and 66 RBI in 144 games. His 54 extra-base hits were the most by a Red Sox shortstop since Rico Petrocelli amassed 63 in 1969.

The contributions of Valentin and Vaughn, and even the presence of three-time Cy Young Award winner Roger Clemens, couldn't prevent the Red Sox from suffering through losing seasons in 1992 and 1993. But the Red Sox were off to a 19-7 start in 1994 when Valentin went on the disabled list for a month. Valentin was hitting .303 with five doubles, two homers, and 10 RBI when his left knee began bothering him in late April and forced him to submit to arthroscopic surgery in early May. While Valentin was out of the lineup the Red Sox lost 15 of their 27 games.

On July 8, 1994, Valentin performed one of the rarest feats in baseball, turning an unassisted triple play against Seattle in front of 33,355 fans at Fenway Park. The Mariners led 2-0 in the sixth and had Mike Blowers on second and Keith Mitchell on first with nobody out when Marc Newfield lashed a line drive that Valentin snagged. The shortstop stepped on second base to double up Blowers and then tagged Mitchell coming down from first. It was only the second unassisted triple play in Red Sox history, previously accomplished by first baseman George Burns against Cleveland on September 14, 1923, and just the tenth unassisted triple play in major-league history.

"Lou Piniella puts on the bunt sign, but Newfield bunts through it for a strike," Valentin recalled. "I can see Lou in the dugout, and he's really ticked. So he puts on the hit-and-run. But I was still expecting a bunt, so I'm playing behind the baserunner to be closer to the bag, and I'm really out of position for a hit-and-run. But Newfield hits the ball right at me, and I catch it right off my shoetops. I thought there was already one out, so when I stepped on second, I thought the inning was over. For some reason I just happened to look up at the sideboard along the first-base line, and there was still a zero up there for the outs. That's when I knew we still needed one more out. The runner from first was still coming at me, so I tagged him.

"I actually left the ball on the field, like it wasn't a big deal," Valentin chuckled. "Someone got it and gave it to me later. Anyway, I'm on a real high. Everyone in the dugout is congratulating me, whacking me in the head, and I've gotta go hit!"

Valentin then led off the bottom of the sixth by socking a 3-and-2 pitch from Dave Fleming into the left-field screen for a home run, triggering a four-run rally that ultimately beat the Mariners 4-3.

Less than a month later, on August 6, Valentin, by now hitting in the top third of the Red Sox batting order, went 5-for-5 with five RBI in an 8-4 win over the Cleveland Indians. He was hitting .316 with 26 doubles, nine homers, and 49 RBI in 84 games when major-league players went on strike on August 12, prematurely ending the season.

The longest, costliest, and most bitter strike in baseball history was not settled until the following April. After three straight losing seasons under Butch Hobson—their worst stretch in 30 years—the Red Sox hired Kevin Kennedy as manager in 1995. With Mo Vaughn putting together an MVP season (.300-39-126) and Valentin fashioning one of the best seasons ever by a Red Sox shortstop, the team surprised everyone by winning the American League East title with an 86-58 record. Valentin hit .298 with 27 homers, 102 runs batted in, a .533 slugging percentage, and a .399 on-base percentage. He led the team with 108 runs, 37 doubles, 81 walks, and 20 stolen bases. His 20/20 season was only the fourth such blend of speed and power in Red Sox history. Jackie Jensen had accomplished the feat in 1954 and 1959, Carl Yastrzemski in 1970, and Ellis Burks in 1987.

On May 2 Valentin and Vaughn hit grand slams to beat the Yankees 8-0, the first time in history two grand slams had accounted for all the runs in a major-league game. Exactly a month later Valentin blasted three homers in a 6-5, 10-inning win over Seattle, becoming only the fifth major-league shortstop to hit three homers in a game. Valentin finished the night 5-for-5 and scored four runs, and his 15 total bases in the game set a major-league record for shortstops. Valentin had six RBI in a 13-3 rout of Detroit on August 1, two homers and five RBI in an 11-1 thrashing of Baltimore nine days later, and five RBI in a 13-6 triumph in Oakland on August 24.

Valentin was selected as the shortstop on the Silver Slugger Team. In the field he led all major-league shortstops in assists and total chances and was second in putouts.

For the first time in five years, the Red Sox were back in the playoffs. But just as they had in 1988 and 1990, they exited quickly. Valentin clubbed a homer off Cleveland's Dennis Martinez in the third inning of the first game, putting the Red Sox ahead 2-0, but it was one of the few highlights of that Division Series. The wild-card Indians swept the three-game series, running the Red Sox' postseason losing streak to 13 games dating back to the last two games of the 1986 World Series.

Three more years would elapse before the Red Sox would get another shot in the postseason. Valentin, meanwhile, continued to be productive despite a left shoulder injury in 1996 that hampered him for much of the season. He tore his rotator cuff and suffered a partial tear of the labrum while diving for a groundball. He hit .296 with 29 doubles but hit only 13 homers with 59 RBI for the Red Sox, who slipped back into third place with an 85-77 record. He did hit for the cycle on June 6 that year in a 7-4 win over the Chicago White Sox.

Valentin underwent shoulder surgery after the season and responded with a strong year in 1997, albeit at a couple of new positions. The Red Sox wanted rookie phenom Nomar Garciaparra to play shortstop, and the 30-year-old Valentin balked at the suggestion he should be the one to move to second base. He walked out of camp for a day during spring training. A decade later, he is still bitter over the way the situation was handled.

His unhappiness did not affect his performance for long, however. After hitting just .160 in April, Valentin hit .335 the rest of the way and finished the season at .306 with a league-leading 47 doubles, five triples, 18 homers, 77 RBI, and 95 runs in 143 games. When Tim Naehring blew out his elbow in mid-season, Valentin moved over to third base and played there for the rest of his Red Sox career.

Valentin's batting average plummeted to .247 in 1998. But he remained remarkably productive and helped the Red Sox return to the playoffs as the wild card. Valentin clouted 23 homers and 44 doubles, scored 113 runs, and knocked in 73. He also had a 65-game errorless streak at third base.

Once again Valentin rose to the occasion in the Division Series, hitting .467 in the four games against Central Division champion Cleveland, which had gone to the World Series the previous year. The Red Sox ended their postseason losing streak with an 11-3 rout of the Indians in Game 1 as Valentin drilled three hits and set an ALDS record by scoring four runs. But the Red Sox lost the next three games and were ousted again.

Injuries limited Valentin to 113 games in 1999, when he hit .253 with 27 doubles, 12 homers, and 70 RBI. He belted a grand slam off Chris Carpenter in a 6-4 win over Toronto on May 22 and beat the New York Mets 3-2 with a 12th-inning single off relief ace John Franco in an interleague game on June 11. He went on the disabled list two weeks later after being beaned by Chicago's John Snyder and was back on the disabled list at the end of August, suffering from tendinitis in his left knee.

Valentin returned to the lineup for the last 11 days of the regular season, just in time for the most memorable game of his Red Sox career.

✚ ✚ ✚

The Red Sox finished the 1999 campaign with a 94-68 record, four games behind the Yankees, and secured the wild card again. For the third straight time in postseason play, however, they drew the troublesome Cleveland Indians as their first-round opponent. Over the previous 50 years, the Indians had ruined many a season for the Red Sox and their loyal legions of fans. Cleveland's victory over the Red Sox in a one-game playoff at Fenway Park for the pennant in 1948 had spoiled the only all-Boston World Series in history. During the late 1970s and early 1980s the lowly Indians had a knack for upsetting the contending Red Sox in crucial late-season games. And now, as the last decade of the last century of the millennium was drawing to a close, Cleveland had twice ousted the Red Sox in the Division Series and was primed to do so again.

"We were good, but we weren't the best team," Valentin said. "Cleveland and the Yankees were the teams of the Nineties in the American League. Cleveland had a great team with Roberto Alomar, Manny Ramirez,

Jim Thome, Omar Vizquel, Kenny Lofton … all those guys. We knew it would be difficult to beat them, and we'd have to play perfect baseball."

But the Red Sox—and John Valentin—were initially far from perfect.

The Red Sox sent 23-game winner Pedro Martinez, who had just completed one of the greatest seasons by a pitcher in baseball history, to the mound in Game 1 at Cleveland's Jacobs Field on October 6. Martinez shut out the Indians for four innings and had a 1-0 lead, courtesy of a Garciaparra home run, when he pulled a muscle in his back and had to leave the game. A two-out error by Valentin, followed immediately by a Thome homer off Derek Lowe, tied the game at 2-2 in the sixth, and the Indians won 3-2 on Travis Fryman's bases-loaded single off Rich Garces with one out in the bottom of the ninth.

The Indians routed the demoralized Red Sox 11-1 in the second game, dealing them their 18th defeat in

> **JOHN VALENTIN**
> **Years with Red Sox: 1992-2001**
> **Other Major League Teams: New York (NL)**
> **Position: Shortstop**
> **Bats: Right**
> **Throws: Right**
> **Height: 6-0**
> **Weight: 170**
> **Born: February 18, 1967**
> **Birthplace: Mineola, NY**
> **Current Residence: Middletown, NJ**
> **Current Occupation: Red Sox TV analyst**

their last 19 postseason games and bringing them to the brink of elimination once again as the series moved to Boston. Their backs squarely against Fenway Park's famous left-field wall, the Red Sox rebounded with a resounding vengeance in Game 3 on October 9.

"We come home, and I felt I really, really had to do something to pick up my game," Valentin related. "I made an error that cost us Game 1, a throw in the dirt that Mo couldn't pick. And I didn't have a hit yet."

Valentin, 0-for-10 in the series, excited the sellout crowd of 33,539 by giving the Red Sox a 3-2 lead with a solo homer off Jaret Wright in the bottom of the sixth. But Valentin gave the run right back in the seventh with an error that allowed Lofton to score and retie the game at 3-3.

The Red Sox loaded the bases with two outs in the bottom of the seventh, bringing Valentin to the plate to face lefthander Ricardo Rincon. Valentin atoned for his second costly error of the series by socking a two-run double to put the Red Sox ahead 5-3, and Brian Daubach followed with a three-run homer. Lou Merloni's RBI single later capped the six-run rally, and the Red Sox won 9-3.

"I was so concerned about making another bad throw that I did it again," Valentin remembered. "The fans were all over me. I'm thinking: 'How much more can I screw up?' Hitting that double was so gratifying."

Employing a controversial strategy calculated to end the series right there and set up his rotation for the AL Championship Series—a miscalculation that would cost him his job—an overconfident Cleveland manager Mike Hargrove brought back his ace, 18-game winner Bartolo Colon, on three days' rest in Game 4 on October 10. The consequence of that decision was the most explosive postseason game in major-league history and the most memorable game of John Valentin's career.

"The reason I picked this game was because of the first three games when I was playing so poorly, and because of the Red Sox' playoff history," he explained. "It was time for some payback. The triple play, the cycle, the three-homer game were nice things. But to be down 0-2 and come back and sweep a team that was probably better than we were and set up a playoff series with the Yankees was awesome."

✦ ✦ ✦

The Indians nicked Red Sox starter Kent Mercker for a run in the first inning on a single by Wil Cordero, momentarily quieting the SRO crowd of 33,898 inside Fenway. Valentin, the runt who had batted ninth at Seton Hall and at or near the bottom of the order throughout most of his minor-league career, brought the fans right back to life.

Jose Offerman drew a leadoff walk from Colon in the bottom of the inning, and Valentin cracked a homer to put the Red Sox ahead 2-1.

"Now I'm on a high and feeling good about myself," he said.

The Indians tied it up briefly in the second on a sacrifice fly by Sandy Alomar, but Colon couldn't get anybody out in the bottom of the inning. Three straight singles by Mike Stanley, Jason Varitek, and Darren Lewis produced a run, and Trot Nixon's double brought home two more. Offerman's two-run homer put the Red Sox ahead 7-2 and chased Colon. Valentin greeted reliever Steve Karsay with a single but was left stranded.

"Colon wasn't on his game, but we were happy to get him out of there because he could still beat you without his best stuff," Valentin said. "Once we got Colon out of the game, we knew we weren't going to lose. It was time to put the pressure on them. We never stopped hitting from that point on."

The Red Sox added to their lead with three more runs in the third off Karsay. Varitek led off with a double, took third on a single by Lewis, and scored on a sacrifice fly by Nixon. One out later Valentin smacked his second homer of the game and third in six at-bats, a two-run shot that upped the score to 10-2.

Valentin and the Red Sox continued to pour it on in the fourth, turning the game into a rout. Steve Reed replaced Karsay and hit the first batter he faced, Garciaparra. Stanley singled with one out, and Varitek ripped an RBI double. Nixon kept the rally going with a two-out walk, and Offerman singled, plating Stanley and keeping the bases loaded for Valentin. This time Valentin slammed a three-run double high off The Wall, putting the Red Sox ahead 15-2 and giving him four hits and seven RBI in just four innings of work and 10 RBI in the series.

"I said to myself: 'There is nothing this guy can throw me that is going to get me out.' I was locked in. Another three feet, I would have had another homer."

Cleveland temporarily made the score a bit more respectable by scoring four times in the fifth. But the Red Sox pounded Reed for three more runs in the bottom of the inning on an RBI triple by Stanley—who had five hits in the game—and a two-run homer by Varitek—who finished the night with four hits and five runs.

Valentin got only one more at-bat in the game, striking out against rookie Sean DePaula in the sixth. A two-run double by Nixon, who finished the night with five RBI, boosted the score to 20-6 in the seventh, and Offerman followed with a single for his fifth RBI of the game. Valentin was scheduled to bat against lefthanded reliever Paul Assenmacher, but manager Jimy Williams sent up Donnie Sadler to pinch hit, and he doubled.

Valentin has no regrets about not batting again with a chance to finish the night with as many as 10 RBI. "I was actually tired. Jimy saw that and said: 'We need you tomorrow. Do you want to come out? It's up to you.' I said okay."

The Red Sox tacked on two more runs in the eighth against Paul Shuey, Cleveland's sixth pitcher of the game. The Red Sox won 23-7, setting postseason records for runs and hits in a game. They obliterated the record for runs set by the Yankees in an 18-4 romp over the New York Giants in the 1936 World Series, and with 24 hits surpassed the record of 22 established by the Atlanta Braves in a 15-0 rout of the St. Louis Cardinals in the 1996 NLCS. Twelve of the hits went for extra bases, another postseason record. Among the other records set by the Red Sox that night were margin of victory (16) and total bases (45).

John Valentin's seven RBI equaled the record for a postseason game, and his 11 total bases were a record for a Division Series contest.

✦ ✦ ✦

The series now tied at two wins apiece, the Red Sox and Indians returned to Cleveland for the deciding game. The Red Sox were attempting to become only the fifth team in baseball history to win a five-game postseason series after losing the first two.

Bret Saberhagen, roughed up for six runs in two and two-thirds innings in Game 2, started for the Red Sox and was again ineffective. He lasted just two batters into the second inning and was charged with five runs. But the Red Sox continued to swing hot bats themselves. A grand slam by Troy O'Leary—who would hit two homers and enjoy a seven-RBI game himself—highlighted a five-run third and put the Red Sox ahead 7-5. The Indians retaliated with three runs off Derek Lowe in the bottom of the inning and retook the lead 8-7.

Valentin tied up the game again with a sacrifice fly in the fourth, and out of the bullpen came the aching Pedro Martinez. Pitching gingerly because of the pulled muscle in his back, Martinez nevertheless threw six courageous innings of hitless relief at the Indians while striking out eight. Valentin started the game-winning rally in the seventh with a single and rode home on a three-run homer by O'Leary that put the Red Sox ahead for good, 11-8. The final score was 12-8, and the Red Sox were headed to the ALCS for the first time in nine years and their first-ever post-season clash with the rival Yankees. Valentin had hit .318 with three homers and 12 RBI in the dramatic upset of the Indians.

The Red Sox lost the first two games in New York, both by one run.

The ALCS moved to Fenway on October 16, and a sellout crowd of 33,190, plus several million more watching on television, were eagerly anticipating the matchup between Roger Clemens, the greatest pitcher in Red Sox history, and Pedro Martinez, the current ace whose back had healed enough for him to start.

John Valentin all but stole the show. Jose Offerman led off the bottom of the first with a triple, and Valentin socked his fourth homer of the playoffs to put the Red Sox quickly ahead 2-0.

"You have to put the pressure on Roger, because he is going to put the pressure on you if he gets comfortable," Valentin said. "And the place went crazy! The momentum was on our side right away. It was like the Cleveland series all over again."

**John Valentin poses with a fan at a Boston Baseball Writers Awards Dinner.** *(Courtesy of Rick Lalime)*

Clemens gave up two more runs in the second, one on a groundout by Valentin, and was gone after one batter in the third, charged with five runs. Valentin added RBI singles in the fifth and seventh innings to finish the day with five RBI, upping his post-season total to 17 in eight games. Martinez, meanwhile, overpowered the Yankees for seven scoreless innings, allowing two singles and fanning 12 before turning the game over to the bullpen. The Red Sox won 13-1, dealing the Yankees the most lopsided defeat in their proud postseason history.

Valentin had two hits in each of the next two games, but the Yankees won them both to win the pennant. Valentin hit .348 in the ALCS, and his 1999 post-season statistics were magnificent. In 10 games Valentin hit .333 and slugged .689 with four homers, four doubles, 17 RBI, and nine runs.

Only 32, Valentin thought he still had more glorious days in front of him. He could not know that his career was almost over.

Valentin played only two games in 2000 before recurring tendinitis in his left knee landed him on the disabled list. He returned to the lineup on May 19 but played only eight more games before rupturing the tendon in that knee while fielding a grounder by Kansas City's Carlos Beltran on May 30.

"Three days before, playing a series against the Yankees, I felt I was in danger," Valentin remembered. "I threw out Scott Brosius on a groundball, and I felt extreme pain. Maybe I should have stopped playing right then and had an MRI. But I never thought that would happen to me. I just thought it would hurt all year."

Valentin underwent surgery and missed the remainder of the season.

He was still rehabbing the knee at the start of the 2001 campaign. He played only 20 games, hitting .200, before going back on the disabled list for good. Valentin became a free agent after the season and signed with the New York Mets but hit only .240 in 114 games. He didn't want to be a role player, and when he saw that's where his career was headed after tryouts with Baltimore in 2003 and Houston in 2004, John Valentin retired at the age of 37.

In 991 games with the Red Sox, Valentin hit .281 with 1,043 hits, including 266 doubles and 121 homers, 528 RBI, and 596 runs. And he was never better than in the games that mattered most, hitting .347 with six doubles, five homers, 19 RBI, and a .639 slugging percentage in 17 career postseason games.

"In a short series there are key guys you have to stop," Valentin said, analyzing his postseason record. "But you can't stop everybody, and I'm one of those guys they fell asleep on. If you don't pitch to me like you're supposed to pitch to me, I'm going to hurt you. That was my big incentive, and I relished the moment."

John Valentin and his wife, Marie, continue to make their home in Middletown, New Jersey, with their two children. Valentin is enjoying taking an active role in the upbringing of his children and currently does some television studio work for the Red Sox.

# Celebrate the Heroes of Red Sox Baseball
## in These Other Releases from Sports Publishing!

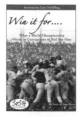